The Wreck of the 'Annie Jane'

The Forgotten Island Disaster
1853, Vatersay, Outer Hebrides.

The Wreck of the 'Annie Jane'

The Forgotten Island Disaster
1853, Vatersay, Outer Hebrides.

Allan F. Murray

acair

The publishers extend their appreciation to all the sources and contributors mentioned individually in the acknowledgements section by the author.

First published in 2017 by Acair Ltd, An Tosgan, Seaforth Road, Stornoway, Isle of Lewis, Scotland HS1 2SD

www.acairbooks.com
info@acairbooks.com

© text Allan F. Murray, 2017

© cover illustration and Sail Plan illustration Rebecca Murray, 2017

Map of the UK and Barra & Vatersay by Margaret A. MacLeod

All rights reserved.

The right of Allan Murray to be identified as the author of the work has been asserted by him in accordance with the Copyright, Designs and Patent Act 1998.

No part of this publication may be reproduced, stored in a retrieval system nor reproduced or transmitted by any means, electronic, mechanical, photocopying or otherwise, without the prior permission of the publisher.

The Cover and interior design by Catriona MacIver for Acair.

A CIP catalogue record for this title is available from the British Library

Printed by Hussar Books, Poland.

ISBN 978-0-86152-412-9

Contents

Maps and Illustrations		viii
Prologue		1
Chapter		
1.	An Introduction to the 'Annie Jane'	4
2.	The First Voyage	23
3.	Repair and Litigation	31
4.	The Second Voyage	43
5.	The Longest Night	52
6.	Vatersay	61
7.	The Aftermath	72
8.	The Ragged School Boy	93
9.	Le Naufrage de 'l'Annie Jane'	106
10.	The Beechey Inquiry and Recommendations	146
11.	The Gray Report and Monument	155
12.	Freight is the Mother of Wages	166
13.	Persecution of a Clergyman for a Peccadillo	173
14.	Songs and Ballads of the 'Annie Jane'	179
15.	The Lean Years	186
16.	Epilogue	195

Appendices:

Lists of those who died, and those who survived

Casualties	**200**
Survivors	**213**
Glossary	**224**
Acknowledgements	**228**
Select Bibliography	**231**

You landsmen all pray lend an ear, to this my dismal tale,

    Concerning the wreck of the Annie Jane, which from Liverpool did sail;

It was for Quebec she was bound, across the raging main,

    With four hundred and fifty souls aboard, the ill-fated Annie Jane.

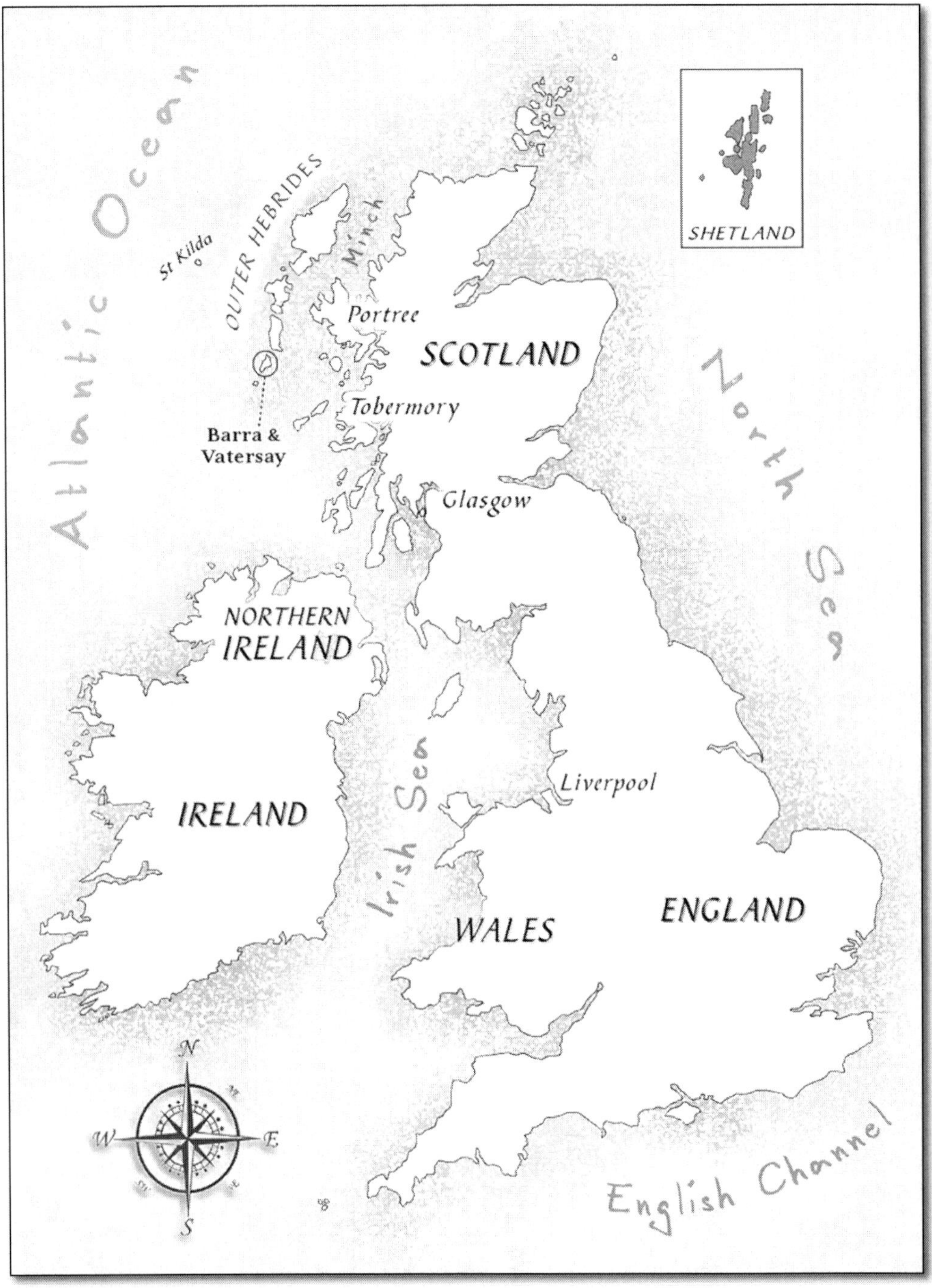
Atlantic Ocean
OUTER HEBRIDES
St Kilda
Minch
SHETLAND
Portree
SCOTLAND
Tobermory
Barra &
Vatersay
Glasgow
North Sea
NORTHERN
IRELAND
IRELAND
Irish Sea
Liverpool
WALES
ENGLAND
English Channel
N
W
E
S

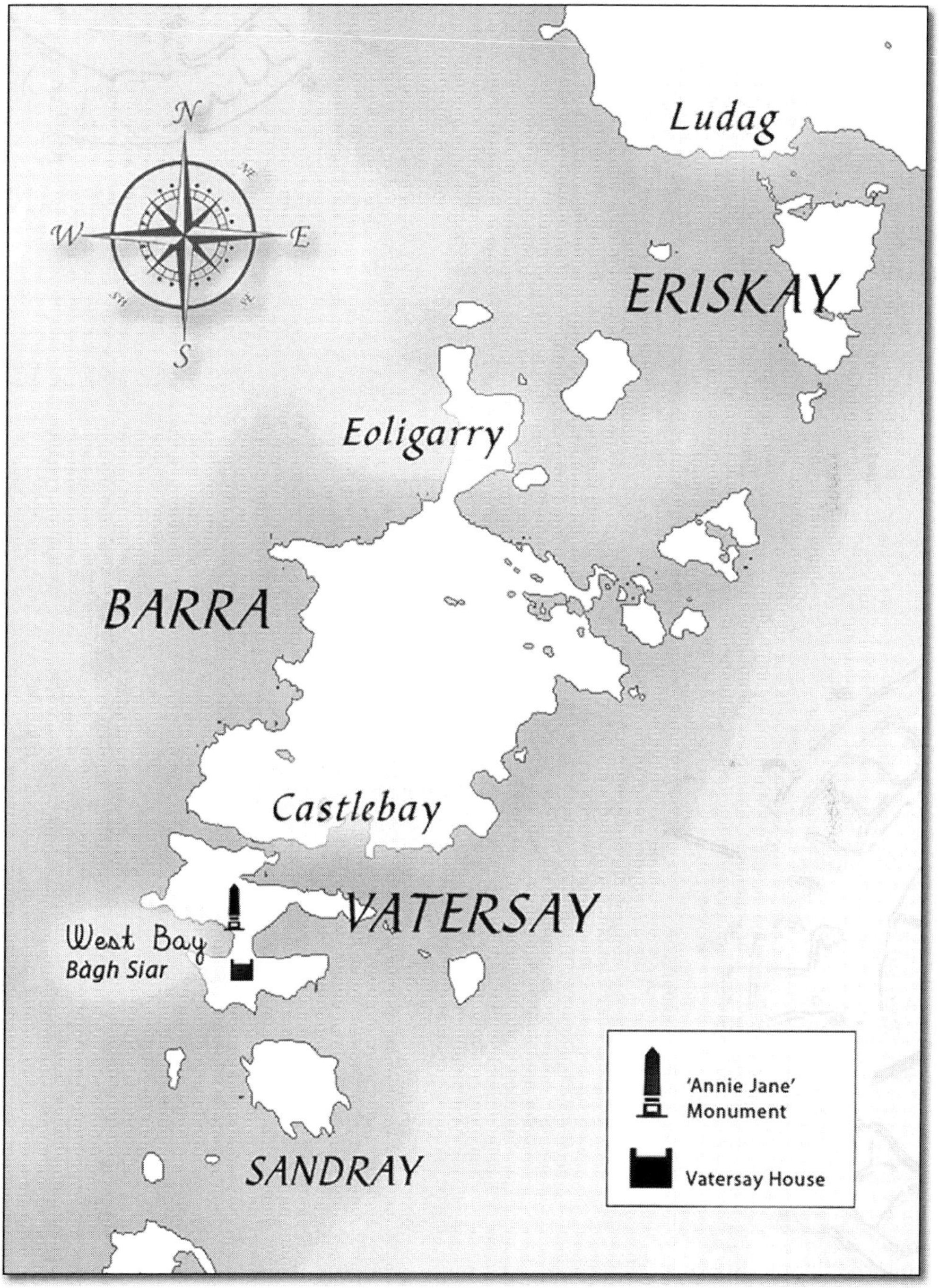
N
E
S
W
Ludag
ERISKAY
Eoligarry
BARRA
Castlebay
VATERSAY
West Bay
Bàgh Siar
SANDRAY
'Annie Jane' Monument
Vatersay House

Crew agreement

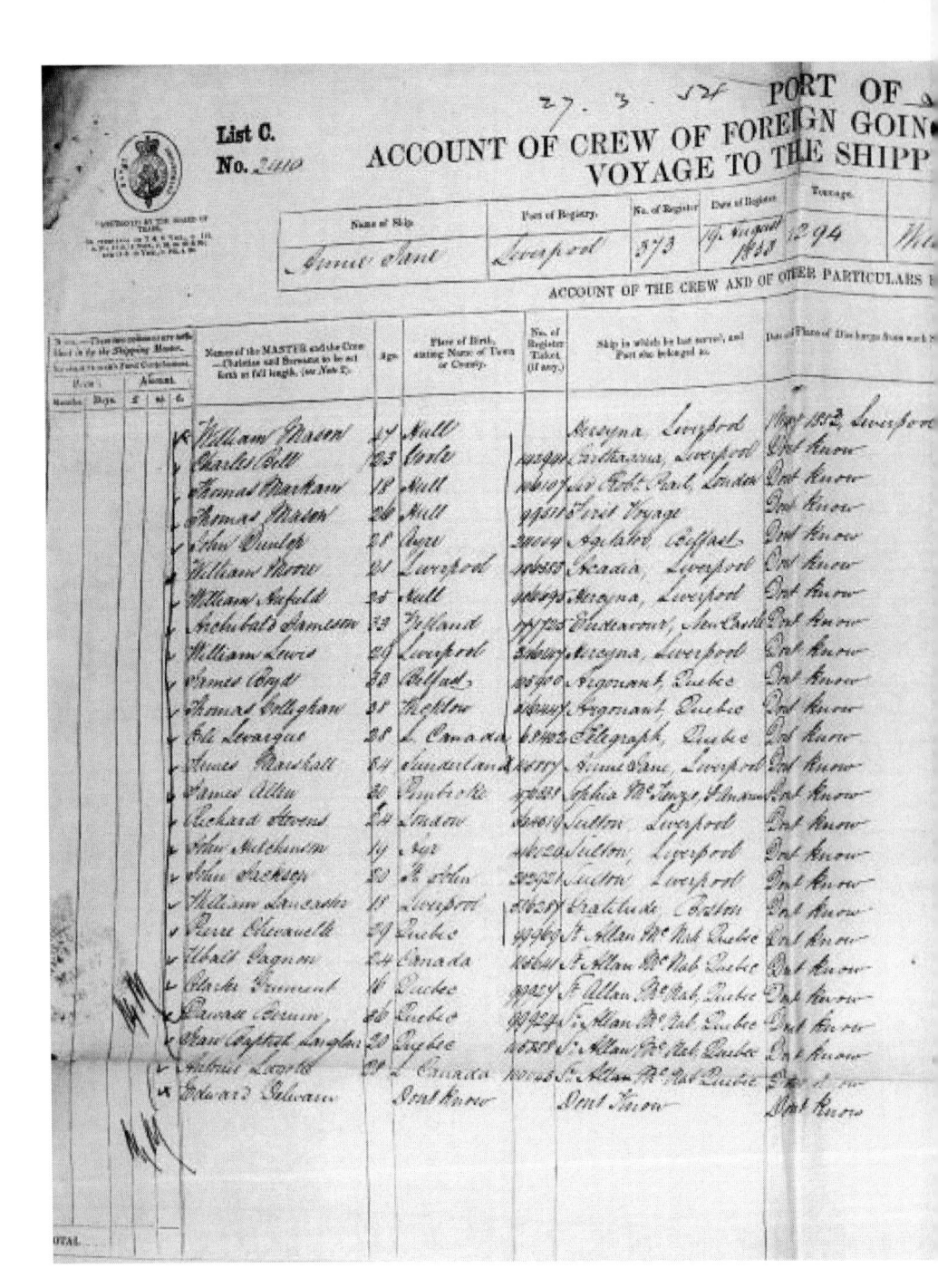

Crew Agreement, which gives the age, register number, previous ship, date of joining the 'Annie Jane', if discharged or believed drowned. With thanks to The National archives.

© National Archives

, TO BE DELIVERED AT THE END OF THE
STER AT THE ABOVE PORT.

Master.	No. of his Certificate.	First Port of Departure.	Date of Departure.	Final Port of Destination in the United Kingdom.	Date of Arrival.
...	51585	Liverpool	21 August 1853	Liverpool	28 Sept 1853

AW, IN RESPECT OF THE ABOVE-MENTIONED VOYAGE.

Place.	In what Capacity Engaged, and, if Mate, No. of Certificate (if any).	Date, Place, and Cause of Death, or Leaving this Ship.			Report of Character (see Note 4.)			Amount of Forfeitures to Owner, under 7 & 8 V., c. 112.	Amount of Fines payable to Shipping Master.	Shipping Office, on Home No. (if any).
		Date.	Place.	Cause (see Note 5).	Ability	Conduct		£ s. d.	£ s. d.	
Liverpool	Master	28 Sept 53	Barra	Shipwrecked						
Liverpool	Mate	28 Sept 53	Barra	Believed to be drowned	V					
Liverpool	Seaman	28 Sept 53	Barra	Shipwrecked	G	G				
Liverpool	Carpenter	28 Sept 53	Barra	Shipwrecked	G	G				
Liverpool	Boatswain	28 Sept 53	Barra	Believed to be drowned	V					
Liverpool	Ordinary Seaman	28 Sept 53	Barra	Shipwrecked	G	G				
Liverpool	Steward	28 Sept 53	Barra	Shipwrecked	G	G				
Liverpool	Cook	11 Oct 53	Liverpool	Paid Off	V.G	V.G				
Liverpool	Carpenter's Mate	28 Sept 53	Barra	Shipwrecked	G	G				
Liverpool	Seaman	28 Sept 53	Barra	Shipwrecked	G	G				
Liverpool	Boatswain and Seaman	28 Sept 53	Barra	Believed to be drowned	V					
Liverpool	Seaman	28 Sept 53	Barra	Believed to be drowned	V					
Liverpool	Seaman	28 Sept 53	Barra	Shipwrecked	G	G				
Liverpool	Seaman	11 Oct 53	Liverpool	Paid Off	V.G	V.G				
Liverpool	Seaman	11 Oct 53	Liverpool	Paid Off	V.G	V.G				
Liverpool	Seaman	11 Oct 53	Liverpool	Paid Off	V.G	V.G				
Liverpool	Seaman	11 Oct 53	Liverpool	Paid Off	V.G	V.G				
Liverpool	Seaman	28 Sept 53	Barra	Shipwrecked	G	G				
Liverpool	Seaman	28 Sept 53	Barra	Believed to be drowned	V					
Liverpool	Seaman	28 Sept 53	Barra	Believed to be drowned	V					
Liverpool	Seaman	11 Oct 53	Liverpool	Paid Off	V.G	V.G				
Liverpool	Seaman	11 Oct 53	Liverpool	Paid Off	V.G	V.G				
Liverpool	Seaman	11 Oct 53	Liverpool	Paid Off	V.G	V.G				
Liverpool	Seaman	11 Oct 53	Liverpool	Paid Off	V.G	V.G				
Liverpool	Seaman	11 Oct 53	Liverpool	Paid Off	V.G	V.G				

Typical Sail Plan of a 19th Century Sailing Ship

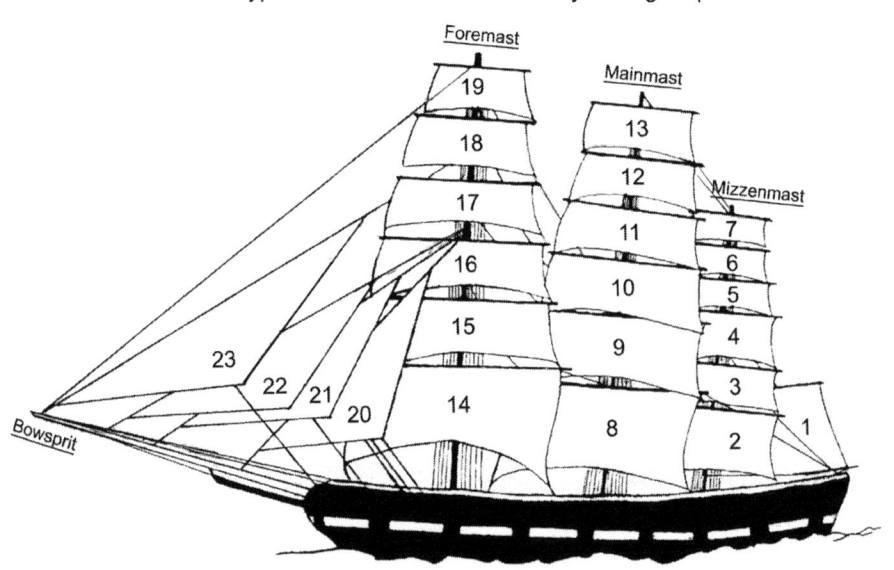

(1) Spanker or Driver (2) Crossjack (3) Mizzen Lower Topsail (4) Mizzen Upper Topsail (5) Mizzen Topgallent Sail (6) Mizzen Royal (7) Mizzen Skysail (8) Mainsail (9) Main Lower Topsail (10) Main Upper Topsail (11) Main Topgallent Sail (12) Main Royal (13) Main Skysail (14) Foresail (15) Fore Lower Topsail (16) Fore Upper Topsail (17) Fore Topgallent Sail (18) Fore Royal (19) Fore Skysail (20) Jib (21) Inner Jib (22) Outer Jib (23) Flying Jib

Monument
Courtesy of Allan Murray.

XIII

Monument Inscription
Courtesy of Allan Murray.

Robert Macfie

Robert Macfie, who commissioned and paid for the monument to the shipwreck.

Courtesy of Appin of Yesteryear. http://oldappin.com/

Vatersay beach
Courtesy of Allan Murray.

Vatersay house today
Courtesy of Allan Murray

Vatersay house internal
Courtesy of Allan Murray.

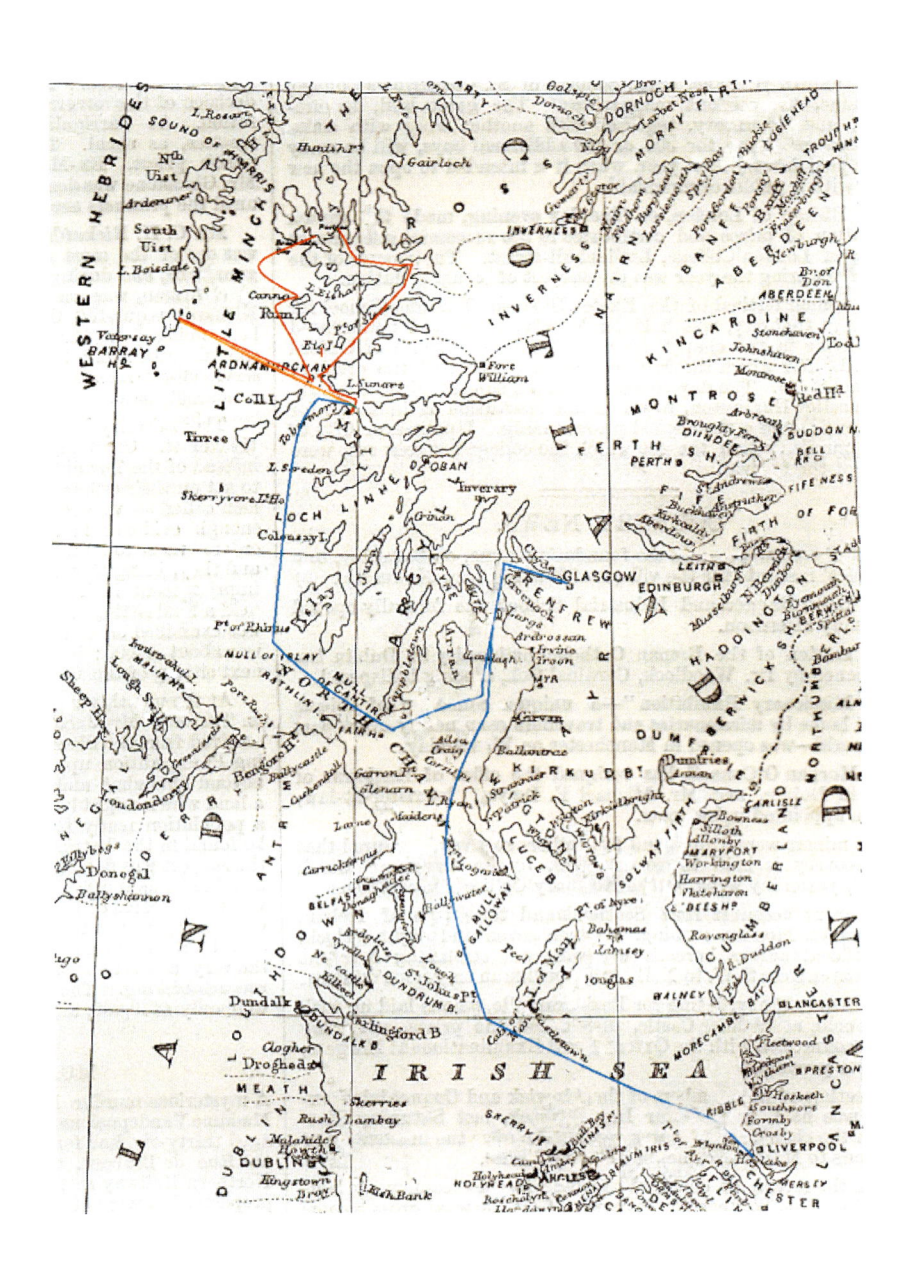

Journey back

Route the survivors took on the way back to Liverpool.

With thanks to Rebecca Murray.

1868 Map, Illustrated London News.

Journey
Approximate route the 'Annie Jane' took on the first and second voyages.
With thanks to Rebecca Murray.
1868 Map, Illustrated London News.

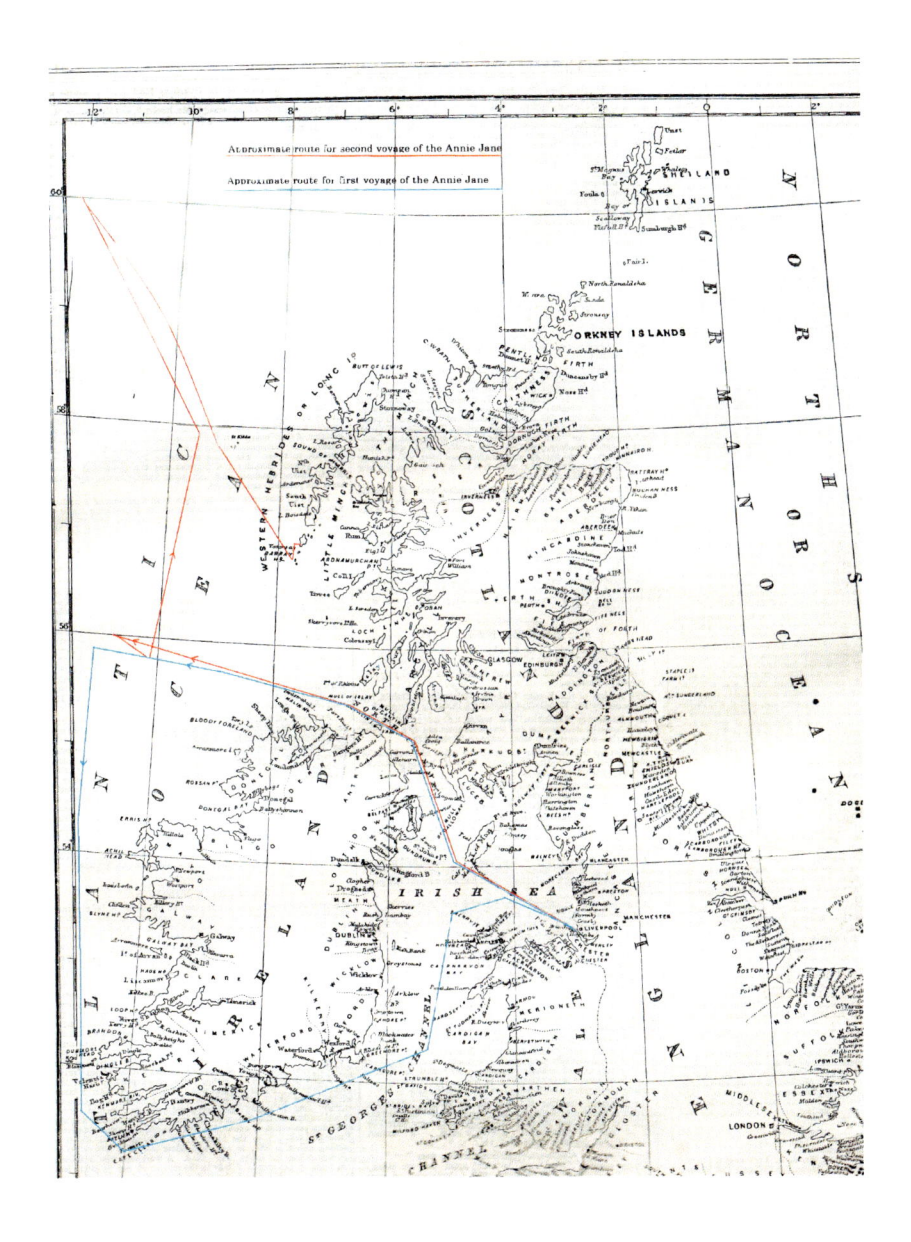

XIX

Alexander Macrae gravestone

Kilchuiman Burial Ground, Fort Augustus.

In affectionate remembrance of Finlay MacRae, Miller of Fort Augustus who died on the 30th Jan 1865 aged 65 years and of his wife Janet Dingwall who died on the 11th Aug 1881 aged 75 years. Also of their 3 sons John of the 79th Highlanders died in 1855 aged 25 years. Alexander drowned by the wreck of the Annie Jane in 1854 aged 23 years. Ewen died in 1848 aged 7 years. This stone was erected by the surviving members of the family.

Courtesy of Allan Murray.

Prologue

In the millennium year I travelled with a companion on a walking holiday down through the island chain that is the remote group of islands called the Western Isles or Outer Hebrides. We crossed from the Isle of Harris to North Uist, travelling southwards through Benbecula and South Uist and finally taking a small ferry to arrive on the island of Barra. As usual I bought a book of circular walks and tried to do as many as possible while exploring the area. I noticed one on the neighbouring island of Vatersay, which had recently been joined by a causeway to the larger island of Barra. This took in some beaches and an abandoned blackhouse village, and finally brought us back to a monument close to where we had parked our car. It was one of those idyllic summer days that make you glad to be alive. As we crossed the crescent of golden sand that makes up the beach to climb our way up over the dunes to the monument, and finish the walk, the sunlight danced upon the surface of the sea. We paused in front of the monument, a tall granite obelisk, and read the inscription:

Prologue

> ON 28th SEP. 1853
> THE SHIP ANNIE JANE
> WITH EMIGRANTS
> FROM LIVERPOOL TO QUEBEC
> WAS TOTALLY WRECKED
> IN THIS BAY
> AND THREEFOURTHS
> OF THE CREW AND PASSENGERS
> NUMBERING ABOUT 350
> MEN WOMEN AND CHILDREN WERE DROWNED
> AND THEIR BODIES INTERRED HERE
> AND THE SEA GAVE UP THE DEAD
> WHICH WERE IN IT REV XX 13

It was intriguing: coming from Lewis, one of the islands that make up the Outer Hebridean group, I was puzzled that I had not heard of an historical event with such a substantial loss of life in my area of the world. Looking round that peaceful place, it was hard to believe that something traumatic had ever occurred there. Walking away from the monument I turned to my companion and declared that I was going to find out the story behind the tragedy.

I discovered there had been one booklet written about the event by a writer called Bob Charnley, published in 1992; it was out of print but I managed to track down a copy, just 34 pages long, entitled 'Shipwrecked on Vatersay'. The story it told intrigued me even more: a new ship; an aborted, disastrous first voyage; a fractious legal case to try to recover passage money; reluctant passengers who had to take passage again because it was that or starve in Liverpool.

Then the second voyage, a near mutiny, and the Captain, William Mason, holding the passengers off with a revolver: '*Quebec or the bottom*', he said. The carnage and chaos of the shipwreck, and up to 350 dead strewn all along that beach, and the 102 survivors being given reluctant hospitality on the small, remote island of Vatersay; some of them for up to a fortnight, being told to mind the pigs, as they slept in the sty. Then came the looting of the wreck and the bodies, the trip back to civilization, with some of the survivors taking a month to return to their homes. Subsequently the public outcry, then an official inquiry in Liverpool, and the controversial result.

Then this accidental monument, not put up by government, emigrant organisation, or relatives of the deceased, but out of the goodness of one individual. Without it, the disaster would have been forgotten.

So here is the untold story of the 'Annie Jane'. During the research for this book, two surviving eyewitness accounts were discovered: one from a 'ragged school' orphan, being sent to Canada to begin a new life, published in late 1853 in the Ragged School Magazine. The other was from the perspective of a nineteen-year-old gentleman with all the attitudes of his times, Marc Ami, a Cabin class passenger, whose memoir was written in 1856, but not published until 1891 in Quebec. 'Le Naufrage de l' "Annie Jane"' is here translated and published in English for the first time.

1

An Introduction to the 'Annie Jane'

1853 was a busy year at the Cape Cove shipyard in Quebec: four vessels were built, one after the other. The two largest, the 1,294 ton 'Annie Jane' and the 1,237 ton 'Argonaut', were for the Atlantic trade. They were almost identical, with the 'Annie Jane' being slightly larger by just a few inches, and were being built by Henry Dinning and William Henry Baldwin, two well-established Canadian shipbuilders. Their Cape Cove shipyard was one of the best in Quebec, covering a large area with two floating docks, houses, wharfs, slips, booms and beaches.

The 'Annie Jane' was commissioned and built for two Canadian businessmen, George Burns Symes and David Douglas Young, and was safely launched on 27th April 1853 and then loaded with a full cargo of timber by the Canadian timber merchants Leavy and Co. to sail to Liverpool. She was to make her maiden voyage without internal bulkheads or fittings, to maximize the lumber that could be carried. An article in the Quebec Morning Chronicle on 3rd June, under *Exports*, shows that she carried: 60 tons of oak; 40 tons of elm; 240 tons of red pine; 1200 tons of white pine; 5200 standard pine deals; 4 million pipe staves and 9 million barrel staves.

In the same paper is an advertisement for passage to Liverpool with superior accommodation for Cabin passengers (First Class), with a Captain Watts in command, departing about 24th June. The crossing seems to have been without incident, with the ship arriving in Liverpool in mid-July. Then they would have begun the total refitting internally as an emigrant ship: a common practice at the time.

However, when she was inspected by Lloyd's of London after her refit they refused their certification. Without this, the ship could not be insured. The keel had been secured with part-iron bolts and then copper sheathing was installed below the water line to protect the hull from worm and marine growth; the fastenings of the sheathing were all copper fittings. The shipbuilders at the yard in Quebec were unaware of the concept of electrolysis: with copper, iron bolts and a solution of salt water there would have been an instant electrolytic reaction between the copper and the iron. The part-iron bolts would have rusted at an extremely rapid rate, with the result that there would have been serious implications for the structural integrity of the vessel.

Deciding to cut their losses, the Canadian owners put her up for sale 'as is'. Traditionally, a broom would have been hoisted up to the top of the masthead to advertise that she was for sale. An advertisement was also placed in *Gores Liverpool General Advertiser* on 14th July 1853.

The firm acting as agent for the ship's owners was called Holderness and Chilton, but the partnership had been dissolved in 1847, with Thomas Hunter Holderness remaining as sole proprietor. He saw an opportunity to acquire the ship for a competitive price. The ship was moved to a dry dock, the graving dock in Liverpool, for the keel bolts to be replaced by yellow metal bolts[1] and the fitting-out to be completed. The ship formally changed hands on 19th August 1853, with ownership being transferred from George Burns Symes and David Douglas Young to Thomas Hunter Holderness, with the traditional allocation of 64 shares to him. He also agreed to purchase the 'Argonaut', under construction in Quebec.

An Introduction to the 'Annie Jane'

The 'Annie Jane' was then re-examined by Lloyd's and was classed as A1 for seven years – the highest grade possible for ships built in the colonies.

For Sale the New Ship Annie Jane

Built by Messrs Baldwin and Dinning at Quebec

of the following dimensions

Length 179 feet

Breadth 31 feet, 4-10ths

Depth 22 feet, 8-10ths

She measures 1145 tons O.M.
and by the new rule 1120 tons, exclusive of 174 tons of poop which runs to the main mast. The ship was nearly 12 months in hand, has not been surpassed in workmanship and fidelity of structure by any vessel from St Lawrence.

She is copper fastened including centre keel bolts which prevented her being marked (Part Iron Bolts) by Lloyd's Registry.

The cabin is fitted and twixtdeck laid. Parties interested in colonial shipping are particularly invited to inspect this vessel.

For particulars apply on board or to
Holderness and Chilton

An Introduction to the 'Annie Jane'

She was to all appearances a well-constructed ship, triple-decked with three masts; her ceilings and beams were constructed of oak with her weather decks of tamarack, and the hull sheathed with elm and oak bands.

Valued for insurance purposes at £9700 sterling (equivalent to £582,000 in 2017), she was built to carry cargo back and forth over the Atlantic, but more importantly, she was first and foremost a people carrier, one of the many emigrant ships of her day. Emigration was a lucrative trade with thousands of Irish, Scottish and English emigrants making their way to the New World, driven by land-hunger, famine, poor social conditions and wages, and all with a burning desire to improve their lives and the future of their dependants. The return journey from Quebec to Liverpool could be supplemented by a cargo of timber as the demand for lumber in European markets from Canada's huge forests was insatiable at the time. If things went well, a ship full of passengers and cargo could clear most of the cost of its construction in a few return voyages.

The steerage (or third class) passengers for the first Atlantic crossing of the 'Annie Jane' as an emigrant ship were a very diverse group of people. Most of the emigrants were Irish – part of the great exodus that had begun with the famine of 1845. The majority departed for the New World using the Liverpool to North America route. There were 100 tradesmen from Glasgow and the west coast of Scotland who had all been recruited and booked in one group on the 'Annie Jane' by the emigrant agents Hamilton Brothers and Co. of Glasgow, to go out and work on the Canadian railway infrastructure. They were a mixture of joiners, blacksmiths, mechanics, engineers and labourers. Some of the better-off men had also booked passage for their wives and children, with the rest waiting till they could afford to send for them. There was also a large number of tradesmen recruited in England, and one group of eleven orphans from ragged schools in London who were being sent to Canada to begin new lives. A number of women were travelling with children to go and join their husbands, who had gone out to North America to prepare a home for them.

The Scots tradesmen were going out to Canada to work on the following railways that were under, or scheduled for, construction: the Quebec and Richmond Railway, 100 miles;

the Montreal and Portland Railway, 31 miles; the Prescott and Bytown Railway, 54 miles; the Toronto and Simcoe Railway, 66 miles; the Great Wester, from Hamilton to Windsor, 180 miles. As for the Irish, labourers were required for railway building and the lumber trade. Some 20,000 to 30,000 were required in the lumber trade alone, earning between £2.00 and £3.00 per month, with board. Skilled lumbermen earned between £3.10 shillings and £4.00 per month.

First (or Cabin) class contained an eight-strong group from the French-Canadian Missionary Society led by a minister, the Rev. J. Vernier, who had been sent on a recruitment drive to Europe to find French-speaking protestant missionaries and teachers. He had recruited Mr. and Mrs Kempf, who were travelling with their two children, and another three individuals: Marc Ami, Jean Francois Cornu and Lammert Van Buren. Also in Cabin class were Captain Charles Rose, RN, and his wife Miriam, who were returning to their home in Quebec. There, Captain Rose was to take charge of Thomas Holderness' second vessel, 'Argonaut', which was just completing construction at Quebec.

There were two more Cabin class passengers, a Mr. John Morgan and a Mr. John Potter Cattely, who appears to have been the servant for Captain and Mrs Rose; he was a thirteen-year-old boy from the north of England, who was probably travelling out to Quebec to take a position under Captain Rose on the 'Argonaut'. There is no exact figure for the total number of passengers and crew aboard the 'Annie Jane' for her first voyage to Quebec, but it must have been over 470 passengers and crew.

To provide some light and a little ventilation along the side of the ship, glass portholes were inserted every seven feet. They were about six inches in diameter. These were the only source of natural light for the tweendeck, except for two skylights set into the main deck. In rough seas or when the vessel rolled severely, the portholes would have to be closed and the skylights secured. The almost 400-strong community of strangers that comprised the steerage class had the whole length of the tweendeck for accommodation. Very little natural light arrived at this area and safety lamps were lit at all times. It was one of the apprentices' jobs to go down twice a day to clean the lamps and fill them with oil. Most of the lamps were extinguished late in the evening and relit at 6.00 a.m., with just enough left flickering to allow a faint illumination for those unfortunate people who had to get up in the night. No naked flames were allowed, smoking being banned completely below decks. Fire was a real and ever-present hazard aboard wooden ships.

The bunks on emigrant ships were described as looking like coffins and just as comfortable, being made of undressed pine boards. They ran the full length of the ship in two tiers, with the lower tier being raised a foot from the deck to allow for ventilation. Passengers had to provide a roll-up mattress and their own bedding, items which were for sale at shops around the port in Liverpool eager to meet the last-minute needs of the emigrants. No record exists for the dimensions of the berths on the 'Annie Jane'. They were probably 6 feet long by 3 feet 4 inches wide, with just about enough room for two adults to lie side-by-side. Those seem to have been the standard dimensions on most other emigrant ships. One of the single men on the ship stated that he shared his bunk with one unrelated man. Bunks placed transversely or across the ship were extremely rare as they caused the passengers a great deal more discomfort in bad weather.

Passengers could hang blankets around their berths, and most people did, to give them some illusion of privacy. There were no ladders to climb up to the top bunks, and for the heavy or less dexterous it was difficult at the best of times; in a moving ship it became almost impossible. Dismounting from the top bunk was always a challenge. Passengers could not sit up as the deckhead was too close above. The minimum height between decks was only six feet, so they had to swing their legs out and lower themselves face-down while they groped with feet for some sort of solid object. It was quite common for there to be shouts of anger and alarm, as a person in the top bunk missed their footing and stood on someone sleeping in the bunk below. For this reason, there was always a rush and a demand to be allocated a bottom bunk – the young very often swapping with their elders.

In the centre of the passenger deck between the rows of bunks, there were tables with high sides (called fiddles) to stop items from falling off in bad weather. On either side of each table there was a bench seat firmly secured to the deck; there were not enough seating places for all the passengers to sit down at the same time. At various points in this area the travelling chests and provisions of the passengers were piled up. These were meant to be lashed down at all times, but as passengers continually accessed them to retrieve items, this was not always the case. Sometimes they would break free and fly from side to side in rough weather, with the attendant risk to life, limb and possessions.

On emigrant ships in this period most emigrants were fleeing an impoverished existence; they were passengers who had scraped the fare of £3 together and had no money left over for any of the necessities that made life aboard ship more bearable, let alone the luxuries. Put something down, be careless with belongings, turn back – and it was gone. There was nowhere to buy a replacement. Depending on how moral a person was, it was borrow, steal or buy, maybe even buy your own article back, at an inflated price. People learnt quickly to be careful with possessions and to mark them in a way that was unmistakable. Disputes over ownership of items on emigrant ships were quite common; at one point on the second voyage a fight broke out on the 'Annie Jane' over a stolen handkerchief.

There were two portable bulkheads across the ship that could be dismantled and moved fore and aft as required, depending on the composition of the passenger group. Following the convention of the time, on the 'Annie Jane' the steerage passenger deck was divided up into three areas in an attempt to segregate the passengers. At the after-end of the vessel were the single women. Midships was the territory of the married couples and children. Forwards towards the bow, in the most uncomfortable area, were all the single men. The Merchant Shipping Act of 1852 stated:

All the unmarried male passengers of the age of 14 years and upwards shall, to the satisfaction of the Emigration Officer at the port of clearance, be berthed in the forward part of the ship in a compartment divided off from the space appropriated to the other passengers by a substantial and well secured bulkhead.

Bulkheads were louvred to assist ventilation on the ship, scandalously allowing men to peek through the gaps.

The poop deck was unusually long – almost reaching the

mainmast. It was divided into an after-cabin and a fore-cabin, with Cabin class passengers and ship's officers travelling in the after part in relatively spacious cabins with a communal mess room. Captain Rose had his own private water closet and saloon. Second class passengers were in shared cabins in the forward part of the poop with a bulkhead dividing the two areas. The Cabin class area was only for the use of first class passengers and the ship's officers; it was strictly off-limits to all others.

The main exits from the steerage level accommodation were situated forward of the poop deck. From there, passengers could exit onto the weather (or main) deck or make their way up the stairs to the poop deck, where the ship's wheel was located.

Cabin class passengers could access the poop deck at will, but steerage passengers were meant to ask for permission before coming onto the poop deck.

Cabin class passengers did not have to worry about provisions or bedding as these were supplied for them. Their food was cooked and served in the mess by stewards. One cook was delegated exclusively for their needs, and they shared meals with the Captain, his First Mate, Second Mate and Surgeon.

Unless they were in large family groups, most people formed themselves into messes of various sizes where they would take turns in cooking their rations. On the 'Annie Jane', the galley was situated halfway along the weather deck. Inside were five boilers capable of heating 380 quarts (432 litres) of water. There were hotplates with nine feet of cooking space as well as a range of different ovens. This was above the legal minimum, but still less than adequate with so many people wanting to cook at the same time. Steerage passengers could also access the galley from below decks. A small number of second class passengers and some crew had cabins in the deckhouse which contained the galley.

Each berth had a number on it which the passengers had to give to receive their daily allocation of provisions from the Bo's'un, sailmaker or ship's carpenter. The person in charge for the day had a set of scales and was supposed to weigh out all the rations, which became a difficult and almost impossible job in rough weather. Each adult passenger on the ship was entitled to a weekly ration of five lbs of oatmeal, two and a half lbs of ship's biscuit, one lb of flour, two lbs of rice, half lb of sugar, half lb of molasses and two ounces of tea.

Rather than depend on the ship's rations, of dubious quality, many of the steerage passengers provided their own provisions for the voyage, normally stored in barrels or sealed jars.

In the Glasgow Herald of 25th July 1853 is an article, *Hints to Emigrants*[2]. It is possible the west coast emigrants on the 'Annie Jane' had read this in preparation for the voyage:

> **Utensils required. If Scotch: a porridge pot, kettle, coffee pot, or a strong iron quart pot, would do to cook anything, but must be made better than those commonly sold, and made to hold two or three quarts, plate, cups, knife, fork, tea and table spoons, spurtle, wooden spoon, strong bags for flour, oatmeal, rice &c., &c. – a number of bags are required, as a week's rations are given out at once, cork screw, mirror, small knife, salt and pepper dish, hook nails, twine, rope.**
>
> **Eatables. Take plenty of jams and jellies, onions, ginger, nutmeg, cinnamon, sago, pease meal, ham, cheese, spirits, wine, ale and porter.**

Porridge made with oatmeal was very much the staple diet of the emigrants as it was quick and easy to make, and nutritious. Water was stored in wooden casks: at the beginning of the voyage the water would be fresh, but as the journey progressed it would become coloured as the wood stained it. On the 'Annie Jane', the casks would have probably been new and unseasoned. This made the problem worse than usual, with the water becoming more acrid and tainted as the journey progressed. Water was rationed and issued twice a day and the emigrants on the 'Annie Jane' were entitled to three quarts a day, almost three and a half litres. This did not include any water needed for cooking provisions but was only for their personal use. The crew had a small hand pump to remove the water from the casks.

And now to the delicate matter of the water closets: for the steerage passengers there were six, three on either side of the galley. There was a receptacle underneath every seat, all interconnected with a discharge pipe over the side. A cistern was on top of the galley. Lead pipes ran from it with valves fitted so the toilets could be flushed. Passengers were encouraged to use the side the vessel was heeling to, for obvious reasons. It was normally the job of one of the youngest stewards to unblock the discharge pipe when required. In rough weather, with a deck awash, the toilets could not be accessed, and the passengers had to make do as best they could by going to the tweendeck and finding whatever discreet corner they could in the cargo hold. Another issue that might seem strange to the modern reader is that women did not want to be seen going to a toilet as people would know what they were doing! Such was the delicate, refined and repressed nature of society at the time.

For those who would not leave the lower deck, they found what privacy they could. A family member would screen them with blankets. They could use buckets with lids or urinate straight into the bilges, the area below the lower deck. This became one of the major problems on the 'Annie Jane'. As with every emigrant ship when severe weather was encountered, days would pass with the steerage passengers shut below without access to the upper deck. With the excessive movement of the vessel the buckets used would fall over, or eventually have to be carried up the steps, overfull, slopping and spilling, to the top deck to be emptied over the side.

The steerage passengers would live in that claustrophobic, poorly ventilated space in the overwhelming stench of urine, faeces, vomit, oil lamp fumes and body odour with a pool of effluent washing from side to side of the lower deck, especially during stormy conditions, till it made its way to the bilges down below, where over time it might acquire a greater degree of potency. Old sailors were said to love the aroma of a pungent bilge, as they knew that the smellier it was, the less sea water was entering: the tighter the ship the more it stank. It should be remembered, however, that while conditions aboard a ship may seem harsh to us, if properly organised, life aboard an emigrant vessel was probably no worse than in the type of cottages and slums that many of the emigrants had escaped from. Possibly they even had more food than some of the more impoverished passengers had been used to in the past. In winter a ship making the Atlantic passage was legally required to carry provisions for all the passengers adequate for 80 days, in summer 70 days.

An Introduction to the 'Annie Jane'

Personal hygiene was rudimentary. It was not unusual for passengers to just wash their faces and hands and to stay in the same clothes for the duration of the voyage. Passengers coming from a rural background had very different standards from city-dwellers. On one vessel full of Highland emigrants the steerage passengers were accused of using the plates they ate off to defecate on.[3]

The Cabin class passengers, who had paid £10 for their tickets, had, for their exclusive use, water closets in the poop area, which discharged straight over the side.

During good weather the ship's surgeon would get all the steerage passengers up on deck and fumigate the lower decks by burning a mixture of tar and sulphur. The crew would also dry-scrape the lower deck clean. Captain Mason, the Master of the 'Annie Jane', temporarily allowed steerage passengers on the poop deck while the fumigation of the accommodation was ongoing. Sometimes the passengers had to be forced out of their berths, especially if they were suffering from sea-sickness. The surgeon would begin the fumigation to encourage passengers to get up. Soon even the most reluctant would get out of their bunks, and head to the top deck for fresh air.

The 'Annie Jane' carried five boats. In the event of an emergency that required total evacuation, this was a totally inadequate number. One longboat was on top of the galley deckhouse; three boats were tied down between the fore-end (break) of the poop and the mainmast. The last one, the ship's gig – the boat used if anybody required to go ashore – was beside a set of davits on the starboard side between the mainmast and the foremast. As was the custom at the time, the upturned boats were well-secured to prevent them filling up with water and getting damaged in heavy seas. There were only two lifebuoys on the ship.

A Captain had very little control of what cargo was loaded on his ship as this was arranged by the owner or the agent, though final discretion and responsibility rested on the First Mate. Certain items, including horses, cattle, guano, animal hides and explosives, were forbidden on emigrant ships. Cargo was mainly stored in the lower holds and tweendeck. On the 'Annie Jane's' first voyage to Canada there were 200 tons of bar iron, 200 tons of pig iron, a quantity of soap in boxes, 30 tons of rice and paper, 205 tons of railroad iron,

An Introduction to the 'Annie Jane'

twenty tons of sheet iron, some machinery, 80 tons of hemp rope, a quantity of tea and pepper, 25 tons of carriage springs, a four-ton boiler, and a large consignment of yellow metal bolts desperately required by the shipyards of Quebec.

It was estimated that the 'Annie Jane' had 1100 tons of cargo aboard, which left her with only 10 feet of freeboard (the measurement between the waterline and the main deck). This was not a big safety margin to cross the North Atlantic so late in the year, but this was well before the introduction, in 1875, of the Plimsoll line – the beginning of huge advances in ship safety.

Unusually, the 'Annie Jane' did not have a below-decks chain locker for the anchor cables. The cable was flaked on deck, with 150 fathoms in length on either side of the foredeck. One end was attached to a windlass, which, with a capstan, was the mechanism for raising and lowering the anchor. There were two bilge pumps on the main deck just aft of the foremast that two men could operate, one at either end of the pump. On a rough sea it was not a task that any individual could keep up for a long period of time.

On her first voyage from Liverpool the crew of the 'Annie Jane' was made up of a mixture of French-Canadian and British crewmen. There were 42 in total, comprising the Captain, William Mason, Surgeon John Page Julina, First Mate Mr. Bell, Second Mate Thomas Markham, Bo's'un, carpenter, sailmaker, two cooks, two stewards, 26 seamen and four apprentices. Seventeen of the seamen were French-Canadians and six of them could speak English reasonably well. For the second voyage of the 'Annie Jane', another six seamen were recruited. Among the seamen were four carpenter/seamen who were unpaid, working their passage back to Quebec. Captain Mason did not have much of a choice about whom he employed; with the increase in international trade and commerce, there was always a chronic shortage of seamen available for hire in Liverpool.

In the year 1850, the nearest year for which figures are available, there were 240,000 sailors employed by the British Mercantile Marine, as well as 70,000 in the Royal Navy.

When desperately short of hands, a shipmaster could resort to 'crimps' who would ply individuals with alcohol and carry them aboard a vessel just as it was about to depart. They then had no choice but to sign on. This does not appear to be the case with the

15

An Introduction to the 'Annie Jane'

'Annie Jane', as all but one of the crew were registered seamen. The average age of the seamen on the 'Annie Jane' was 24. Nowadays we would not consider this an experienced crew, but during that period a seagoing career would begin in the early teens. It was said that by the time a seaman reached 40 he would be prematurely aged and only fit for retirement.

Accommodation for merchant seamen, even in a brand-new ship, was always very basic. As far as status was concerned, they were on the bottom rung. The position and quality of their sleeping and living quarters had not changed for hundreds of years and the vast majority of the crew were crammed in to the forecastle, or fo'c'sle, deckhouse if fitted, in the forward part of the ship. They slept in two-tier bunks in one of the wettest, most uncomfortable positions to be in a ship. In contrast to the steerage passengers, there was a demand for the top bunk as it tended to be the driest. There was no room for tables and chairs so the tops of their sea chests, which contained all their worldly possessions, were substituted for both these items; there were normally lashing points on the deck to facilitate the tying down of the sea chests. In the fo'c'sle, the sailors slept, ate, dressed and washed.

The only consolation was that they were away from the officer class and passengers, as far apart as they could physically manage on a ship. At least they had a place to relax and gossip about events among the steerage passengers, and discuss the personal qualities and parentage of the ship's officers. From the fo'c'sle, they could access other areas of the ship only along the weather deck, whatever the extremities of wind and wave. In poor conditions, lifelines were rigged fore and aft.

Once a sailor had signed on to a vessel, jumping ship could earn him a prison term of up to three months. There was a system of registration in place to discourage sailors from deserting: each seaman had a unique number, which he had to give on joining a new ship. Upon desertion, the Master of the ship would enter it into the ship's log and then a certificate of desertion would be forwarded to the Registrar General in London. The law would eventually catch up with the offender when he tried to obtain employment again. Any seaman giving a false name, or misrepresenting the last ship he was on, was also deducted £5 from his wages as well as enduring whatever legal proceedings he had to face. Once the voyage had begun, the working day for seamen was four hours on, four off, except for the two dog watches. These were only two hours long, from four to six in the afternoon and from six to eight in the evening. Their purpose was to allow for the variation of night watches so that no one was stuck in the same schedule. At any time you could be roused from your sleep by a cry of *'All hands on deck!'* when a crisis occurred that needed more than one watch. The seamen were divided into two groups: the First Mate's Port and the Second Mate's Starboard watch. The exceptions to this were the cooks, the carpenter, stewards and sailmaker who worked a twelve-hour day shift and were called 'the idlers' by the ordinary seamen just for that reason. Though when the call came for all hands, with the exception of the stewards, they acted like everyone else. Many of them were skilled seamen in their own right.

We might today look at the incomprehensible mass of ropes that make up the rigging of a tall ship. But in that period the rigging on every ship followed an internationally accepted standard, so experienced sailors transferring from one ship to another would 'know the ropes'.

Food was basic, consisting almost entirely of inferior cuts of salt pork or beef, which at most times were hard and unpalatable. Freshly baked bread would be available at the beginning of the voyage until the flour got mouldy. Then it was ship's biscuit/hardtack, which you had to soften in water before you could even attempt to eat it. It was notorious for its toughness.

At all times living quarters were foul and suffocating. In bad weather, the water that was washed about the weather deck would enter the fo'c'sle, going into all the corners, creating a permanent smell of dampness. This was not helped by the seamen going to bed 'all standing' (fully dressed), sometimes in damp clothes, so as to be ready to turn out at a moment's notice. Below, everything was damp in the winter months and stayed that way. Precious possessions tarnished and rusted, fabrics mildewed and rotted away. In rough weather in the fo'c'sle there would be the constant noise and crash of the waves as the ship pounded through the seas, with the creaking and groaning of timbers as the vessel's structure 'worked' (or flexed) to meet the demands of crashing through Atlantic breakers.

An Introduction to the 'Annie Jane'

Merchant seamen might have been full of tales of the joys of a maritime life as they celebrated the end of a voyage at the nearest inn. However, it's doubtful that they experienced much comfort on a ship journeying to North America in the later months of the year. Very few did at that time.

---

1. Yellow metal bolts were of an alloy construction.
2. British Newspaper Archive, Copyright British Library.
3. Harper, Marjory, *Adventurers and Exiles: The Great Scottish Exodus*, Profile Books, 2004.

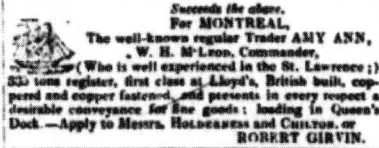

An Introduction to the 'Annie Jane'

> For SALE,
> The splendid new Ship ANNIE JANE,
> Built by Messrs. Baldwin and Denning, at Quebec, of the following dimensions:—
> Length .... 179 feet.
> Breadth .... 31 ,, 4-10ths.
> Depth .... 23 ,, 8-10ths.
>
> She measures 1145 tons o.m. and by the new rule 1120 tons, exclusive of 174 tons of poop, which runs to the mainmast. This ship was nearly 12 months in hand, has not been surpassed in workmanship and fidelity of structure by any vessel from the St. Lawrence.
>
> She is copper-fastened, including centre keel bolts, which prevents her being marked (part iron bolts) by Lloyd's registry.
>
> The cabin is fitted, and 'twixt deck laid. Parties interested in Colonial shipping are particularly invited to inspect this vessel.
>
> For particulars apply on board, or to
> HOLDERNESS and CHILTON.

'Annie Jane' for sale

Gore's Liverpool General Advertiser 28th July 1853.

With thanks to The British Newspaper Archive (www.britishnewspaperarchive.co.uk);

© The British Library Board.

> LINE of PACKETS for HAVANA.
> Now loading in George's Dock, and will be despatched in a few days.
> The fine new Spanish Brig SEBASTIAN, Captain URRECHAGA;
> A 1, and coppered, 160 tons register, and an excellent conveyance.
> Succeeds the SEBASTIAN.—With very early despatch, The very favourite-trading Barque ANONIMA, M. A. de OZINAGA, Master;
> A 1 at Lloyd's for nine years; 300 tons, and coppered: loading in Prince's Dock.—Apply to
> PARTRIDGE, FLETCHER and Co.
>
> First Vessel.
> For HAVANA.
> The Spanish Brig LEON, Captain PEREZ;
> Burthen 208 tons, not two years old, coppered and a swift-sailing craft. Her last passage hence to Havana was accomplished in thirty-six days: loading in George's Dock.—Apply to Messrs. RICHARD SOBEL and Co.
> or to J. T. NICKELS.
> The regular-trading Spanish Brig AMALIA, now in the Prince's Dock, will follow.
>
> For MATANZAS.
> The regular-trading British Brig AMELIA HILL, Captain W. HILL;
> Burthen 307 tons; coppered and copper fastened, and a good conveyance: loading in George's Dock.—Apply to
> J. T. NICKELS.
>
> Succeeds the above.
> For MONTREAL,
> The well-known regular Trader AMY ANN, W. H. M'LEOD, Commander,
> (Who is well experienced in the St. Lawrence;) 553 tons register, first class at Lloyd's, British built, coppered and copper fastened, and presents in every respect a desirable conveyance for fine goods; loading in Queen's Dock.—Apply to Messrs. HOLDERNESS and CHILTON, or
> ROBERT GIRVIN.
>
> For MONTREAL and QUEBEC.
> The very fine new clipper-built Ship ANNIE JANE,
> WILLIAM MAGGS, Commander,
> (Late of the HERCYNE, and who is well acquainted with the navigation of the St. Lawrence;)
> Classed at Lloyd's A 1 seven years, and is in every respect a superior conveyance for fine goods: now loading in Prince's Dock.—Apply to Messrs. HOLDERNESS & CHILTON, Owners, or to ROBERT GIRVIN.
>
> Early 1st Ship.—Will have immediate despatch.
> For MONTREAL,
> The fine A 1 British-built Ship PARAGON.
> JOHN PAYNE, Commander,
> (Well known in the trade;)
> 425 tons register, coppered and copper fastened: now loading in Salthouse Dock.—For freight or passage apply to Captain Payne, on board; to Messrs. CLINT and Co.; to
> KENNETH DOWIE and Co. or FORBES BROTHERS.

'Annie Jane' Voyage

Gore's Liverpool General Advertiser 28th July 1853.

With thanks to The British Newspaper Archive (www.britishnewspaperarchive.co.uk);

© The British Library Board.

An Introduction to the 'Annie Jane'

EMIGRANTS AT DINNER.

"THE OCEAN MONARCH," OF LIVERPOOL, BUILT AT QUEBEC.—(SEE NEXT PAGE.)

Immigrants below deck and Ocean Monarch
The 'Ocean Monarch', a similar ship to the 'Annie Jane', built by Baldwin and Dinning at the Cape Cove shipyard in 1854.
(both) Illustrated London News.

EMIGRATION FROM LIVERPOOL IN 1853.
WHENCE IT IS SUPPLIED.

The following interesting table, for which we are indebted to the obliging head-clerk at the Government Emigration office, shows the number of emigrants who have taken their departure from this port for all foreign ports during each month in the past year, with a classification of the countries to which they belonged. The numbers under the head "by short ships" refer to those who have proceeded in ships which have not come under the inspection of the Government officers. It should also be stated that the classification applies only to steerage passengers, cabin passengers being exempt from the operation of the law in this respect:—

Months.	Cabin.	English.	Scotch.	Irish.	Other countries.	Total.	By sh ships.
January	31	1344	340	4153	112	5980	864
February	22	2237	694	10025	274	13322	1110
March	471	5128	1549	12297	1758	21149	860
April	212	4318	321	20003	3081	27935	1128
May	251	3519	950	16649	2833	24202	1001
June	144	1516	520	13906	2617	18748	1627
July	512	2352	490	12396	2041	17691	1114
August	512	2206	624	14122	1130	18594	1744
September	283	2225	269	17227	2508	22512	1945
October	266	1880	635	12413	2278	17472	1066
November	113	1684	628	1313	1225	12963	1766
December	91	585	395	1606	480	3157	1514
Totals	2924	28939	7415	144110	20337	203725	15747

It appears, from this return, that the total number of passengers who took their departure hence, for all ports, during the past year, was 219,472, of whom 2,924 were cabin passengers, 144,110 Irish, 28,939 English, 7,415 Scotch, 20,337 other countries, (principally German,) the remaining number, 15,747, being composed of those who proceeded in "short ships." It will be seen, therefore, that more than one-half of this full flood of emigration was supplied by Ireland. The majority of the Irish emigrants go to America, comparatively few being amongst the adventurers to our gold colonies. In the conveyance of this multitude of people 947 ships were employed, of an aggregate tonnage of 844,058 tons, manned by crews to the number of 7,837 men.

Emigration from Liverpool in 1853
Glasgow Examiner 4th February 1854.
With thanks to the staff at the Mitchell Library, Glasgow.

An Introduction to the 'Annie Jane'

PROVISIONS, STORES, &c., to be found by the OWNERS.

Rations, according to the following Scale, are to be issued during the voyage to each Male and Female Passenger of 14 years of age and upwards; Children between 10 and 14 are to receive two-thirds; and Children between two and ten years of age, one half of such rations:—

DIETARY SCALE.

	Biscuit.	Beef.	Pork.	Preserved Meat.	Flour.	Oatmeal.	Raisins.	Suet.	Peas.	Rice.	Preserved Potatoes.	Tea.	Coffee, weight when ground.	Sugar.	Treacle.	Butter.	Water.
	oz.	oz.	oz.	oz.	oz.	oz.	oz.	oz.	Pint.	oz.	oz.	oz.	oz.	oz.	oz.	oz.	Quarts.
Sunday	8	–	6	6	6	3	–	1½	–	–	4	¼	–	1	2	–	3
Monday	8	6	–	–	6	3	2	–	1	–	–	–	½	–	–	2	3
Tuesday	8	–	6	–	6	3	–	1½	–	4	–	¼	–	1	–	–	3
Wednesday	8	–	–	8	6	3	2	–	1	–	–	–	½	–	2	–	3
Thursday	8	–	6	–	6	3	–	1½	–	–	4	¼	–	1	–	2	3
Friday	8	–	–	8	6	3	2	–	1	–	–	–	½	–	–	–	3
Saturday	8	6	–	–	6	3	–	1½	–	4	–	¼	–	1	2	–	3

Mixed Pickles } Weekly { One gill
Mustard } { Half an ounce
Salt } { Two ounces.
Pepper } { Half an ounce.

Children between four months and two years old are to be allowed 3 pints of water, and a quarter of a pint of milk daily; also 3 oz. of preserved soup, and one egg, every alternate day, and 12 oz. of biscuit, 4 oz. of oatmeal, 8 oz. of flour, 4 oz. of rice, and 10 oz. of sugar, weekly. To infants under four months old, the surgeon may issue such nutriment as he may, in any case, think necessary, with any quantity of water, not exceeding one quart, daily. He may also, if he thinks fit, issue three times a week, to children between two and seven years of age, 4 oz. of rice or 3 oz. of sago, and one egg, in lieu of salt meat.

Atlantic Dietary scale.
Taken from: The Select Committee on Emigrant Ships. Published 6th April 1854. With thanks to Google Books.

2

The First Voyage

Problems started for the 'Annie Jane' passengers almost immediately. Having said goodbyes to family and friends, the 100-strong group of Glasgow tradesmen and dependants gathered on the banks of the Clyde to catch the steamer to Liverpool on the morning of Wednesday, 17th August. They arrived in Liverpool on the evening of Thursday 18th. They had arranged to spend the first night on the steamer that had taken them from Glasgow. On the morning of the next day they were to hire carts and arrange transportation of their provisions and bulky sea chests, containing the precious tools of their trade, and all the worldly possessions they had thought important enough to take with them. They were brought from Clarence Dock to Sandon Dock, to where the 'Annie Jane' was moored waiting for them, with a departure date that had been set for 19th August.

After this, they should have taken up their berths on the 'Annie Jane' and done some last-minute shopping or just wandered around enjoying the unaccustomed leisure time and soaking up the sights and sounds of Liverpool docks. Having been fed a host of exaggerated stories about the dangers of Liverpool docks and the con men, crooks and pickpockets that would exploit the unwary, the Glasgow tradesmen probably wanted to spend as little time as possible there. But all was not well. When they turned up at the docks with their luggage, it was to find an unpleasant surprise: the sailing had been delayed.

The sailing had been put back four days till the following Tuesday because of the late arrival of some cargo, not an unusual circumstance for emigrant ships. It was quite common for ships to be delayed waiting for cargo, undergoing repairs or even struggling to recruit enough crew to man the ship. A deposit was required to secure a place on an emigrant ship, with the rest of the fare paid before departure. Liverpool lodging houses were full of disgruntled people who were having to get by on the shilling a day they were given for expenses by the ships' agents, as they waited for the ship they had already bought tickets for to depart. Delays of up to a fortnight were not uncommon. The cost of lodgings at that time was fourpence a night, with the use of a fire for cooking. Emigrants claimed that being away from home they easily spent more than the allocated shilling.

The Glasgow men were angry and reluctant to spend any of their hard-earned savings on accommodation, but they were forced to separate and spend a night in some of the numerous lodging houses scattered around the docks. To add to their irritation, they had to leave their sea chests and barrels of provisions uncovered on the docks. On the Saturday morning they went to the agent and with much abuse and the threat of physical violence, forced him down to the 'Annie Jane', where he finally instructed the crew to allow them aboard the ship. This was to their advantage. It would allow them to be the first passengers on the ship, and let them explore and acclimatise to the place that would be home for the next four weeks. Some of the joiners took one look at the dark space where they were allocated berths just below the forward hatch and immediately asked to be moved to second class, paying an extra five shillings for the privilege.

It was Tuesday 23rd August before the 'Annie Jane' had received all her cargo and was ready to sail, but there was one more hurdle before she could cast off her ropes and set to sea. Before an emigrant ship could set sail, it was a legal requirement that it be inspected by the Government emigration agent at the port of Liverpool, or one of his deputies. In this case, it was a Lieutenant Prior RN. Agents had considerable powers at their disposal, as they were responsible for checking all the equipment and the facilities on emigrant ships. They had to inspect the stowing of cargo, emigrant berths (which they were supposed to inspect and confirm that every one of the passengers had an allocated berth), the provisions supplied for passengers and, finally, the crew, whom they would line up and examine. To Lieutenant Prior's annoyance, one of the French-Canadians answered to two names on different occasions, for which he was reprimanded.

The only major fault that Lieutenant Prior found was the state of the water closets. He refused the 'Annie Jane' the clearing certificate without which an emigrant ship could not leave Liverpool docks. He declined the certificate because the six steerage water closets were dirty, badly designed and shoddily constructed, and he informed Captain Mason that he would issue the certificate when this was rectified.

Some of the Glasgow joiners were put to work to put stronger hinges on the doors and they increased the incline of the discharge pipe. It was in everybody's interest that this work was rapidly finished, and the modifications did not take them long. Lieutenant Prior returned, made a second inspection, declared himself satisfied, and issued the clearing certificate.

Captain Mason, now in a hurry to begin the journey, issued instructions to cast off. There would have been a gathering on the dock of people to say their last goodbyes. The usual collection of spectators and hawkers were shouting out their wares. There was lots of noise and waving of handkerchiefs with the steerage passengers on the main deck all excited, and cheering themselves hoarse. At last a steam tug took them in tow at 3.00 in the afternoon on Wednesday 24th August. They had to pick a time to leave when the current in the river was slight, as the river Mersey ran fast: up to nine or ten knots on a strong tide, making a ship difficult to control. The tug released them at 10.00 in the evening clear of the North Channel, and out in the open sea. By the morning of 25th August the 'Annie Jane' had left Liverpool well behind and was going by Rathlin

The First Voyage

Island, off the coast of Ireland, on a heading of north by northwest. The wind was favourable and the sky was clear: everyone must have thought they were in for a pleasant journey. But even in those benign conditions the vessel had a peculiar motion, with a pronounced roll in a cross sea. Many of the sailors later stated that she rolled more than any other ship they had been on, even in calm conditions.

As always at the beginning of such a journey, many of the passengers were overcome by seasickness and stayed in their beds; the Irish and the Scots, having already made at least one long sea journey aboard a vessel, may have been less troubled than the first-timers. They all knew they were in for a long voyage: with favourable winds it was possible to reach Quebec in under 30 days but the average voyage time was 40 to 45 days. The first sight of land, bringing joy to all hearts, would normally be the coast of Cape Breton.

Problems immediately began to surface with the food distribution system. Although many of the passengers who had already taken to their bunks feeling unwell did not require feeding, for the others it seemed a disorganised affair. When over 400 people are trying to get fed at the same time, the system has to run like a well-oiled machine, but on the 'Annie Jane' it was anything but. Rations were distributed by the Bo's'un, John Dunlop, the ship's carpenter, Thomas Mason, or the sailmaker, William Moore, who reluctantly took it in turns to carry out that unpopular duty. An apprentice also assisted whoever was carrying out the task. There was a system in which passengers had to give their name and berth number to be issued with food or water; a tick was then made in a ledger book to say that they had received their allocation for the day. For whatever reason, people were turning up to find their names already ticked off. The crew were meant to weigh out the amounts, and had a small set of scales for that purpose, but in a ship with a constant rolling motion, that was proving almost impossible.

The passengers began to complain that they were not getting their full entitlements of tea, biscuits, bread, oatmeal, rice, and, most importantly, water. The small galley was totally chaotic, with everybody turning up at the same times to prepare meals; queues were inevitable and tempers frayed. Anyone not in the first group would find that all the hot water had been used up, and they would have to wait till another boilerful reached temperature. Some of the passengers on this first voyage later complained that they could not get breakfast before midday. Under an act of parliament in 1852 provisions should have been issued cooked. Ship owners ignored this, claiming, probably with some justification that emigrants preferred to cook for themselves.

On most emigrant ships a rota was made up, allocating passengers to a mess and giving them a time slot for getting into the small galley and preparing food. After this, there was another time slot for a space to sit down at a table to eat it. It does not seem to have occurred to anybody on the 'Annie Jane' to put this into practice, on her first voyage with passengers.

On Friday morning, three days into the voyage, the wind began to pick up, and around noon a squall came. According to witnesses, neither the wind nor the sea was particularly violent at that point but the vessel laboured fearfully with a peculiar motion, rolling violently from side to side. The wind increased at last into a full gale that the 'Annie Jane' seemed incapable of sailing in. Captain Mason ordered the reduction of sails, with the royals, the very top sails on the three masts, taken down. But it was not enough. An hour later, there was a sudden stronger gust, and with a massive lurch and a loud cracking noise the three topmasts broke. Two topgallant sails and three whole topsails, rigging and spars came crashing down onto the deck, narrowly missing members of the crew and passengers, a sailor diving to pull one of the London orphans to safety under a boat. The vessel became disabled immediately, with masts and sails hanging over the side. She went broadside to the sea and began to roll more violently. The fore-hold hatch, where the Glasgow joiners were, had only a loose covering of planks. These were damaged or disturbed by the falling spars, leaving the passengers down below subject to torrents of freezing sea water and falling timber.

In that half-light of the tweendeck, the sea water that had entered swept under the bunks with all the debris that could be carried along with it. Passengers' chests broke loose and were thrown about from side to side. With the smell of vomit, the shrieking of the wind in the rigging, the creaking of the ship's timbers, the cries and screams of the children and women, the cursing of men, it must have seemed that the night would never end. Nobody slept

The First Voyage

at all. They were all in fear of their lives. During the chaos below decks, many passengers' chests and the barrels which they had purchased to store provisions in had been damaged. Their contents were contaminated with sea water or destroyed.

With an unsteady platform and in the teeth of a full gale, the crew took ages to restore order to the deck, and a new problem emerged as many of the French-Canadian crewmen only had a rudimentary grasp of English. It was later claimed in the press and at the inquiry by the passengers and crew that the French-Canadians weren't around when required, struggled to understand simple instructions, and showed a marked reluctance, and even fear, when ordered to climb the rigging. Because of the excessive rolling motion, it was dangerous to attempt to climb the rigging or the masts. The men had to hold on at all times as the ship attempted to throw them into the turbulent sea. They could not, or would not, understand the orders given to them.

The Captain of a vessel would consider a number of issues before he gave the order to shorten sail. If Captain Mason was under any illusions that he was in command of a good crew, he would have been brought back to reality when they had first set sail. A more able set of sailors could have all sails set in about five minutes. Nobody commented on how long the crew had taken to set sails as the steam tug cast them off, but given their subsequent performance, it is doubtful if that would have been impressive.

Most experienced sailors keep one eye on the horizon, looking for cloud formations and indications of an increase in wind strength. Before night falls, even more care has to be taken, with the sails reduced if a sailor suspects a change is coming in the weather. For whatever reason, Captain Mason was caught totally unprepared. He was very lucky that none of the crew was up in the rigging at the time the masts broke, and that no passengers had been injured. Either he had seriously underestimated the wind speed that night, or he had overestimated the 'Annie Jane's' ability to handle that strength of wind.

By morning, all the damage had been cleared away and the vessel had resumed its journey to Canada on reduced sails, but she was still labouring with the same uncomfortable motion through the heavy seas. The Bo's'un refused to issue any provisions to the passengers that day, not even water, though it would, in any case, have been impossible to cook anything, as no fires were lit in the galley. So, for another day the ship continued ploughing on towards North America. With constant sail changes, adjustments and running repairs, all the crew were required on deck and the needs of the passengers were completely ignored.

Most of the women and children, and many of the men, would not brave the dangers of the main deck, which at times was awash with sea water, to get to the steerage toilets. Conditions continued to deteriorate down below, with the lower hold, tweendeck and bilges getting more squalid by the hour.

Dissension was growing, with the passengers concluding that with the damage she had sustained the ship would never make Quebec and they were headed for total disaster. Resolutions were being made, with many individuals declaring that they wished they had never set foot aboard the 'Annie Jane'. If they got another chance, they would never do so again. Others went further, promising God and themselves that if they got out of this, they would never set foot on any ship in the future. Individual passengers went up to complain to the crew and to express their desire to turn back. By all accounts, they were only met with insults.

A general meeting was called by the steerage passengers, probably instigated by a Glasgow engineer called William Hendrie. A petition was drawn up, complaining about the deteriorating conditions on the steerage deck and the failure to issue provisions or water, and pointing out the disabled condition of the ship and the dangers of continuing on the voyage. William Hendrie volunteered to give it to Captain Mason and went to the poop to present it to him. Upon receiving it, Mason read its contents, consulted with his First Mate, Mr Bell, and went down below to see the passengers and the conditions that they were living in. He spoke to them, and all aboard said *'For God's sake, return'*. He agreed to turn back to Liverpool, at which the assembled passengers gave a huge cheer of relief.

The 'Annie Jane' was turned around and began to head south, still encountering challenging conditions along the way. The crew were so hard-pressed that on one day at least they again forgot all about the passengers. This hardened the resolve of those aboard like William Hendrie, who said they would never set foot again on the 'Annie Jane', under any circumstances. The vessel continued to struggle southwards, passing along the west coast of Ireland. As they drew alongside Cork, the wind died to nothing. The harbour pilot intercepted them, as they were almost becalmed, and offered to send for a steam tug to meet them. Mason declined this, declaring they could manage very well by themselves. On 30th August, as they drifted along in light breezes, one happy event occurred. A small group gathered on the deck and a baby girl who had been born on board during the voyage was baptised by the Reverend Jean Vernier. The proud parents were Hugh Munro, a rail contractor and builder, and his wife Margaret, who had somehow given birth to their child during these difficult few days. Finally, the 'Annie Jane' arrived at the mouth of the Mersey in the late afternoon of 31st August, docking in Liverpool on 2nd September after a nine-day, 1000 mile, round trip, back exactly where she had started.

After saying all their goodbyes and putting the old country behind them, the would-be emigrants were unhappy to be back in Liverpool, a place they must have thought they would never have to see again. Some began to make plans that did not include another voyage in the 'Annie Jane'. Others reconciled themselves to the understanding that they were not entitled to get their passage money back. Having sold everything they owned in preparation for a new life, they had either to risk another journey on the 'Annie Jane', once repairs were carried out and she was ready for sea, or starve on the streets of Liverpool.

3

Repair and Litigation

When the relieved passengers on the 'Annie Jane' streamed excitedly down the gangway and on to the dockside to look for lodgings in Liverpool while the vessel was being repaired, many of them had made up their minds that they would never sail on her again, even if this meant losing their passage money. The owner, Thomas Holderness, was to give them four shillings each as subsistence for their stay in Liverpool, but was under no legal obligation to return to them the passage money. Others were determined to go to the law to make a formal complaint against the owner of the 'Annie Jane'.

They did not waste time. By that morning, Friday 2nd September, they had been in touch with the chief emigration officer for the port of Liverpool, Captain Frederick Schomberg, and presented him with a list of their grievances. He agreed to meet a deputation of passengers the next day, on one condition – that Captain Mason and Mr. Holderness, the owner of the vessel, would be present.

According to witnesses, the passenger complaints were numerous and varied. The meeting was boisterous, with the passengers not scared to voice their opinions, and Captain Schomberg struggled to keep control of the proceedings. The first of their principal complaints was that during the time the vessel was at sea the quantity of provisions served out to the passengers was not in conformity with the relevant Act of Parliament. In particular, instead of ten pounds of oatmeal each for that period, they received only one pound four ounces each and no flour or salt (the penalty for not serving out the full quantity of provisions on board of emigrant ships was from £5 to £50 for each individual emigrant). Secondly, they claimed that the provisions had been served out in a haphazard manner. There were complaints, too, about the general squalor of the ship and that it seemed to be overcrowded, with not enough berths for all the steerage passengers.

The deputation also demanded their passage money back. They stated that they did not wish to re-embark on the ship, refusing on the grounds that she was not properly fitted out and their confidence in her seaworthiness had been completely destroyed.

Having organised the petition aboard, William Hendrie described the meeting at the subsequent inquiry. He stated that the Government inspector asked them to say what complaints they had against the Captain and owner. The first who spoke up was an engineer from Manchester who said *'We were all used like pigs'*. Thinking him rude and insolent, Schomberg stopped him and said *'Enough of that'*. He called upon another witness, who replied by desiring him to read the articles of grievances placed before him the previous day, as they all still adhered to the same statement. Schomberg declined this request. He asked a further witness who declared:

We complain about the filthy and overcrowded state of the ship, and a great number having paid their berths in full, had no berths but had to lie on the deck on top of the chests.

The witness also mentioned a case of two young boys and a girl, brothers and sister, who had no berths. When the tickets were examined, it was found the numbers had been duplicated. They were the same as berths occupied by another pair of individuals. On complaining to the officers of the ship, they responded by saying *'It had nothing to do with them'*. Schomberg's response to this was:

Do you expect to be as comfortable in a ship as at home, and as for the ticket having the same number, that is not right.

Another passenger complained he had not obtained his share of oatmeal while on board. Several passengers also raised the matter of the different proportions of oatmeal which they had received during the voyage, complaining that they had not had the exact quantity and that it had not been served with scales. Schomberg then asked Captain Mason why the law had not been carried out on this point. Mason replied, saying that the oatmeal had been served all day long, that two barrels had been standing on deck, and that the people were too lazy to come from their berths and take it. As it appeared they had brought oatmeal back, it was very evident that they were '*not very hungry*'. One man then said that he had brought it and kept it to prove the case against the Captain.

As owner of the vessel, Mr. Holderness then stated:

I am ready Mr. Schomberg to do anything that is reasonable for these passengers. I have paid them four days' subsistence money, and am ready to give them the price of a week's provisions, provided they choose to receive it. I consider this a fair remuneration.

One of the passengers responded by announcing he would go to the law over the matter. Schomberg replied in a theatrical way to this point, declaring '*I am a captain in the navy, who is ready to listen to you or any other person making a complaint, but I am not a lawyer and if you wish to see a lawyer there is the door.*' He accompanied these remarks with a flourish of his hand, pointing to the entrance to the room.

After this, Captain Mason turned directly to Hendrie and asked:

What do you have to say against me?

As one of the leaders of the group, Hendrie continued his attack.

Seeing the dangerous position the passengers and ship were in, with the loss of the masts, why did you not return before the passengers petitioned you? And also, how did you not accept the services of the Cork pilot when he offered them? Or allow the pilot to go and arrange a steam tug?'

Schomberg interjected, '*If I had been master of the ship, I would not have turned for you*'.

Hendrie once again replied to this interruption:

The provisions are the principal matter in which we allege breach of contract; first, in not giving them by weight as per agreement. Secondly, we can prove having received one pound four ounces in lieu of ten pounds, for the last ten days, which we produced and no flour being served out.

Schomberg answered, '*Do you think this gentleman* (pointing to Holderness) *would try and cheat you out of your provisions?*'

Hendrie replied:

'*I do not care if it was his intention to cheat or not. All that we wanted to prove is that we were cheated in quantity and quality*', he declared. '*We also said that we wanted our passage money back, or be provided with a better ship.*'

Schomberg's response to this was firm and unequivocal:

You appear to settle the matter yourself, but you must know that I come here to settle these matters, and you must submit to what I say.

At this point, there was a call from one of the group: '*We are quite willing to submit to your decision if you would give us justice, but if you do not we will try it in the civil courts.*'

Again, Schomberg revealed his force and authority. He summoned one of his officials and turned the individual out. From this stage in the proceedings, matters became more ill-tempered and troubled. Hendrie even admitted threatening the Inspection Officer.

'*We told Schomberg that we would publish his name in England, Scotland and Ireland*', said Hendrie.

The meeting ended acrimoniously at that point. Before he left the room, Hendrie complained to Schomberg about the conduct of the Second Mate, Thomas Markham, who '*came down one night drunk to the poop, and wished to fight with the passengers, using language that ought not to have been used before females*'.

Schomberg listened to Hendrie and promised to have his officers investigate the allegations if Hendrie would only give him the witnesses' names. The passengers who intended to sail again in the 'Annie Jane' wanted no part of it, and nothing came of his complaint.

Repair and Litigation

Despite the questions over his conduct, Markham remained as Second Mate for the subsequent voyage.

Over the weekend the passengers had a meeting and wrote a petition to the Lord Mayor of Liverpool. This was delivered to his office on the Monday morning:

> To the Honourable the Lord Mayor of Liverpool[1]
>
> *Liverpool, September 5, 1853*
>
> My Lord – We, a number of the passengers per the ship Annie Jane, which sailed from this port for Quebec on Wednesday 24th August last, beg leave to lay before your lordship the following statement in reference to the treatment we received since going on board the said ship. After being ten days at sea the ship again landed in Liverpool, being compelled to put back with the loss of her three topmasts, sails &c. Before and since we proceeded to sea we received no regular allowance of provisions or water, as stated in our printed contract. Instead of receiving 5lb of oatmeal weekly, we can prove that during these ten days we only received about 1lb 4oz, and no salt or flour whatever, as mentioned in our printed tickets. Your Lordship will observe that the owners or agents of the ship have failed in implementation of their contract with the passengers, besides the other arrangements of the ship were conducted with no kind of order or regularity. We, therefore, wish to be guided by your Lordship in reference to the mode in which we ought to proceed for return of our passage money and the loss of time we have thus sustained. At present the ship is in the course of being repaired, which the owners propose to send to sea again with the passengers. Now, your Lordship after the dangers we have already experienced aboard the said ship, we assure you that one and all of us unanimously agree in considering our lives in imminent danger should we again have to proceed with the same ship. Trusting you will be pleased to give the matter your

earnest consideration, with the view to a return of our passage money and compensation for the loss of time, – we leave the matter in your Lordship's hands; and have the honour to remain, your most obedient servants,

James Maxwell, John Rogers, William Thomas, William Brown, John Stranger, Henry Bayly, David Rees, David Davies, George Williams, William Hughes, George Taylor, John Taylor, William Gallatly, Thomas Johns, Charles Smith, Lawrence Campbell, Fredrick Treadwell, John Treadwell, John Scott Chalmers, Johnston Dowler, James Edmonson, Thomas Young, Andrew Anderson, Benjamin Powhes, Peter Macpherson, Daniel Leahy, Shem Richards, Samuel Elliot, Rees Williams, John Rogers, Henry Thomas, David Jones, John Storry, Daniel Thomas, David Thomas, David Williams, John McDougall, David Gunn, Thomas Campbell, Augusten Lloyd, Thomas Thomas, Archibald Clark, James Driver, Michael Lane, Dennis Driscon, Thomas Galbraith, Thomas Gourlie, Alexander Macdonald, John K Weir, John Curr, Angus Matheson, James McLymont, James Wood, James Rodgers Sr, John Rodgers, James Rodgers jr, Thomas Lee for self, wife, and child, Jane Tenlin, Charles Tenlin, James Tenlin, Michael Tenlin, William Chisholm, Alexander Kerr, Thomas Hawkins, Thomas Hodges, Patrick Kelly, William Davis, William Owen, Edward Mockluyer, David Divisers, John Power, James Kelly, Jeremiah Porter, Denis Disrael, Jeremiah O'Brien, John O'Brien, John Cristopher, Edward Donelley, Edward Chainhen, John Parker, John Stobie, George King.

Hendrie was determined not to let the matter go. Both he and Thomas Thomas, another of the Glasgow tradesmen, went to see a solicitor on the Monday after having returned to Schomberg's office on the Saturday and again gained no satisfaction from him. The solicitor, James Owen, told them to call back the next day, when he took down a list of their grievances in writing. He was then asked if he thought they could recover the passage money, and he said there was not the smallest doubt of that. At the same time, he required two sovereigns to commence this action, and another two if he would recover the whole of the passage money of the subscribers. They began immediately, went round the lodging houses, obtained as many subscribers as they could among the passengers, raised the money, went with it to the solicitor that same day, and paid him. He told them to call next morning at the court house, as he would have the Government inspector and the owner, Mr. Holderness, summoned there, when he would have an opportunity of proving the case before them.

They met at the court house on Wednesday morning. Mr. Owen, the solicitor, read over the statement of the grievances which were as follows: that instead of ten pounds of oatmeal they received four ounces, and no flour or salt whatsoever. Thomas Holderness did not deny the above statement, but said to Hendrie:

You received two shillings yesterday as compensation for provisions not given according to agreement. All the other passengers have received the same sum, and are well pleased.

Taken by surprise by this statement, Hendrie remained defiant. He said '*I never received two shillings yesterday, nor would I take it on any account and as they had broken the agreement, we want our passage money back*'.

Mr. Owen's response was to read out the Act of Parliament regarding serving out the full quantity of provisions on board of emigrant ships to the emigrants.

'*These fellows want to stop our ship*', Holderness said.

Hendrie's reply was sharp and angry. '*We are not fellows, and have as good a character as him.*'

The retort from Holderness was a reminder of his position as the ship's owner:

We will give these two men their money back, if they will give up their tickets.

Hendrie shook his head: '*We have no more right to our passage money back than the other subscribers who had signed this subscription sheet.*' Hendrie later stated proudly that he was told to be silent by the Government inspector as they could not reason with him.

In his response to this, Mr Holderness became even more petty and personal. '*The reason why these men did not get their provisions*

Repair and Litigation

served out, is that they could not get out of their bed at half past six o'clock.'

Hendrie might have shrugged his shoulders at this stage in the proceedings, aware that the entire case was becoming more and more out of control, with personal abuse becoming a substitute for reason and argument. He said that *'he was quite willing to submit to the doctor's evidence on that point, as he could prove that they were all out of bed at that time.'*

Mr. Holderness seemed to recover his dignity for a moment. He reached for a solution that might prove, at least, advantageous to himself. He stated that *'he would come between the captain and all damages, so that the vessel might sail on the morrow'.*

As a result, it was decided that only William Hendrie and Thomas Thomas would get their money back and the case was dismissed.

Hendrie did not leave it there. They went back to the solicitor, Mr. Owen, and asked him why the other subscribers had not been given their passage money back, as all had been equally defrauded. Mr. Owen said he could do no more till they gave him another two sovereigns, and assured them that he would recover all the subscribers' passage money. They subscribed again and raised enough money to provide him with this sum. Yet for all that, though Mr. Owen promised to get the case settled each day for the space of eight days, no solution was achieved. Truth and justice were – as they sometimes remain till this day – elusive and evasive. Owen's excuse was always that the Government inspector could not be found.

At last the case was taken in a civil court before a magistrate, who dismissed the case, on the grounds that Thomas Holderness had paid out the handsome sum of two shillings for each passenger, as compensation for the manner in which they had been cheated out of their berths and provisions.

By that time the 'Annie Jane' had been repaired. On 9th September, after a delay of seven days, she had slipped her moorings, with the vast majority of the passengers totally oblivious of the court proceedings that were taking place. The berths that had been abandoned by those who refused to sail on her again were quickly filled by some of the hundreds who were in Liverpool desperate for a ship to cross the Atlantic to North America. They were even offered at a reduced rate as an extra inducement.

Given the length of time it took, a total of just seven days, repairs must have been hurried. New pitch pine topmasts were fitted with the replacement spars supplied being even more substantial than the original ones. Seasoned rigging that had only been in use for a month was removed from another ship and fitted to the 'Annie Jane'. This was considered pre-stretched and thus better than new. Two spare sets of sails were put aboard. There were also a number of spare spars, and one spare topmast.

The general consensus was that the ship's instability, the tendency to roll heavily, had been caused by her heavy cargo being stored too low. The solution was proposed that the cargo should be removed and reloaded carefully, so this was done, with the heavier items as high up on the tweendeck as possible. This would ease the motion of the ship. The vast majority of the iron cargo remained in the hold; sheet iron and railway iron were in the tweendeck, stowed in as elevated a position as possible.

The exact number of those who had made up their minds not to re-embark in the 'Annie Jane' for their voyage to North America is not known. Of the Glasgow tradesmen, we know about thirteen refused to embark on her again. About 30 steerage passengers later took the more expensive but safer option of passage on the 'Sarah Sands', a steamship that left Liverpool on 16th September and arrived safely in Quebec in mid-October. The passengers who chose this option paid a fare that was more than double that on the 'Annie Jane': the handsome sum of 6 guineas for a steerage ticket and 20 guineas for Cabin class.

Some individuals were so terrified by their experience that nothing would induce them ever to attempt a transatlantic crossing again. Contemporary sources say about eighty individuals in total turned their backs to the 'Annie Jane'. How many times must they have reflected as they grew older, that it was one of the best decisions they had ever made? A twenty-year-old mill worker, Mary Cassidy, wrote to her mother in Kilmarnock:

My Dear Mother[2]

I was on my way to America but am turned back to Liverpool again. We sailed on the 24th *August and after two days, a storm arose, and we were all nearly to the bottom; the cargo was not right put in and it made the ship rock from side to side. I am in lodgings but we could not get out our beds. My money is nearly done if I could get it back I would come home again, but they will not give it back. I do not know when we will sail, but you can write to me on receipt. Little Daniel has not been very well since I left, but he is getting better. Now I wish I was at home again I would like very well; but I will have to go if I do not get my money. I would not have thought it so bad if Daniel had not been with me. You can write by return of post, and tell me if I should go or return without my money. I wish I had never left you mother, for I think it would have been better. Address my letter to Mr Bell, mate aboard the Annie Jane, Sandon dock, Liverpool. Be sure and write by return of post.*

Good bye.

A reply, if there was one, did not arrive in time and Mary reluctantly re-embarked with her five-month-old son Daniel, for the journey to Quebec. The crew could not leave the ship: having signed the ship agreement they were legally bound to complete the voyage. One member was not constrained from leaving and he had had enough of the 'Annie Jane'. Nothing would have persuaded John Page Julina, a newly-qualified surgeon on his first sea voyage, to repeat the experience he had just gone through. He left the ship as soon as she docked in Liverpool, established a practice on land and never took to the sea again.

A replacement had to be found quickly. Unlike cargo ships, in which the Captain carried a set of medical books and stood in as doctor, an emigrant ship with more than one hundred people and allowing no more than 12 square feet of space per person, had to provide a doctor. Rather strangely, if there was 14 square feet of space per person they did not have to carry a doctor. Some smaller ships got round this requirement by only carrying ninety nine emigrants, to avoid the extra expense. In order to fulfil this legal requirement, Surgeon Francis Goold, from County Cork in Ireland, was recruited as surgeon for the voyage.

Another member of the crew made a run for it as soon as the coast was clear. Thirteen-year-old Joseph Cove, an apprentice on his first voyage, had decided that a nautical career was not for him, and abandoned ship. The ship agreement has his name and the date of his indenture, 17th August 1853, then the date of 2nd September with the comment 'Deserted'.

His family would have forfeited the substantial sum they would have paid for his five-to-six-year indenture; given subsequent events it is doubtful they would have been too hard on him. The position he vacated was taken by another apprentice, the one crew member for whom, unfortunately, we do not have a name.

Thomas Hendrie later said '*When they were repairing the ship, I saw they were not getting her properly repaired. They were not taking sufficient time because they were hurried. I am not a carpenter, but at the same time, I have a knowledge of a job, when it is done and I consider they were not making a good job of it. I consider it was a mere patch, and they were not taking sufficient time for the repairs, for the men were hurried, and making a patch of it. I saw that it was not well completed as it ought to be. In repairing the mizzenmast, they put on three rings that were not a fit. The two jaws were not a fit nor anything like a fit*'.

And, for all his failure in the law courts, he would have the last word on the subject. He claimed to have gone down to the 'Annie Jane' before the departure with a carpenter and a sailor whom he claimed had been to Quebec thirty times. The man who had been to Quebec said '*I know the road to Quebec well; I have been there thirty times, and that vessel will never get there.*' Hendrie said '*They both told me if I valued my life not to go in her, that she was too light and that her damned cargo would sink her to the bottom*'.[3]

1. Glasgow Examiner 14th October 1853. This list of petitioners is only partial. The newspaper stated that it would publish the full list the following week; unfortunately, events had moved on, and it did not do so.

2. Glasgow Examiner 14th October 1853.

3. Minutes of evidence, Beechey Inquiry.

4

The Second Voyage

On the evening of Thursday, 8th September, word spread that the repairs to the 'Annie Jane' were completed at last. The passengers left their lodgings and headed down to the docks. Many of them even took up the same berths as they had occupied before, in preparation for departing at first light. There were no hitches this time: the Government inspector came down to the vessel and issued the clearing certificate promptly, finding no other problems. So, on the morning of Friday, 9th September the 'Annie Jane' cast off. On the dock there would have been a few relatives, possibly some new acquaintances made during the stay in Liverpool, and the usual bystanders and hawkers. Those aboard who were doing this for the second time were probably not cheering as enthusiastically as at their first departure. No doubt they had some apprehension in their hearts. A steam tug had been chartered to set the ship on its way as gently as possible. This was to allow the rigging and new masts to bed in with the least possible strain. It even remained with the

'Annie Jane' longer than normal, finally releasing the tow rope just off the Isle of Man.

The ship's course was the same as on the first voyage. The sea was calm. Dolphins sported in the sea around them. There was even a slight breeze from the right direction – the southeast – which made progress seem effortless, and the ship surged ahead with full sails. All the signs seemed promising. The old hands among the passengers from the first voyage enjoyed showing all the newcomers where everything was, explaining the feeding arrangements and recounting the horrors of the first voyage, which must have seemed by now a distant memory. The passengers began to assume a peaceful routine. Nobody made any complaints about the issuing of provisions or overcrowding on the second voyage. There would have been some musical instruments aboard and they would have been taken out. Steerage would have echoed with popular songs and the songs of exile that have been sung by every generation as they left the shores of their homeland. Blankets would have been hung around bunks and the numerous children would have played what games they could around the decks.

However, three days out, on the morning of the 12th, the wind changed direction, picking up strength from the southwest. All on board were about to get a reminder of the frailty of the 'Annie Jane'. The ship started rolling heavily: the rearrangement of the cargo had failed to cure any of her faults. According to Captain Mason:

We were running under double-reefed topsails when the foreyard broke, and a part of the mainmast.

They were almost precisely at the same place where the first accident had happened. Running at about 8 knots, they were at about longitude 11 degrees west, latitude 50 degrees north. The wreckage of the foremast struck the bow of the ship with such force that some of the timbers were damaged and seawater began to enter the ship. At some point a decision was made to cut the heel lashing of the jib boom to allow the spar to go overboard, but this action broke off the head of the bowsprit, leaving them unable to set any headsail and forcing them to lie to. The wind then blew so strongly that they were prevented from doing any repairs for two days, the ship rolling so violently that the main deck was constantly under water. The wind finally moderated on the 15th. Repairs were carried out to the masts. The carpenter was sent over the bow of the ship to nail on some boards and canvas, and do what he could to repair the bow. Then the ship's head was turned westward into the Atlantic again.

Dissent was growing below decks. There had been some sort of disturbance that day: a fight among the steerage passengers over a missing handkerchief. Captain Mason had gone below to sort out the problem – a duty that would normally be undertaken by the ship's officers – and told them to 'Hush up'.

'Damn it, if you do not leave me alone you will have to find your own way', he announced.

In late afternoon, all the steerage and second class passengers had a meeting. Thomas Hendrie might have left the ship, but there were plenty of worthy successors to him: Scotland has never been short of individuals who are willing and able to stand up to authority. The person who led the passengers this time was Abraham Brooks, a twenty-one-year-old joiner from Stirling. The passengers all thought the ship was in a disabled state, but many of them did not feel they were qualified to say so.

Brooks went to see Charles Bell, the First Mate, and had a discreet conversation with him. Bell told him he could not give them any advice, but, according to Brooks, said *'From the state that the ship is in, she will never arrive in Quebec'*. When Brooks returned and relayed the First Mate's comments, the passengers all agreed that the ship was not in a fit condition to proceed. A petition was hastily drawn up by Brooks and a joiner called Robert Murray. It was signed by all the steerage and second class passengers, except for five people who refused. Cabin passengers, as was the case with the first sailing, were not even asked to sign the petition.

Twenty-five-year-old Alexander Ross, an engineer from Glasgow, volunteered to present the petition to Captain Mason. It simply stated *'We the passengers by the "Annie Jane" humbly request the captain considering the disabled state of the ship, to return back to Liverpool and we will consent to forfeit all claim to passage money'*. Mason read the petition and threw it down on the deck, where it promptly blew over the port side. He said he had put back for them before and they had tried to do him an injustice.

The Second Voyage

He would not give them the satisfaction of telling them where he was going.

Half an hour later the Captain came down among the passengers and told them to keep their minds easy, that he would run for the nearest port. The ship was turned and, to all appearances, they were headed back in the direction of Liverpool.

When night came, Mason gave instructions to the helmsman and the vessel was headed again for Quebec. It was later claimed by many members of the crew that there were high words and raised voices between Captain Mason and Captain Rose, who it seems was desperate to get to Quebec to take command of the 'Argonaut'. He eventually convinced Mason that once they had carried out repairs with the materials they had aboard, they could easily make it all the way to Quebec.

The passengers, having been informed that the 'Annie Jane' was on its way back to Liverpool, now found out from crew members that they were en route to Quebec again. Becoming agitated, a group of them rushed up to the poop deck to confront Mason, led by a sawyer from Liverpool called John Parry. Mason is reported to have asked *'Do you know how to manage a ship better than me? I have turned for you once, that I would now have the satisfaction of carrying you forward'*.

'That would be poor satisfaction', John Parry said.

Mason's only response to this was to become melodramatic, announcing his ultimatum. He said that it was *'Quebec or the bottom'*, and that he would shoot the first man that tried to take the ship from him. He called for his pistol and handcuffs as the crew gathered protectively around him.

'That would only be one life lost', Parry shouted.

Mason replied that he would serve the others with two ounces of lead in the same way. For a few minutes the passengers held their ground, sizing the situation up, but the sight of the pistol in Mason's hand and the handcuffs seemed to change their minds. They backed down from the confrontation. Mason followed them and told them to get off the poop or he would blow their brains out. No doubt as the passengers retreated they debated excitedly among themselves what to do. None of the passengers had any experience of sailing a ship; supposing they had rushed the Captain, what could they have done? Later they spoke to the sailors, and were told not to mind the Captain as any mutiny would go against all of them when they reached the shore. Captain Mason later claimed that the gun was not even loaded.

Shortly afterwards Mason had a change of heart. He maintained at the inquiry it was because of individual passengers' urgent entreaties. He went among the steerage passengers on the poop deck, and informed them that he would put back to the nearest port when the wind was favourable.

On 18th September, almost a week after the ship was initially damaged, they set some extra sails, turned the ship round and steered a southerly course in the direction of Londonderry, the nearest port. Shortly after, the wind shifted to the southwest, forcing Mason to turn the vessel to windward to keep offshore. The wind began to rise yet again on the following day. Mason seems to have had problems with the crew at that point, with some of them claiming that with the extreme rolling of the vessel even in calm weather, it was too dangerous to climb the rigging to work on the sails. Suddenly the main topsail sheet broke. In response to this, members of the crew again maintained that nobody could get aloft. Mason tried to shame them, told them to follow, and climbed up the mainmast to furl the sail, with crew members reluctantly following his example.

While he was up the mainmast, the Captain noticed that the rigging seemed to be slacker than it should have been. Thinking the mast had sunk into its step (the socket the mast sits in) he summoned the ship's carpenter, who confirmed his suspicions. They both knew there wasn't much they could do about it. The sailors re-tensioned the rigging as best they could, but the 'Annie Jane' was still rolling heavily. That night the foreyard gave way and was lost with its sail. The deck was repeatedly swept by large waves; the forward boat, the ship's gig, was washed over the side complete with davits; the anchor chain and spare spars broke free, and began to roll about the forward deck. It was impossible to stand on the decks to do any repairs. The wind was later described by Mason as blowing a hurricane.

On the 20th the mainyard, main-topmast and mainmast head also went over the side: with the movement allowed by the mast having shrunk or settled, the chain-plates – the metal fittings used to tie the mast stays – had pulled free. For three days the vessel was driven north, with no land in sight. Somewhere during this period a heavy sea struck the ship on the starboard side, carrying away the binnacle completely, along with the compass, making it harder for them to maintain a course. On the 22nd the wind at last moderated; there was a brief period of respite and the crew managed to put up some sails. At that point the vessel was at longitude 12 degrees West, latitude 60 degrees North, over 60 miles north-northwest of the island group of St Kilda.

During the lull, a party was sent up to secure the anchor chain, which had been rolling about for almost a week. The ship was still rolling uncontrollably when the attempt was made: one of the French-Canadian sailors got his leg caught between the bulwark (the side of the vessel) and the chain, and broke his ankle. Shortly after that the ties were cut completely and the chain and cable allowed to go over the side.

On 24th September, the crew managed to make some repairs and put up sails, including a jib, a foresail, two jibs between fore– and mainmast, a topmast studding sail, (set for a mainsail), a topsail, and a mizzen. They were able to get those sails set successfully but it was very much a jury-rigged, makeshift arrangement. They began to travel at about five knots in a southerly direction, the winds at this time being from the northwest.

During that time there was an attempt to get life on the vessel back to normal. Hot food was prepared for the first time in days. Every two days, when the weather conditions allowed, passengers were encouraged to get up on deck so the surgeon could fumigate the lower decks, as they had got into a terrible state when the passengers were kept below by the bad weather. At one point the passengers refused to leave their berths, and Captain Mason responded by threatening to stop the water ration for everybody. The steerage passenger water closets out on the main deck had been damaged, first of all by falling spars and then by casks that had broken loose. They were now completely demolished, so the passengers had no choice but to make what toilet arrangements they could down in the lower decks. Conditions on the steerage deck worsened by the hour.

Because of the exaggerated rolling of the vessel and the weight of all the iron internally, the seams between the planks had now opened, as the internal woodwork flexed to withstand the pressures that the extreme weather conditions were putting on the vessel. The Scottish and English passengers, along with the crew, had been put to work on the pumps, the Irish refusing except for two or three of them who were willing to help, the rest described (by Donald Fraser) as paralysed by fear and seasickness. They now had to pump night and day to keep the bilges dry. They could be heard by all the other passengers as they sang rhythmically through the night. One of the survivors later said that because of the uncomfortable motion of the deck of the 'Annie Jane' he could only keep pumping for three minutes at a time.

The excessive and uncomfortable movement of the 'Annie Jane' had prevented many of the passengers from recovering from seasickness; after two weeks at sea they were still ill, unable to keep any food down, and growing weaker by the day.

On the 27th they were surrounded by a thick fog, and then on the morning of the 28th the islands of the St Kilda group were sighted about 15 miles off the starboard side. This was the first land they had seen for two weeks. That would not have meant much for most of the passengers; but one at least would have felt very close to home and even have despaired about the journey taking her close to the location where she was born and brought up. Catherine Oates, a steerage passenger who was travelling with her six-month-old daughter, Margaret, was from the parish of Barvas on the west side of Lewis, and would have heard about the islands of St Kilda, and known exactly where she was.

At midday, a breeze came from the west, and then at about 2.00 p.m. they saw a land mass on the port side. The passengers were informed by the Captain that it was the Isle of Barra in the Outer Hebrides. The passengers were exultant: land had appeared at last! Relief took hold, and they rejoiced as if they were already in port. Everybody seemed happy, except for Captain Mason and Captain Rose, who spent a lot of time looking at the land getting closer, looking serious, speaking in hushed voices to each other, and taking sights with their instruments to confirm their position. Sometime in that period the First Mate, Mr Bell, turned to Captain Rose and said

The Second Voyage

'Anything that happens to the ship, you are to blame for it'.

As evening approached, all on deck could make out the light of Barra Head lighthouse, built twenty years before on the island of Berneray, the last and the most southerly of the Outer Hebridean chain of islands. The wind from the west continued to rise in strength until by evening it was storm force; at about seven o'clock at night they could see the breakers of the Atlantic waves on the many reefs surrounding the island. All efforts were made by the crew to get past to windward into the open sea beyond, but the weight of the cargo, the high seas and the wind direction made this impossible. The island could not be weathered, they could not sail past it.

Captain Mason had no choice but to turn the ship one last time. For him it was every sailor's worst nightmare, caught against a land mass with a strong wind blowing him on to a lee shore. He would have known that, barring a miracle, the ship was doomed. Square-rigged sailing ships would sail at their best with the wind behind them, but their upwind sailing ability was just about non-existent. With a full set of sails and a good crew they could manage to sail up to 20 degrees into a wind, but with reduced sails and a heavy cargo the 'Annie Jane' did not stand a chance. The other manoeuvre that square riggers could only perform in lighter winds and seas was to tack or turn through, nose into, the wind. When carried out successfully in perfect conditions, it required the coordination of all the seamen. Any turn in severe weather and high seas had to be a gybe or wearing round, changing course to swing the stern through the wind, losing them valuable sea room every time they had to change direction. In the darkness and confusion, shouting to be heard above the screaming wind, Captain Mason gave the order to wear round. There were a couple of possible routes, reef-strewn passages between the islands below Barra and the island of Vatersay, but none that anyone would attempt to navigate in storm conditions, total darkness and in a large disabled vessel.

The storm had now risen in intensity, later described by survivors as a perfect hurricane. Captain Mason had looked at his charts and studied all the options available to him. There really was only one: Vatersay's Traigh Siar or West Beach, also known as Bagh Siar, or West Bay. He called all hands to the poop and directed the First Mate, Mr. Bell, to go down below to warn the steerage passengers that the ship was about to go aground; he also instructed him to take an axe and to knock down the bulkheads, to give the steerage passengers an unimpeded route through the ship. When he was clear of the rocks at the south side of the bay, he wore the 'Annie Jane' round and directed her downwind towards the beach, in an attempt to save as many lives as possible, staying on the poop all the time and giving directions to the men at the wheel.

By that time the ship had lost most of her sails and was being driven along on bare poles; four men were on the wheel, two on either side, trying to keep some kind of control. They could see and hear, even in the storm conditions and the darkness, the white breakers directly ahead of them pounding ashore on the beach. At 11.45 p.m. on the night of 28th September the 'Annie Jane's' nineteen-day, second attempted voyage to Quebec was over. She touched the ground softly and stopped gently and easily, huge breakers running past her and foaming round her stern. Up to that point the worst injury aboard was a broken ankle, but all that was about to change.

5

The Longest Night

Captain Mason sent the First Mate, Charles Bell, down below 15 minutes before the ship struck, to let the steerage passengers know about the impending disaster. Bell was also given instructions to take an axe with him and knock down the bulkheads to give steerage passengers an unimpeded run through the deck. Unfortunately, he does not seem to have done that. The second steward, James Taylor, said that he had come into the pantry and asked for a bottle of whisky; William Moore, the sailmaker, saw him there with a bottle in his hand and later going in to his cabin to take to his bunk. That would be one of the last times he would be seen alive.

Although the 'Annie Jane' struck the sea bed gently, that state of affairs did not last very long. The vessel rose on the next large wave and lurched further in towards the beach, this time stopping with a massive shock that threw everyone off their feet. Just before the ship struck, Captain Mason had positioned two parties of seamen at the hatchway doors on either side of the exits from the forward part of the poop cabin, to stop the passengers from coming out on deck.

The Longest Night

A few of the passengers had been woken up by friends who had been out on deck and who were aware of the events taking place. Those who were awake had now gathered there, but were prevented from going any further. They were also stopped from entering the Cabin class passenger area. Those who were still asleep, the vast majority, were rudely awakened by the concussion of that second impact. Then came the first casualty of the night. As the ship struck, the whole of the foremast was wrenched forward, toppling into the sea, partly driven by the remains of the tattered sails that were still on it.

There was a young apprentice up in the rigging at the time, a last-minute replacement for Joseph Cove, the apprentice who had deserted the ship. He would also have been about 13 years old. For a moment he could be seen clinging on to the rigging, then he was gone, into the turbulent sea. Unfortunately, he would soon have plenty of company.

The foremast struck the side of the ship, smashing through the bulwarks and making a hole in the side of the ship that the sea would surge into to accelerate the break-up and destruction of the vessel. Driven by the enormous white breakers thundering towards the shore, the ship then began slowly to turn broadside, her port side to the oncoming sea. Then the whole vessel was lifted with each incoming wave and pounded down onto the seabed, the shock reverberating through every timber on the ship. The awakened passengers raced up the steps of the companionway, the weakest being trampled and suffocated in the narrow opening as everybody tried to get out at the same time. A large group pushed past the seamen and rushed out on to the main deck, many described by survivors as half-naked in their nightclothes. Some screamed and cried while others were mute with shock, wives holding on to husbands, and children to their parents.

Frantic passengers ran to the three boats just in front of the cabin before the mainmast. Others scrambled to the boat on the galley roof and they began to try to untie them; what use they would have been to them in conditions like that is questionable, but it was the only hope that they had left. Suddenly, out of the darkness, a massive wave bigger than all the previous ones hit the ship, foaming, surging irresistibly over the deck, taking just about everybody and anything that was on it, including the galley, wrenched from the deck in its entirety, with all who were still in their cabins or who had sheltered inside it.

A mass of humanity, estimated by survivors at over 100 of the passengers, was swept into eternity, gone in one minute. Their screams filled the air. For a brief moment afterwards, their cries could be heard above the screeching of the wind, and then they were quiet, voices and lives extinguished forever. The powerful wave had taken all four of the boats away as well, along with all the remains of the ship's bulwarks. Only two individuals had survived the onslaught of the wave on the deck. When the water drained away, a joiner called Charles Smith was still there, arms wrapped round and latched on to the mainmast. Julia Macarthy was hanging on as well. Travelling with four-month-old twins, she had strapped one on her back, and the other one was held tightly in her arms, but the large wave had ripped one baby away, cruelly snatching it from her grasp. The three of them retreated to the forward poop cabin.

Two of the young Scottish tradesmen, desperate to survive, grabbed the ship's two lifebuoys, stepped into them, jumped into the sea on the sheltered starboard side, and were swept out of sight into the darkness in seconds.

The forward cabin was getting more crowded now, and there was hardly room to move. Survivors were still trying to make their way up from below decks but the sea was pouring in, filling up the vessel, and the companionway was now jammed with bodies. The combined weight of the iron aboard the ship and the action of the waves was smashing the bottom to pieces as it pounded up and down. The centre of the ship began to collapse, and break up into three sections. The main- and mizzen- masts went over at that point, one of the spars violently decapitating a young woman who was standing on the poop deck.

Meanwhile, the forward part of the poop cabin, where everybody had taken refuge, began to fill up with water as it leant over at an extreme angle. There was no space left in the cabin and the water level was rising rapidly, forcing the terrified survivors to squeeze together into a smaller and smaller area. A Canadian seaman called James Boyd fetched an axe. Abraham Brooks grabbed it and began to smash his way through the dividing wall between the two areas, helped by others. They tried first at the bottom but failed because of the ropes and blocks lying there. They then tried at the top, making a large hole in the partition. One of the first through the hole was a joiner by the name of Thomas Galbraith. He later claimed that Captain Mason throttled him, and tried to push him back. Other witnesses named Mr Bell, the First Mate, and Dunlop, the Bo's'un; but with the others pushing past, whoever was in the way gave up and let them all through. Donald Fraser described grabbing his brother by the collar and pulling him through the hole after him. After this, they all crammed into the cabin area.

The French-Canadian Missionary group had gathered in Captain Rose's stateroom, praying. As the other passengers began to fill up this space, being driven in by the rising water level, the ship completed its separation into three parts. The middle part was submerged by another huge wave, collapsing on itself as the weight of the iron tore it to pieces. The deck came down on the passengers still below, perhaps mercifully putting them out of their misery and bringing to an end their struggles to survive. The forward part of the ship now broke away and floated free; the after part, including the rear part of the cabin, also broke away from the centre section and, unknown to the terrified survivors, began to float in towards the beach.

As the vessel tore itself apart, the cabin into which everybody was crowded suddenly lurched and dropped deeper in the water, lying at a more extreme angle. The survivors had some light from oil lamps up to that point, but now suddenly they were all extinguished and they were plunged into complete darkness. The sea water was already up to their waists and rising. Some scrambled for the skylights. Others grabbed floating objects – tables, barrels, whatever they could find – and climbed on top of them, trying to get out of the water. Some of them were caught by collapsing bulkheads. One of the survivors described listening to one of his friends who was trapped by wreckage and unable to break free, conversing with him until finally the water rose over his mouth. Many drowned in those frantic minutes. Survivors escaped the cabin, many making their exits through the skylights and the stern windows. Then they joined others who were huddled in groups for warmth on the poop deck. Waves and spray soaked them as they tried to stay on the deck, grabbing whatever they could hold on to. Thomas Markham, the Second Mate, described beating surgeon Francis Goold's back all night to try to keep him alive. Many died of hypothermia during that long night inside the cabin and outside on the exposed deck. Captain Mason, with others, stood on top of a table with his head out of the cabin skylight, giving instructions and what encouragement he could.

The poop finally grounded close to the beach about 4.00 a.m. As the sea began to moderate and settle down, high tide had passed. The worst was over. It was only a question of hanging on until daybreak.

It was a beautiful morning as dawn broke. The sun was shining without a cloud in the sky and the wind had dropped to a mere whisper. At about seven o'clock in the morning, the sixty people who had survived out on the open deck saw movement on the shore. There were six people standing shouting and waving to them. The mizzenmast had fallen towards the beach and was still attached by the shrouds to the ship, making a makeshift bridge in the direction of the shore. As it was now low tide, William Moore, the sailmaker, walked along the mast carrying a rope, and waded ashore. When Moore had made the rope fast to the wreck of a longboat that had been cast up the beach, the male survivors dragged their bruised and battered bodies along the mast, dropping into the waist-deep water, and then making their way to the beach.

The people on shore, seasonal farm employees, had a horse and cart with them. They had heard the screams and cries of people in distress over the sound of the storm, and come to see what assistance they could give. They backed the cart up to the remains of the poop and took all the women ashore in it.

The ones who had survived in the cabin made their way out of the skylight or exited any way they could, leaving behind them a cabin full of corpses. There were other survivors on the fo'c'sle, the forward part of the vessel: four sailors had been huddled together on it all night. This section of the ship had also remained intact and floated in till it grounded.

The scene that was revealed to them on reaching the beach was beyond human understanding and took away any relief or joy they might have felt on surviving. The golden crescent of the beach was

The Longest Night

strewn with the bodies of the dead in their hundreds, most of them greatly disfigured. Many were without heads and limbs, crushed and mutilated by the weight of the iron cargo crashing down on them. The vast majority of the bodies were naked, gashed and torn, the clothes they had been wearing ripped off them by the ferocity of the sea and encounters with the mangled wreckage of the ship. Giving mute testimony to how little warning the steerage passengers had received, most of the bodies that were clothed only wore nightclothes: they had no time to prepare for the coming catastrophe.

In groups, small and large, or sometimes pathetically alone, the corpses were scattered all along the beach. There were some still floating in the sea, slowly making their way ashore. Mostly they were face down, but some stared up sightlessly at the still blue sky of that morning. More bodies were being released from the wreck all the time, as the remains of the wreck they were entangled in released their grip. Mixed up with the bodies all along the beach were the shattered pieces of the ship: the lighter parts, barrels, bits of wood, personal possessions and unidentifiable debris. Two of the bodies, the young men who had grabbed the ship's lifebuoys and jumped overboard, were still attached to them as if they could still bring about their salvation. In the ferocity of the storm, they had served no purpose but to delay the moments of their deaths by a few minutes.

The survivors who had lost family members searched among the bodies for their loved ones. Pitiful cries, shrieks, screams filled the air and tears flowed copiously. As they found loved ones, they would gather them together and cover them with what they could find. The more stoic kept control of their emotions, many still stunned by the events of the night, but inwardly their hearts must have been scarred forever by the experience they had just gone through.

Captain Mason gathered them all on the beach and made a head count and a list of the survivors. Of the crew, there were 36 survivors: 12 had drowned. Of the 12 Cabin passengers, only four had survived, and of the steerage passengers 46 men, 16 women and one four-month-old baby had survived. According to Mason they numbered a total of 101, plus the baby who, for some reason, they did not count as a survivor. Assuming there had been the full complement of 385 emigrants aboard, then strewn along the beach and still caught up in the wreckage were 329 bodies in total, but children under ten travelling with parents were not even listed as names on the passenger list, so the real figure would have been much higher. The wreck of the 'Annie Jane' remains, even today, one of the worst maritime disasters in British peacetime history.

As one family, the Kellys from Bellaghy in the north of Ireland, embraced on the beach, it must have been sinking in how lucky they were: not a single family member out of four was lost. They were a rare exception. Jane Farrel was with them and clung to them. From the same village, she knew them all well. Jane had become separated from her family in the chaos, but found them again, along the beach. All six of them were dead: she was the only survivor.

Julia Macarthy, from Crookhaven in County Cork, walked along the beach, her surviving child in her arms, hoping against all reason that her other baby would still be alive, but she was to be disappointed.

Hugh and Margaret Munro from Glasgow who had so joyfully baptised their first child on the 'Annie Jane' while returning to Liverpool after the first voyage, perished along with the minister who had carried out the ceremony, the Rev. Jean Vernier. He was leaving five children and a widow behind him, waiting for his return to Quebec. Another four of his party, the Kempf family from the canton of Uri in Switzerland, had all perished inside the cabin as the water level rose. Captain Charles Rose, who was blamed by many for persuading Captain Mason to carry on to Quebec, perished along with his wife, Miriam.

At least ten of one family perished: of the Townleys from Belfast, County Antrim, only one, John survived; there is no record now that they ever existed.

Catherine Oates and four-month-old Margaret did not survive. She would be buried nearer her home and family than all the others, just a few islands down from where she had spent most of her life. Bernard Oates would wait for her ship to arrive in vain. Bernard was a surveyor from Ireland. They had met and fallen in love when he came to the island of Lewis to do the first Ordnance Survey map of the area in 1851.

Mary Cassidy, who was the author of the poignant letter to her mother in Kilmarnock, pleading for help to leave the 'Annie Jane', also died along with her son Daniel. Perhaps a letter was still lying in Liverpool saying *'Come home'*.

Thirty-six-year-old Jessie McKechnie from Paisley was travelling with her five children to re-join her husband Malcolm who had travelled ahead of them to Canada: Catherine aged thirteen, Mary aged eleven, Jessie aged nine, Eliza aged five and lastly the long-awaited boy, two-year-old Malcolm; all perished.

Of the Scottish tradesmen who were in the centre of the vessel, out of a total of about 87, described as strapping young men in the prime of their lives, there were 11 survivors: George Lennox of Portobello, Edinburgh, Abraham and John Brooks of Stirling, Donald and William Fraser from Inverness, David Caulder of Edinburgh, Charles Smith of Grantown on Spey, Angus Mathieson of Dornoch, James Rodgers from Kilbirnie and his sons James and John; another of his sons, William, was lost.

Not a single one of the Scottish wives who had set off from Glasgow with such high hopes and expectation survived. Of the children, only the two Rodgers boys stepped ashore on Vatersay.

Of the crew, 12 in total had drowned, including the First Mate, Charles Bell, and the Bo's'un, John Dunlop. Eight of those who drowned were the much-maligned French-Canadians.

From the party of eleven orphans from London ragged schools, only two survived: John Grogan and Robert C Walters. As part of his rehabilitation, Robert wrote an articulate and well-crafted account of the voyage and shipwreck, reproduced in Chapter Eight. He subsequently, and bravely, emigrated to Australia to join his sister, who could empathize with him as she had been shipwrecked on the way to Australia, only escaping with the clothes on her back: a reminder, if one were needed, that these were risky times to travel.

In Britain at that time there was no legal requirement to register a death; that did not become compulsory until 1855. There was never an accurate list of the casualties compiled. The list of survivors that Captain Mason compiled on the morning of 29th September did not stand up to serious examination either. He struggled with the names of the French-Canadians and the Irish, obviously facing the double difficulty of a language barrier and the strong accents of both groups. In the discharge document for the surviving sailors, only four of them could sign their own names; the rest made their mark. Among the steerage passengers the same problem would have arisen. If you can't read or write, can you even spell your own name?

Mason, bruised and battered and probably as much in shock as anybody, did the best he could under the circumstances.

6
Vatersay

After Captain Mason made a head count and took the names of the survivors, they all walked in the direction of the only settlement on the island, some of the badly injured requiring assistance. The cabin passengers, Captain, ship's officers and most of the surviving women went to Vatersay House, the only substantial house on the island, while the steerage passengers and most of the crew had to take what comfort they could in the outhouses and barns.

The following statements, made by the crew and passengers at the subsequent Inquiry, give an idea of the contrast in conditions the survivors experienced. The steerage passengers were left to look after themselves as best they could. The last group did not leave the island till almost a fortnight after the shipwreck.

Thomas Markham, Second Mate

Were you well treated by the natives? *Very indifferently treated.*

Describe how? *Captain Mason, the cabin passengers, the women, myself, and all the other petty officers, we all went down to Mr. McLellan's office, and the rest of the passengers and crew were all sent down to a farm-stead and cow-houses, and were put in there; and what they got to eat and drink I do not know. Captain Mason and myself never got anything to eat until eleven o'clock at night. They gave us a glass of whisky when we got ashore, and that was all we got until eleven o'clock at night.*

Did you ask for anything? *We asked for something to eat, but they kept saying they would "give it to us directly".*

Was there anything to eat in the house? *Yes. It was not the proprietor of the house, that was there, but his brother. Mr. Donald McLellan he was away, and when he came back we were a little better treated.*

Were there any provisions on the island? *Yes.*

How do you know? *There was plenty of cattle and sheep.*

Did you offer to pay for them? *Captain Mason offered to pay for them.*

Was there any bread? *There was barley meal cake.*

Did they offer you any of that? *No; they did not offer us anything till eleven at night.*

When the master came home? *No.*

What did they give you at eleven o'clock? *Some tea, some barley meal cakes, some salt herrings and potatoes.*

How many of you? *Captain Mason, four cabin passengers, two stewards, a sailmaker, three boys, myself, and twelve women I think.*

Charles Brown, Seaman

When you landed did the natives treat you very well? *Well they would have treated us very kindly, only I do not know if they had anything to give us. The first they gave us was well enough, but the next day they would not give us anything, and we had to go down to the beach and pick up our own salt meat and cook it; we came across a cask of oatmeal, and we took the heart of it out and made some soup.*

Then they did not treat you very well? No; the people in the island treated us very well; the governor of the island told us when we went on shore first, to go down to the other house and there we should have plenty of potatoes and herring. They gave us about a pint of milk the first time we came on shore, and then we had some potatoes, and the two days after we got potatoes once more.

Were the passengers a contented, orderly sort of people? I do not know, some of them came to me sometimes, and said they had nothing to eat; they felt pretty hungry.

Thomas Mason, carpenter

Where did you go when you were wrecked; to what house? To Mr. McClellan's.

Were you well treated there? I had many a hungry belly when I was there, and for sixteen days and nights, I was never in bed, and never had my clothes off.

But perhaps there was not a bed to be given? I do not know.

How many people are there on the island, it is a small place is it not? The island is plenty big enough, but there are not many houses on it.

How many houses in the bay where you were wrecked? A little distance off there were a few of those queer turf huts. There were some people lived in them, but they were queer people.

And they were not able to do much for you? Not they, only Mr. McClellan.

They were the people who worked for this Mr. McClellan. He was the Laird of the island I suppose? I do not know.

He was the principal man there? Yes.

When Mr. McClellan came back, he treated you kindly enough? I hope I shall never any more have suchlike treatment. We had to go on the beach and see if we could find a bit of salt beef, or anything that was washed up from the ship, and they ran away with everything we had belonging to us.

Your clothes? Yes, every rag.

Who were they? *The islanders, the people who were working at the wreck.*

Where did they come from? *I do not know.*

They did not live on that island? *No; they came from a neighbouring island, I think there were only eight men on that island.*

And then, as always, there was the class divide, the difference between how the bulk of the crew and steerage passengers were treated and the treatment of the cabin passengers.

John Morgan, Cabin passenger

What did you get to eat when you landed; did any one give you anything to eat or drink? *Yes; we had some barley bread and herrings, and then we had some mutton the following day and plenty of potatoes.*

Did all the people get that? *Only the cabin passengers, the doctor, the captain, the mates and the stewards.*

Where did the others go to? *They were down in some cottages that they had on the farm.*

What cottages? *Some cottages built up with stone and thatched, and a fire in the middle of the floor.*

They gave you what they had? *Yes.*

Treated you well? *As far as I know of, I can only speak about myself there.*

And all the cabin passengers were treated very well? *Yes; they had all the same as me, I do not know if they were pleased or not, I cannot say, I was pleased.*

Donald Fraser was interviewed when he reached Glasgow by the North British Daily Mail, published on 17th October 1853. Originally from Inverness, Donald would at least have had a rudimentary knowledge of Gaelic and have been able to communicate with the locals.

When daylight came about 5 a.m. she remained steady, it being then ebb tide. About 7a.m. we saw we could walk ashore; when all the survivors left the wreck and waded to land, the water being about breast high. Before we left the ship a number had died from cold and fatigue during the night. They had been on the poop. When we came to land we found the beach strewed with dead bodies of persons we had seen on the wreck; and there were a few country people there, some of whom told us to go to Donald MacLellan's farmhouse and all would be right, and all our things would be saved. When we went there we got some warm milk, and were accommodated in the outhouses, where many of us had neither blankets nor straw. We recovered none of our luggage. Fishermen came down in great numbers to the scene of the wreck, where they drew the dead bodies out of the water, stripped them in some cases of their clothes, boots &c., and in other cases cutting open their pockets with knives to obtain any money that might be there, and also taking the gold rings off the fingers of some female passengers. The bodies to the number of 160 to 180 were laid out on a row on the beach, and on the second day were buried in large pits dug in the sand about 100 yards from high watermark. We had nothing to eat, and on the 29th we went to a field to dig potatoes, but were stopped by MacLellan's grieve. We then went to the brother of Mr MacLellan (the latter being absent) who told us there were plenty of potatoes, and to go and dig them. The grieve again interfered, when the brother came and scolded him, and we were never troubled afterwards. When Mr MacLellan himself came home, he consented to our digging a field which was threatened with disease. We had nothing but potatoes and a little oatmeal, and salt hock, which had been washed ashore. Owing to the bad provisions, a number of us were attacked with a bowel complaint. About a week after, we went to the captain, who was staying in the farm-house, and got a barrel of herring.

The outhouses the steerage passengers stayed in were nothing more than traditional 'blackhouses', which were low squat crude stone built buildings with thatched roofs, possibly with two small windows to let in a little light and a low door, past which you would have to stoop to enter. Any fire would be in the middle of the floor without a chimney, the smoke left to find its own way out through the door and permeating through the thatch.

Normally at that time of year only the milking cows would have been present in the outhouses, and then only in the evening, but, from the passengers' descriptions, the pigs at least were at home.

Once the passengers had been accommodated, Captain Mason's next duty was to raise the alarm. He wrote a letter to Thomas Holderness, sending it with the first group of survivors who left Vatersay on 3rd October. It was subsequently reprinted in full in many of the newspapers, being published in the Glasgow Herald on 10th October:

> **Dear Sir, – I am sorry to inform you of the total loss of the "Annie Jane", with about three fourths of the passengers and crew aboard; which happened on the night of the 28th of September, during a heavy gale from the Westward, and which prevented me from clearing the land on either tack, the ship having been dismasted 36 hours after leaving Liverpool. I three times got up spars on the stumps of the lower mast, but lost them shortly after, owing to the violent gales, which have continued ever since I left Liverpool. I was drifted as far as lat.60N. One hundred and two are all that are saved on board; only three cabin passengers remain. Capt Rose, Mrs Rose and the boy servant have been found and interred. About 230 in all have been washed ashore. I have engaged boats to take the survivors to the mainland. By one of them I am sending this note. The ship was broken to atoms in five minutes, and all the cargo of the ship rolled out. It was six hours before I came ashore on part of the poop deck, very much bruised. Some of the cargo has been washed up, but nothing of much value, but the islanders are saving all they can, and have been very kind to all of us. I will write to you more fully by the next**

post that comes across, which will be in two or three days. Yours, &c "Wm Mason"

P.s.-I sent a list of passengers saved three days ago, by a different route. Anfield and Markham are both saved.

The Church of Scotland minister, Henry Beatson of the parish of Barra, came over to Vatersay to offer what consolation he could, writing a letter on 30th September to a friend on the Isle of (North?) Uist. Barra having no direct postal service at that time, all official mail had to come through the town of Lochmaddy on the island of North Uist. The other letter Captain Mason mentioned went by this route. Events would prove its journey to have been a great deal slower, with Holderness receiving the passenger list later than the letter that the first group of survivors took with them.

Manse of Barra

30th Sept. 1853

A shipwreck awfully calamitous in its result, took place yesterday morning, at two o'clock, on the West side of Watteray island, in this parish, about ten miles from the Manse. The emigrant ship 'Annie Jane', belonging to Messrs Holderness & Chilton, of Liverpool, was driven on the rocks there, and out of four hundred and thirty lives aboard only about sixty are saved. This ill-fated vessel was going to Montreal. Her steerage passengers were principally Irish, and the majority of those in the cabin, French-Canadians. She had been quite disabled during the late gales, and drifted to the N.W of Barra Head, which could not be weathered. Her commander, Captain Mason, and all his relatives on board are saved, also the surgeon, steward and three Swiss students connected with the French Protestant mission in Canada. The mate, Mr. Bell, perished, and among the cabin passengers lost were M. Vernier, one of the French Protestant pastors at Montreal, Captain and Mrs Rose and two Canadian ladies whose name I did not obtain. All their bodies have been found, and about two hundred other corpses are washed ashore. The captain is anxious to send a boat direct to Tobermory, but lest that should be prevented by the weather, he requested me to communicate these facts via Uist, to any friend who would give them publicity. Perhaps you would also write to one of our clergy at Montreal, that M. Vernier's family and congregation may know the sad event. The Swiss students, who were under his charge, are overwhelmed with grief, but I hope they will be able to attend the funeral, which takes place tomorrow. I will again write you but must now return to the scene of this heart-rending calamity.

Henry Beatson

The Reverend Beatson seems to have carried out a number of funeral services on Vatersay as the bodies were gathered by MacLellan's workers and interred. The nearest graveyard was on Barra, but the laborious process of transporting so many bodies there was thought to be impractical. The other issue that seems strange to us nowadays is that there were separate Protestant and Catholic cemeteries on Barra. God forbid that you would inter people in the wrong place. Labourers were taken to the scene by William Mcgillivary, a Justice of the Peace and farmer from Barra, brother-in-law of Donald MacLellan of Vatersay Farm. On arriving on the island, he took over organising the unpleasant task of interring the bodies. Barra native Ann Sinclair recounted how her father was taken over to Vatersay as a seven-year-old, where he was told by her grandfather to lay his hands on a corpse so he would never be afraid of the dead again.[1]

The location of the two large pits dug for the bodies has always been subject to dispute. A map in the 1860's shows them in one place; the first Ordnance Survey map, surveyed in 1878, shows it in another location. The survivors' accounts all say the pits were dug at the shoreline, except for Donald Fraser who says 100 yards from the shoreline. Newspaper accounts at the time say only two coffins were constructed, one for the Rev. Jean Vernier, and one for the First Mate, Charles Bell. Marc Ami of the French-Canadian Missionary Society said Captain Rose and his wife had coffins, as well as the Rev. Vernier. Lammert Van Buren, also of the French-Canadian Missionary Society, said that Mr Kempf was buried in a coffin with his son, and that Mrs Kempf was in another coffin with the daughter. These are not the sort of details they are likely to have made up.

Like many other impoverished communities on the edge of the sea, Barra's inhabitants looked upon any wreck as heaven-sent and regarded it as their God-given right to descend upon it and help themselves, driven as they were by poverty and need. If they could salvage barrels of salted meat, oatmeal, flour or any provisions, a successful foraging expedition could mean the difference between a family doing well that year or starving through the winter. With the property of the emigrants coming ashore with every tide, it was irresistible. Barra women were described by visitors as wearing a strange mixture of clothes: some homespun mixed in with beautiful shop-bought garments. One can only imagine they were well-wrapped against the elements in the winter of 1853. Inevitably, more boats arrived as word spread through Barra and South Uist: *'There's a wreck on the shore at Vatersay'*. The wreck was systematically looted, with many of the survivors subsequently complaining that the locals prevented them approaching the site of the wreck to try to recover their possessions.

However, others left with their sea chests. One of the groups, the last to leave Barra, needed four carts to carry the injured and their property.

Holderness replied to Mason, probably as soon as he received the second letter, in a communication dated Liverpool, October the 8th 1853:

> **Dear Sir, – It is with the greatest concern that we received your letter of the 3rd, with the distressing account of the loss of the Annie Jane, and such a fearful loss of life. We can give you no instructions whatever, not knowing if this will reach you before you have left, but will be glad to know you and the poor survivors are in all respects cared for as well as possible. Any draft you send on us will meet due honour, and you will do all you think can and ought to be done on our part towards the passengers. So long as we have been ship owners**

we have never been so much distressed or had such an awful accident. We shall be willing to return the amount of passage to the survivors to such as wish it, and the rest we will forward with as little delay as possible. The loss has created profound regret in Liverpool. We shall be glad to see you, and remain, yours faithfully.

Holderness and Chilton

Just two days later, he obtained even greater familiarity with the nightmare of the sinking, as the first of the survivors arrived at his door.

---

1. http://www.tobarandualchais.co.uk/en/play/79975;jsessionid=E68063E08F02A2CB08424A030269C118
Contributor: Annie Sinclair. Reporters: Mary Macdonald and Dr Emily Lyle. Collection: School of Scottish Studies.

Blackhouse image.
A typical blackhouse, similar to the structures in which the shipwrecked steerage passengers would have stayed on the island of Vatersay.
Courtesy of Màiri Ceit MacKinnon of the Barra Heritage Centre.

7

The Aftermath

News of the disaster was first broken when a telegraph was sent from Tobermory to the Lloyd's office in Liverpool, arriving on the evening of Friday 7th October.

The newspapers published the first articles on Monday 10th October. As always, the press excelled itself with lurid headlines and graphic descriptions. The Glasgow Herald was one of the first to break the news on that day, and, as was the accepted practice at that time, other papers re-printed the articles and some added their own small flourishes, mentioning any locals caught up in the event.

The headline was:

The Aftermath

> **APPALLING SHIPWRECK ON THE COAST OF BARRA.**
> **NEARLY FOUR HUNDRED LIVES LOST.**
>
> It is our painful task to announce one of the most mournful shipwrecks which has ever occurred on the coast of Scotland.

It then followed with a series of reports from various correspondents about the first voyage, the second voyage and the disaster, with lurid descriptions of the 300 dead on the beach, *'greatly disfigured, many of them without limbs and heads, and nearly all naked'*.

The tone of the newspapers' coverage changed quite rapidly over the following days, as the survivors made their way back to 'civilization'. Initially sympathetic, they were soon looking for somebody to blame. The North British Daily Mail printed one article castigating Holderness for not publishing the list of the drowned, writing *'his name has become hateful enough in many a household'*, and calling at the last for an impartial investigation and stern retributive justice to be rendered.

By now the Captain was being described as moody, ill-conditioned and a cruel man, drunkenly tearing up the petition to return with the phrase *'Quebec or the bottom'*, one statement he must many times have wished had never left his mouth. Thomas Hunter Holderness, replying to an attack in the North British Daily Mail, wrote this reply:

THE FATAL WRECK OF THE ANNIE JANE

> To the editor of the North British Daily Mail
>
> Sir, – A friend has just placed in my hands your journal of yesterday's date, and, in reply to your article on the loss of the Annie Jane, I would wish to correct a few of the statements, so far as the same is in my power, not having any further letters from the captain, and which I am sure will afford some satisfaction to yourself, as well as your readers.

The Aftermath

The ship was owned by myself, built, under special contract and survey, by one of the best builders in Quebec, and was in build, materials, fitting, and class surpassed by no ship that has left that colony. She was only four months old, had the highest possible class given her by Lloyd's, both in Quebec and Liverpool, and was fitted under the inspection of her Majesty's Emigration Agent here. I state the foregoing to show, in the first place, that as regards the class of the vessel, about which you make no remarks, nothing could be more desirable or satisfactory; and now devolves upon me the painful duty of contradicting distinctly some points that might reflect on the owner.

The ship was only what is considered two-thirds laden. She was by register 1294 tons, and would have taken as a full lading 1700 tons of weight or upwards. You state she had 1500 tons. She had of railway iron and materials not over 250 tons; and in all, including a large quantity of rope, soap, and other goods, a little over 1050 tons weight, and a little measurement freight; and so far from this being stowed in the lower hold, the whole space between the foremast and the mainmast was filled with cargo, say to the extent of about 350 to 400 tons weight.

By an inference most unpardonable you would lead your readers to believe that owners would prefer to risk the lives of either their crews or passengers, rather than a ship put back and not become a total loss. Surely only in the mind of a base man could such an idea of his fellows have ever found a place; and for your information, so far as my pocket is concerned, it would have been much more to my advantage had the ship put back again; for, even if I had been fully insured, I could recover every portion of the loss, as the ship was on her first voyage and, therefore, the underwriters pay all, and have not to share it with the owner as you state.

Again, you would infer that the list of survivors is kept back by the owner, when God knows I have been most anxious to obtain it, and publish the same; and to the friends of those who are saved, so far as I can get information from the crew, I have sent word. The list has not yet come to hand, and it would only have been kind and honest to give me the benefit of this doubt rather than write as you did.

With regard to Captain Mason having made the remark named in the Albion, I do not believe it ever passed his lips; he will, however, I hope, soon be here to give an answer on that head, but it is some consolation to know that he had with him, besides most efficient officers and crew, Captain Rose, who has for some years commanded vessels to this port, and who held a commission in her Majesty's service, and with whom, I doubt not, he would consult in his difficulties. Captain Mason is well known out of Liverpool – much respected – and never did a word of complaint reach me from either crew or passengers on any former voyage; and therefore, for the present, I credit my experience of the man rather than the assertion of an unknown person.

The loss of life is awful indeed, as you will see below; but, amid the depression of mind and deep sorrow for those bereft of families and friends, it is a great consolation to feel that no exertion or expense was spared on my part to fit the ship for her voyage, and no point of duty was omitted by either her Majesty's Emigration Officer or Lloyd's Surveyors of the ship.

The number of souls who sailed in the ship was, including infants

(Counted by H.M. agents as 263 adults)	337
Crew and officers	46
Four apprentices and eleven cabin passengers	15
	<u>398</u>
Total number saved	102
Souls drowned, including children	296

The Aftermath

I remain, Sir, your most obedient servant,

THOS. H. HOLDERNESS,

Liverpool, Wednesday Evening, October 12, 1853

William Hendrie fuelled the fire. He had returned to Glasgow and from there he fired off letter after letter to the press, about the first voyage of the 'Annie Jane': the chaos and instability of the ship, the morose and difficult nature of the Captain and the overcrowding. He told of his court case, the failures of Captain Schomberg and his search for justice. One of his letters, reprinted in the Falkirk Herald on 20th October, asks:

> **How does it come, that when poor people are driven back shipwrecked, and their contracts have been broken by owners, and they have nothing but starvation before them, and that too, in the face of a Government inspector with the act of parliament in his hand – I ask, where is justice to be found, when the man who is commissioned by Government, and paid by the public, to see justice done to all, cannot let a man speak the truth, but will order one of his officers to put him out of his presence?**

As for the Barra and Vatersay folk, they were receiving a bad press as well:

> **We regret to learn that the survivors of the "Annie Jane" are unanimous in stating, that they were most shabbily treated by the natives of the place where they were shipwrecked. No efforts whatever were made to administer to their comfort in any way, and food of even the meanest kind, was rarely vouchsafed to them. Their clothes and any articles the survivors could save from the wreck were pitilessly taken away, so that they were left destitute in some cases even of clothing.**[1]

The journey back to the mainland from the island of Vatersay is not an easy one even in the present day. Back in 1853 a sailing vessel could leave Vatersay and be in the harbour at Tobermory, the main town of the island of Mull, within about 12 hours. This would be very much the route of choice at the time. From Mull to Glasgow, there was a scheduled passenger ship, a brand-new paddle steamer, the 'Chevalier'. The survivors would expect to take this route, and, if they wished to continue their journey, another steamship would take them to Liverpool where they could approach Thomas Holderness's agent to recover the fare money, and make decisions about what to do with their lives after the traumatic experience they had just undergone.

Captain Mason had no choice but to organise small cargo vessels to take the survivors away from Vatersay, for the first stage of their journey back to Liverpool. The first one seems to have been mainly sailors: 26 of them, along with six steerage passengers.

Steerage passengers

George and John Kingston, County Cork; James Edmundson, County Antrim; Alexander McCormick, County Armagh; Mathew Toumaway, County Cork, Timothy O'Donovan, West Cork.

Crew

William Anfield, 25, steward, Hull; Archiebald Jamieson, 33, cook, Shetland Isles; James Boyd, 33, joiner/seaman, Belfast; James Marshall, 34, joiner/seaman, Sunderland; Edward Durray, joiner/seaman, Quebec. All the rest were seamen: James Hood,19, Dundee; Charles Brown,23, New York; Charles Garret, 23, Quebec; Pierre Damaise Berniez, 36, Quebec; Francis Walsh, 20, Dublin; John Hutchinson, 19, Ayrshire; Theodore Charest, 21, Quebec; Antoine Lizotte, 28, Lower Canada; John Jackson, 20, St Johns Newfoundland; James Allen, 30, Pembroke; Charles Burnett, 26, Forfar; Thomas Halcrow, 20, St Johns Newfoundland; William Lancaster, 18, Liverpool; Christopher Kelly, 22, Dublin; Richard Stevens, 24, London; Jacques Faillow , 19, Quebec; Joseph Dion, 21, Quebec; Joseph Leuniel, 24, Quebec; Odulphe Lemieux, 25, Quebec; Jean Baptiste Langlois, 20, Quebec; Celestin Gruimont, 16, Quebec.

The Aftermath

They left on Monday 3rd October, on the sloop 'Maria', landing that night in Tobermory, where they were hospitably received, and looked after by the agent of the Shipwrecked Fishermen and Mariners' Royal Benevolent Society, till the Wednesday, when they were granted free passage aboard the 'Chevalier' for the trip onward to Glasgow. They were described as having lost everything, some of them without shoes or jackets. The first port of call was Oban where they were fed and cared for and then re-embarked onward to Glasgow. A collection made on the ship raised the sum of £7 for the shipwrecked sailors and steerage passengers. They arrived on the River Clyde at two o'clock on Saturday morning; by then the news had broken to the press, with many of the survivors being interviewed. They then left for Liverpool aboard the 'Princess Royal' on the Sunday, arriving on the afternoon of Monday 10th.

The next morning the sailors went to see Thomas Holderness. There were no witnesses to the meeting, but unlike the others on the boat whose pay-off date was 28th September, the night that the ship was wrecked, their pay-off date was 11th October. There is a question about whether or not they received wages up to that date. A sailor during this period might get paid for the voyage up until the point he was shipwrecked, if he could prove negligence by the owner or master. Legally they would not even have been entitled to wages for the 29th as the ship touched ground just before midnight. By law they were not even entitled to any wages at all, and would lose any they had earned up to the point of shipwreck. Sailors in that period lost their income in the event of a wreck. So even though they would have been struggling to save others' lives and preserve their own all through that desperate morning, they would not even have had the consolation that they were getting paid for the experience. The logic of the owners was that if you paid the sailors when they were shipwrecked, they would not fight so hard to keep a ship afloat. Owners could insure their ships and freight so that they would lose nothing, but the sailor was not allowed to protect himself by insurance for loss of wages. His loss was total.

There might have been a good reason for Thomas Holderness to make an exception in this case. We know he had only heard about the wreck of the 'Annie Jane' on 8th October, and would presumably still have been reeling with shock with the news. Today we would probably be angered if the passengers were left behind and the first people returned to 'civilization' were the crew, but given they were a group of fit, angry, unpaid young men, Captain Mason was probably glad to see the back of them as quickly as possible.

The next group of 42, composed entirely of steerage passengers, arrived in Tobermory on Thursday 13th October. Captain Mason had given them written passes which he said would entitle them to a bed, a meal, and passage onwards when they reached Tobermory. They found that the passes were worthless, and reported to journalists that they were treated as paupers on arrival. This group comprised the following:

> John, farm servant, and Abraham Brooks, joiner, Stirling; Donald, joiner, and William Fraser, Inverness; George Lennox, potter, Edinburgh; Charles Smith, joiner, Grantown on Spey; Angus Mathieson, smith, Dornoch; Thomas Galbraith, joiner, Scotland; Timothy, James and John Rodgers, Kilbirnie, Ayrshire; David Caulder, rope maker, Edinburgh; John Grogan, London; John Parry, sawyer, Liverpool; William Reynolds, mason, Lyme Regis, Dorset; Thomas Macarty, labourer, Ireland; Gerald, labourer and Mary Clifford, County Kerry; Alexander Walker, labourer, County Antrim; Thomas Kavanagh, labourer, Ireland; Thomas Hawkins, labourer, London; Patrick Donnelly, labourer, Ireland; Edward Donnelly, Balincary, County Kilkenny; Patrick, labourer, and Ellen Kelly, County Waterford; Cornelius Mahoney, labourer, County Cork; Michael Barry, labourer, County Cork; John Townsley, labourer, Belfast; Edward Shanehan, labourer, County Waterford; Walter Farrier, labourer, County Waterford; John Macnamara, labourer, County Tipperary; Martha Donohoe, Cahersiveen, County Kerry; Mathew Hayes, labourer, County Clare; William Shack, labourer, County Tipperary; John O'Brien; James Kelly; Alexander Allen; Patrick Shea; Mary J Getty; Catherine Burke, servant, Tipperary; and, finally, Julia Macarthy from Crookhaven, County Cork, and her unnamed surviving baby boy.

They, too, were looked after by the agent of the Shipwrecked Fishermen and Mariners' Royal Benevolent Society, whose agent,

The Aftermath

Mr. Pirie, stayed with them all night and again paid for their passage on the 'Chevalier'. The agents were authorised to forward all shipwrecked seamen and passengers to their destinations, the cost being refunded by the parent Society in London. They were taken on to Glasgow by the steamer 'Islay,' arriving at Broomielaw Quay on the Clyde late on Saturday; they had to spend Saturday night in what was described as a shed at the 'Islay's' berth. 32 of them were then accepted into the Town's Hospital, the others, who had relations or friends in Glasgow, making their own arrangements. All who wished to, took passage to Liverpool on the Monday.

The last group to leave Vatersay for Tobermory in Mull were not as fortunate as the others. It comprised 27 individuals, including 12 women, three men of the steerage passengers, four cabin passengers, and eight of the crew.

Cabin Passengers

Lammert Van Buren, Holland; Marc Ami, Switzerland; Jean Francois Cornu, Switzerland; John Morgan.

Steerage Passengers

William, Amelia, Mary and Rachael Kelly, Bellaghy, County Antrim; Jane Farrell, Bellaghy, County Antrim; Catherine Stanley, Dublin; Martha Marrah, County Cork; Margaret Macaulay; Elizabeth Bridget Sullivan; Mary Jane Carruthers; Mary Sheridan; Rosina and Johanna Cohen; John Häberli, Switzerland; Robert C Walters, London.

Crew

Thomas Markham, 18, Second Mate, Hull; Thomas Mason, 26, carpenter, Hull; William Lewis, 29, carpenter's mate, Liverpool; William Moore, 21, sailmaker, Liverpool; James Taylor, steward; Mathew Irwin, 13, apprentice, Liverpool; Charles Lea, apprentice; Edward Roberts, apprentice.

They travelled in the 'Alarm', a small cargo vessel, leaving early in the morning of Thursday 13th October. It was a fine day when they left, with only a light breeze initially. Unfortunately, they made only eight miles the first day. When darkness fell, they were forced to spend the night bedding down where they could on the boat out on the open sea. The next morning, and well within sight of Mull, the wind began to rise and a sudden gust tore the sails apart. They were forced to sail away from Tobermory and head in a northerly direction towards the Isle of Canna, and try and put in there for shelter, but did not reach the harbour before darkness fell. Once more they were forced to spend a night on the open sea, on the northerly side of Canna, drifting in total darkness among the rocks, in the pouring rain. Some of them later described the whole experience as more terrifying than their voyage in the 'Annie Jane'.

When daylight dawned, they headed initially for North Uist, but conditions being favourable they turned in the direction of the Isle of Skye and sailed into Bracadale Bay, a natural harbour on the west coast of Skye, anchoring there on the Saturday morning. They tried to get some sleep in the boat as they had not slept the night before. By then, hunger pains were getting the better of them, as they had taken nothing to eat, expecting just a short crossing, not a two-day ordeal. They had a miserable time tossing and turning. The sails were now too damaged to risk any further voyage in the vessel. They eventually went ashore about 4.00 in the afternoon, and were directed to the house of the local minister, Reverend Neil MacKinnon, where arrangements were made for them all to be fed at houses on the shoreline. Then Reverend MacKinnon arranged four carts to carry their possessions and the injured, and also provided a guide to take them on to Portree, the main town and port on Skye. The short cut they were guided to was a ten-mile walk. Nowadays the B885 follows roughly the same route: a single-track road with passing places, still precipitous, twisting and steep at the beginning of the journey. The road crosses over the middle of Skye with stunning views back over Bracadale Bay and the Minch on a good day. It is unlikely that the bedraggled travellers were in any mood to enjoy the scenery. They departed Bracadale in the late afternoon. It started to rain heavily, and by the time they got to Portree in the darkness, after trudging through the bleak moorland and wading across two rivers, it was about 10.30 on Saturday night. They were soaked through, tired and footsore.

They were well-received in Portree. All of them put up in Mrs Ross's Hotel[1], and they were hospitably entertained by the inhabitants of the town under the guidance of Mr Donald Mackenzie, the Procurator Fiscal. They described the inhabitants of Portree as being extremely caring and a huge contrast to the Vatersay experience, with the local people not being able to do enough for them. Before they left Portree, a collection was made for them and 25 of the 28 were presented with four shillings each, the three Swiss missionaries declining. They had already been given a substantial sum of money by a fellow countryman called Albert Necker[2], a retired professor of Geology from Switzerland who had been living a secluded life in Portree for ten years. He insisted they travel first class all the way to Liverpool, and gave them the funds to do so.

They were taken away by the steamer 'Chevalier' on Wednesday 19th October, all being granted free passage, and a collection was taken aboard ship. All male passengers received the sum of six shillings each, and the women seven shillings apiece. The missionaries again declined the offer.

Arriving on Thursday night in Glasgow, the steerage passengers were taken to the Town's Hospital to be accommodated, accompanied by a police constable, but they were refused entrance and were redirected from there to Barnhill, the poorhouse. They demurred at this, conferred amongst themselves and refused to go, returning instead to the 'Chevalier' to spend the night in steerage.

Continuing their journey to Liverpool on the first available steamer, the 'Princess Royal', this group of passengers might have thought that their troubles were over, but it wasn't to be. The ship they were on got caught up in yet another storm, and was forced into shelter near the Isle of Man, where it waited for the waves to die down before proceeding to Liverpool, arriving on Saturday 20th October, over three weeks after the shipwreck. They were then restored their passage money and given 15 shillings each to cover expenses incurred.

In Glasgow, the sum of fourteen pounds thirteen shillings and sixpence was raised up to Saturday, the day of their departure, for the relief of this group, but only eight pounds three shillings and sixpence was received before the steamer sailed. This was distributed among the steerage passengers and the balance was then telegraphed to Liverpool, but arrived too late, as the passengers had dispersed. A member of the group, one of the ragged school orphans, had been taken to hospital in Liverpool, and some of the funds were given to him.

Following this, the survivors slowly returned to their homes. Some of the Irish did not even make it home until a full calendar month after the disaster. There were many poignant individual stories. The Belfast News Letter reported on 2nd November 1853:

The wreck of the Annie Jane – Return of some of the Survivors to Ireland

Bellaghy, October 28.

The Kellys and Jane Farrell arrived here today, after a series of disasters and hardships that have scarcely had any parallel in the annals of shipwreck. Crowds of the country people surrounded them, anxious to hear their melancholy tale: and they went from house to house describing the sad particulars. I had an interview with them. Poor Jane Farrell who lost all – father, mother, brothers, sisters – appears quite bewildered and stupefied. She is dressed in deep mourning. She states that she owes her safety to having clung to the Kellys when the vessel was parting asunder. Her family was attending their little boy who was ill, when she was borne towards her friends, she knows not how. The passengers were trampling over and suffocating each other, when a brave fellow called Carty drew the Kellys to the poop, whilst the waters were rushing both below and above them.

There follows a brief description of the wreck and the scene on the beach in the morning. It continues:

The survivors remained at Barra for three weeks, their only shelter being a shed, their only bed a heap of straw. Their food almost entirely consisted of boiled herrings, potatoes and cheese, and sometimes a little coffee; bread being a luxury unknown to the majority of the inhabitants of Barra. Gaelic is the language universally spoken on the island, whose inhabitants

The Aftermath

the survivors describe as being wild, coarse looking creatures, apparently subsisting on the spoils of the ocean, for they unmercifully plundered what the sea had spared. The sufferers left Barra in a smack, in which they then encountered so severe a gale that the master of the vessel despaired of her safety. They were driven to the Isle of Skye, at a spot about 24 miles from Portree, from which they walked thirty miles over rugged mountains to Tobermory[3], whence they sailed to Glasgow. But not yet were their perils at sea at an end for, while on their passage from Glasgow to Liverpool, they had to put in at the Isle of Man, the vessel being in great danger. After thus once more encountering the perils of the sea, they were restored their passage money, and allowed 15 shillings each besides, which did not cover their additional expenses. They then started for Belfast, which they reached this morning, and before evening they had the happiness of seeing their native village again.

A similar report appeared in the Exeter and Plymouth Gazette, 5th November:

THE "ANNIE JANE" – A young man by the name of Reynolds has just arrived here, who with his father, mother, sister and a brother aged seven years, were passengers on the ill-fated emigrant ship 'Annie Jane'. It is indeed a tale of woe. He states that his little brother was drowned in his arms, while what became of the other members of his family he did not know, until the tide had receded, when he found their lifeless bodies cast upon the shore. A subscription is being raised for Reynolds, and we do not doubt that a goodly sum will be forthcoming, for the inhabitants of Lyme are ever ready to assist the unfortunate.

There were a few obituaries, very few, as working class people did not have the money to spare for such gestures. As for all the Irish people who died on the 'Annie Jane'? They should be placed

The Aftermath

in their grim and cruel context. One million Irish people starved to death during the potato famine; another one and a half million people emigrated from Ireland in the period just before 1853: the ones who perished along the way vanished un-mourned.

One obituary added two names to the casualty list. Children under a certain age, sharing their parents' berth, did not even appear on the passenger manifest, but the Glasgow Herald, 21st October 1853, carried the following:

> Drowned on the 29th ultimo, off the coast of Barra, by the wreck of the Annie Jane, Mr William Corbet, Smith, late of Glasgow; also Catherine Reekie his wife; and Helen Millar aged 9 years, and William aged 7 years their children.

Another newspaper report added six names of a family who did not even appear on the passenger manifest at all. The Bury and Norwich Post, 2nd November 1853, reported:

> The loss of the Annie Jane – The following names of sufferers lost in the Annie Jane are to be added to the lists that have already appeared: Mrs Jessie McKechnie and her five children, Catherine, Mary, Jessie, Eliza and Malcolm from Paisley.

Mrs Mckechnie was going to join her husband Malcolm who had preceded them to Quebec; he had arrived in New York on 10th March 1853, and when he was ready sent for his wife and family.

And then, the Glasgow Sentinel, 12th Nov 1853, reported what those of a cynical disposition might deem a public relations exercise:

> The Annie Jane – The owners of the Annie Jane lately wrecked at Barra, having been applied to by a gentleman in Kilmarnock, on behalf of the widow Cassidy, whose daughter and grandchild were drowned aboard that unfortunate vessel, remitted to her last week, the sum of 30 shillings, which, though in no sense an equivalent to the loss she had met with, is nevertheless a great help to the poor woman, and was by her accepted in the most grateful manner.

The Aftermath

At that point there were only two of the survivors remaining on the island of Vatersay: Captain Mason and Surgeon Francis Goold. Mason seems to have set himself the task of disposing of the wreck. The survivors reported that he had realised £450 from the sale of the wreck and cargo, all of them saying bitterly that he had given them nothing to assist them on their journey, except £1, with the instruction to drink his health with it.

Captain Mason had sold the complete wreck to Neil Macdonald, the receiver of wrecks in Uist. This was something he had no right to do, as the wreck and all its contents, except for the possessions of the passengers, belonged to the underwriters.

On 24th October, an interim interdict was granted in Edinburgh, requested by various merchants who had shipped cargo aboard the 'Annie Jane', and Lloyd's, the underwriters, to prevent Mason and Macdonald and all others *'from interfering with and carrying away any portion of the cargo, or from interfering and carrying away any parts of the chain, and anchors, cordage and rigging, oakum or any part of the hull of the said vessel "Annie Jane"'*.

It accused the Captain of being *'unskilled and reckless and showing an obstinate disregard of all consideration for the passengers on board'*. It went on: *'The other respondent Neil Macdonald is Lloyd's agent at Barra, and instead of protecting the remains of the wreck he appears determined to make a profit out of it by means of the said pretended sale.'*

Captain Peter Nichol was appointed by the underwriters as their agent and sent to secure and protect what was left of the wreck and cargo.

In late October Neil Macdonald and Captain Mason organised a public sale, or roup, of all the remaining cargo of the 'Annie Jane'. Many people flocked to the sale, with boats arriving from as far as Glasgow and some items achieving the full market price. The purchasers then went to considerable expense to arrange uplift of the items from Vatersay.

The Glasgow Sentinel of 12th November 1853 carried this article:

Wreck of the Annie Jane

Tobermory, Nov. 1

Mr. Munro, messenger at arms, from Glasgow, and Mr. Nichol, Crinan Canal, proceeded from Tobermory in the smack Dream, on the 29th ult, for Barra, to take possession of the materials saved from the wreck of the Annie Jane. They met the smack Alexis Kerr, in Canna harbour, and took from her, above four tons old and new cordage, which she had on freight for Glasgow, being part of the wreck of the unfortunate Annie Jane. The above was bought and paid for at the public sale of the said wreck.

The purchasers took legal advice but discovered that Neil Macdonald and Captain Mason had no legal authority to dispose of the items and that the sale was not good in law. They tried to recover the expenses they had incurred, but the underwriters refused to indemnify them for this or even repay the expenses that they had incurred prior to the sale. Captain Nichol then continued to Vatersay to secure the wreck and cargo, recovering any items that had yet to be removed. One newspaper report states that he arrived in Vatersay and interrupted an ongoing sale, much to the consternation of the buyers and the mirth of the onlookers.

Captain Mason had begun the erection of a neat wooden fence around the burial place, the timber being taken from parts of the wreck which had been washed ashore. Captain Nichol put a stop to the use of timbers from the wreck for that purpose, and the fence was never completed. What had been erected was eventually dismantled, and nothing was left to mark the site of the graves of over 300 people. As has been noted before, its exact location remains a mystery.

The storm that wrecked the 'Annie Jane' was not an isolated incident. Huge damage and loss of life were inflicted throughout Britain on 27th September, as this contemporary newspaper report describes, with remarkable prescience:

North British Daily News,
Glasgow, Wednesday, September 28, 1853

EQUINOCTIAL GALES

The destructive storms known as the equinoctial gales, which are generally experienced at this period of the year, have set in with more than usual violence. They commenced from the South-West early forenoon, and by the telegraph messages that were received by Lloyd's in the course of Monday, it seems that the storm has visited all parts of the coast. Towards evening the wind veered round to the North-West, and at midnight raged with the fury nearly of a hurricane. The fearful character of the gale, however has led to the anticipation that to-day's (Tuesday's) mail will furnish details of some catastrophe during the night.

In the vicinity of the Downs, between the North Foreland and Dungeness, most terrible weather was encountered. Outward bound ships, which had sailed from Deal on Saturday, were caught by the gale while making their way down channel. They made short work of it in running back. Some, when brought up, were driven from their anchors, and lost cable and all, besides being exposed to great peril when drifting. Several distressed vessels were, after much difficulty, got into Ramsgate Harbour. A ship called the Barnard, Mr Delano, bound to London, from the St Lawrence, while endeavouring to ride out the gale, had a narrow escape of being lost on the Goodwin. While the wind was raging with its greatest force, the Barnard went from her anchors. Her destruction was almost inevitable, and as a last expedient, her main and mizzen masts were cut away. This had the desired effect, and ultimately she was brought into Margate roads and securely brought up. The Margate and other boatmen report, that no fewer than 15 ships were blown away from under the Foreland. Their names could not be gleaned.

Lower down the channel the gale is described as being equally, if not more severe. Numerous disasters

The Aftermath

are looked for on the French coast. The eastern coast is also reported to have suffered much from the storm; and Harwich and neighbouring ports are filling with vessels that have lost anchors, cables, spars, &c. Most of the seagoing steamers which arrived in the river on Monday were late. They speak about experiencing very boisterous passages. The gale had a curious effect upon the midday tide of the Thames. It should have ebbed at London Bridge, according to the tables, until nearly 2 o'clock. Instead of going over to that time, the water suddenly began to flow shortly before 12 o'clock, nearly two hours before its time. This remarkable occurrence is attributed to the circumstance of the gale driving an immense body of water up channel, and so up the numerous rivers.

Liverpool – Loss of Life – This town and port were visited on Sunday evening and Monday morning with one of the most violent hurricanes experienced for many years. In the town, chimneys, tiles, scaffolding, and windows were blown down in every street, and the time ball on the summit of the electric telegraphic office was much strained, and would eventually have been torn away, had it not been secured by ropes as soon as the danger was perceived. Communication by electric telegraph was for some time suspended, and we have learned that the driver of one of the engines of the London and North Western Company was considerably injured by one of the poles falling upon him while the engine was going up one of the inclines on that line. The river throughout the day was very rough, but in the evening it lashed itself into a perfect fury. Some parties had the temerity to attempt to cross to Cheshire in the Woodside ferry-boat from the landing stage at half-past five, but after buffeting about for two hours found it impossible to proceed, and the boat had to return to land her passengers at the Prince's pier, and whilst making fast snapped no less than five hawsers. At six o'clock all the ferry boats ceased to ply. The accidents on

The Aftermath

the river have been numerous, and it is feared that very bad accounts will be received from the various ports along the coast. The American packet ship Nova, which sailed on Thursday, put back through stress of weather, and arrived in the river on Sunday evening. During the gale she dragged her anchors, and went ashore near Sandon Dock-basin. She had on board 191 passengers, and when she went ashore, several attempted to jump from the ship to the pier head, but fell into the river and were drowned. The Joseph Walker, from New York, also went ashore near the same place, and sustained considerable damage. The brig Caroline, from Prince Edward's Island, got ashore of the Nelson Dock, and lost masts and bowsprit. The captain, fearing the vessel was in imminent danger jumped ashore, and the crew and a woman with five children passengers, were shortly afterwards rescued. At high tide the ship came off and drifted up the river, and got ashore at Pluckington Bank. Two small vessels were seen to founder off the North-West lightship during the gale, and all on board perished. The Intrinsic from Prince Edward's Island, is ashore off the Bramley Moore dock, with loss of foremast, Bowsprit, rudder, &c. A flat sunk in the Huskisson dock, and with great difficulty the crew were saved. The American, from this port for San Francisco, got ashore near Southport, and at one time it was feared she would go to pieces. The lifeboat went out to her, and remained with her all night. The William Ward, from Quebec, was put on shore above the New Ferry, having parted her anchor. The clipper ship Shooting Star, discharging in the Huskisson dock, lost all her top masts during the gale. The Stephen Glover, from St John's N.B., at anchor of the rock, with loss of main and foremast, bowsprit, &c. A small pleasure boat capsized off the rock, at New Brighton, but three persons who were in her were saved with difficulty. At the Prince's Pierhead some of the persons who had ventured imprudently too near the edge of the river, were blown in, but rescued by the

timely intervention of the police, &c. The Hinds, from Quebec, was in contact with the Elizabeth, from Smyrna in the river, and both vessels lost their bulwarks, &c. The Rhydland Trader, (flat) was driven ashore at Rhos bay: the crew were saved. It is feared that the shipping off the coast and in the Channel will have suffered severely. The gale having lasted about 16 hours, died away.

---

1. Still called the Royal Hotel and open for business; there is a photo on the wall close to reception (illustration on page 92) with the name 'Ross Royal Hotel' on it.

2. Professor Louis Albert Necker, 10th April 1786 to 20th November 1861, Interred in Portree Old Cemetery, where his gravestone still stands.

3. If anyone walked from Portree to Tobermory, they would clearly be performing an impossible task – they are on separate islands.

The Aftermath

Ross Royal Hotel

'Mrs Ross's Hotel', now The Royal Hotel in Portree on the Isle of Skye, as it would have looked when the survivors stayed there. It is still open for business, and this original poster is up on the wall close to the reception desk. With thanks to the manager and staff.

8

The Ragged School Boy

Within this book, there are several references to the 'ragged schools', as eleven of the passengers were inmates. These were charitable organisations dedicated to providing free education to destitute children in nineteenth century Britain. The vast majority of these institutions were in the working-class districts of rapidly expanding new and old industrial towns. They were called 'ragged schools' because the students attended in whatever clothes they owned, sometimes literally in rags. Robert C Walters was one of those who attended a ragged school, and took ship on the 'Annie Jane', bound for a new life in Canada. His account was published in the Ragged School Magazine of 1853, and is reproduced in an unedited form here. At the end of the article are comments from the editor of the Ragged School Magazine about Robert Walters and his character.

1. The first voyage

In presenting this narrative of my misfortunes or adventures, whichever the reader is pleased to term them, I feel as if a great responsibility were imposed upon me however light others may look upon the matter. The fear of incriminating certain parties has prevented me from giving any account before; still at the urgent request of those whose duty it is to inquire into such matters, I have laid aside all notions of delicacy, and determined to furnish my benefactors with as correct an account as it lays in the power of my poor imagination to render. I became an inmate of Bloomsbury school about the 15th of March 1853. I will pass over that portion of the time from my first entering the school as an orphan to the time I left to go to Canada, merely remarking that I and my companions experienced every kindness that our benefactors could bestow upon us.

We started from London on the 19th of August 1853, for Liverpool where we arrived the same night, we formed a merry party and were in the highest spirits, and the day being fine we were much delighted with our day's journey; that night we took a stroll round the town and took up our quarters at the Emigrants home[1], where we stayed till our departure. The next morning we paid the ship a visit, and spent the rest of the day in visiting different parts of the town, accompanied by a gentleman from London who kindly officiated for us, and rendering all the assistance in his power. We embarked on board the "Annie Jane" in the Sandon dock on Tuesday, August the 23rd and slept on board that night. The next day we lay in the river and were towed out to sea at three o'clock P.M.; the tug left us about ten o'clock the same night. We slept soundly that night, but upon waking the next morning I felt very sick, and was obliged to keep to my bed the best part of the day; but I was not the only one who did so, some laid in their berths for several days. The next day Friday, being the second after leaving Liverpool, a strong wind blew, increasing at last into a complete hurricane, and carried away at one swoop the fore, main, mizzen-topmasts, spars, rigging etc thus the vessel became in a few minutes disabled; All the time she was rolling fearfully, and the boxes belonging to the passengers got loose and rolled from side to side, thus endangering persons' limbs to a fearful extent. At the time the foretopmast fell, two of my companions were standing near the galley and had it not been for a seaman who pulled one of them under a boat, he would in all probability have been killed on the spot. Nor were these our only misfortunes: beside the misery we had to suffer hunger – the Bo's'un refused to serve out the provision, and on the other hand it would have been impossible to have cooked anything, if we had had it. As night came on, the rolling increased fearfully, and we were all in darkness. Chests flying about, children screaming, seamen cursing– in short it was such a scene as must be seen to be believed. One part of the vessel, the fore-hold hatchway, where the Glasgow joiners were, was covered with a few loose planks which when she lurched, all fell down in the lower fore-hold, which not being covered left them in imminent danger of their lives; the majority of the crew being French-Canadians, and not understanding the English language, left the ship in great danger, and were not at hand when required.

Some of the passengers spoke individually about bringing the ship back, but these only met with insults. The next day a petition was made out with the names of the passengers affixed, and handed to the captain which induced him to turn back.

Upon our arrival at Liverpool after being at sea nine days, a number of the passengers went to the government inspector and stated their grievances, but nothing particular was done for us.

Having arrived at Liverpool on the 2nd of September some of my companions made up their mind to start to London, and were going to write to London for that purpose, but upon further consideration it was agreed that I should write one letter for the whole lot, upon which Mr L---- came down and settled all matters satisfactorily. While staying here a great many disputes arose between the passengers and owners, some declaring they would not enter the vessel to go to sea again after the usage they had received; others adopted the more safe but expensive plan of forfeiting their passage money, rather than risk their lives a second time; Three of our lads held out till the last, upon which the same gentleman who had engaged our berths sent to London for a corresponding number to take their places. These came and then the others kept their places, adding three more to our company.

II. Second voyage and shipwreck

The vessel underwent repairs and sailed on the 9th of September from the Mersey, after being towed to the outside of the Isle of Man. The weather continued fine till Sunday the 11th. About the middle of the day it blew a violent gale, which carried away the foretop-mast and main-topgallant-mast, besides damaging the bowsprit. The gale increasing to a storm, and the ship from the heavy cargo, being chiefly railway iron, this caused her to roll in a fearful manner. By some accident the chain cable broke adrift and rolled about the quarter deck for a week after, at last an effort was made to secure it in some way, and a number of the crew were ordered to stow it; one of the number, a French-Canadian had his leg broken by the chain jamming it against the bulwarks.

One morning soon after leaving Liverpool me and G----- were sitting in our berths talking about those we have left behind, when he took a letter from his box and requested me to read it to him. I read it aloud to him, and upon perusing it, I found it to be from Mr W---- the secretary of the school he left. He cried very much, and putting the note away he said, "*Ah! I shall never see Mr W---- again*". I tried to comfort him as much as I could, but I am afraid I proved a sorry comforter, being much in need of consolation myself. At the time the crew having got up some spare spars, the ship's head was turned for England. Upon coming on deck the next morning I noticed a disturbance among the passengers, upon enquiry I found the ship had been turned again during the night, and it was the intention of the captain to prosecute the voyage to the St Lawrence. A number of the male passengers then formed themselves into a council, and proceeded to the captain to demand an explanation, and upon requesting to know where they were going, the captain called out to one of the mates to hand him his revolver, then levelling the piece at them, threatened to shoot the first man that interfered between him and his duty.

One night, whilst I was asleep in my berth, I was awoken by a passenger calling out that the ship was in danger, and that the aid of the passengers was required to pump the ship. I went upon deck, and found everything in the greatest confusion, and nearly all the male passengers were up; the Second Mate requested the passengers to lend their assistance to the pumps, which they did;

I took my station the same as the others, although I was only half dressed; but from the dreadful nature of the sea it was impossible to stand to it more than three minutes. The pumps were kept at work all that night, and for several days after. The crew cleared away the broken spars and replaced the foretop-mast; the ship's head was again turned, and we learned to our dismay that it was still the intention of the captain to continue the voyage.

We now held to the West and North West, the wind blowing chiefly from the South West for several days. During this time I was very ill, and was consequently obliged to keep my berth.

On the 21st of September a strong wind sprung up from the South, which gradually wore into a complete hurricane, which lasted till the 28th. The crew were now ordered to close-reef the topsail, and a number of them were aloft for that purpose, but found it impossible to do so; at length by dint of great effort the ship was brought to.

The passengers were again ordered to the pumps, the next day the weather-mainsail was carried away, as the sea was running very high and the ship rolling fearfully; orders were given to cut away the maintop-mast and throw the chain-cable overboard, which was done.

At this time the life-boat, which had been lashed to the starboard quarter, was washed overboard; the foretop-mast which had been only temporarily replaced, was again swept away. It was now deemed necessary to turn back, and the ship's head was again turned for the nearest port in England or Ireland. We ran about three days before the wind; on the morning of the 28th it was reported that they could see land[2], which afterwards proved to be correct. Towards night the wind increased in violence; some of our lads dressed themselves and went upon deck; I still kept below being very ill at that time. As the night advanced a rumour was spread through the ship that we were approaching a reef of rocks, but we paying little attention to it, having become so used to seeing danger that we thought the person who told us must be labouring under some extraordinary delusions at the time. At length, after having slept for some time, I was awoken by one of my companions, who requested me to put on my clothes and come upon deck. At first I was inclined to treat his advice with contempt, and tried to persuade him that his fears arose from a weak imagination; but at that moment another boy verified the other's assertion and said, "*He had seen some of the sailors shake hands*". Upon receiving this information I got out of my berth, and went up the after-hatch-way into the fore-cabin, where I found most of the passengers assembled; At that instant I heard someone crying and upon turning round I recognised George. I tried to persuade him there was no danger, and pointed out the folly of showing such weakness; but I soon found out I was wrong, for at that juncture I heard the screams of some of the females. The poop of the vessel being a remarkably long one it held the greater part of the passengers, who, upon hearing the ship was in danger, crowded to the doors on each side, but they were prevented from going any further by two parties of seamen, who seemed posted there for that purpose.

I tried to force my way through one of the crowds that were standing on the Larboard[3] side to get out upon the deck, but was prevented. At this crisis I saw a sailor pushing his way through the crowd, he had just come of the poop deck and I could see that he wished to be heard but from the shrieks of the affrighted creatures it was impossible to hear him. At length the clamour ceased and taking advantage of the pause, he told them that there was no danger if the vessel remained where it was till morning – we should be able to get off in the boats at daylight. Scarcely had this intelligence been communicated to us, when I noticed another sailor come in from the deck, and I saw the old passenger cook[4] – go up to him and enquire about the vessel; the other one said, "*It's all over with us*". Upon hearing this the cook threw his arms into the air, and walked up and down like a man deprived of his senses. I saw no more of the poor fellow after this; I tried again to get out on deck, and while in the act of so doing the vessel struck the sands, I was thrown upon a number of boxes, and nearly smothered by the others landing upon me. I regained my feet, but had scarcely done so when she again struck the sands, and I was precipitated a second time. At last I contrived to stand on top of the boxes and cling to an iron stanchion; while standing there a number of persons clung to my clothes for support; by this time the bulwarks were stove completely in, and the water was rising to a considerable height. At length, abandoning my post on the boxes, I removed to a greater distance; the chests had by this time got loose, and were floating about. I clung to a berth for support. Presently I heard a voice that I knew, and went in the direction from which it proceeded, and found it to be one of my party; upon recognising me, he put out his hand and exclaimed, "*Oh Walters we shall all be drowned*".

Presently a young woman, who had occupied a berth opposite ours, came upon deck, and inquired of me if I had seen any of her children; upon my answering in the negative she turned away and rushed down the hatchway, where she must have perished. There must have been at this time as many as three hundred persons in this part of the vessel. The ship had now become a complete wreck, the greater part of the fore-cabin was broken up, and I was standing on a large chest, expecting every moment to be my last. As nearly as I can remember I stood for about twenty minutes, kept in a dreadful suspense between life and death, or, in a more classical language, I seemed to be the mute spectator of the awful sacrifice of human life.

At length, as if by the goodness of the Almighty, in answer to my prayers, I was to be delivered, but not before going through a great many more trials. The greater portion of the passengers were now crowding towards the partition which separated the fore-cabin from the after-part, so that we were completely hemmed in an all sides, without the least chance of escape. A seaman who was standing among us volunteered to go in search of his hatchet, to break through the partition and thus give us an opportunity to escape to the after – part of the cabins. He at length returned, and a place broken, a great number availed themselves of it. I was just in the act of climbing through when I perceived three of our lads; I sprang through the aperture, and then assisted the others.

When we got in the cabin we found it crowded mainly with male passengers and seamen; the captain was standing in the midst, and in answer to their inquiries whether there was any hope, said, "*Let me go upon deck and attend to my duty*". G---- went up to him, and shook hands with him; and then turning to me, said, "*Walters, shake hands with the captain, and thank him for what he has done for us*". I obeyed mechanically; the captain said, "*God bless you my dear boys*". We four managed to get into a private enclosed berth, to shelter us from the water, but we had not been there many minutes when the partition of the cabin gave way, from the pressure of the crowd outside, and we narrowly escaped being buried in the timber. We came again into the open cabin, and I was just leaving to go back again through the partition when I felt a fearful jerk, the water rose nearly to my waist and the light was extinguished, thus leaving us in total darkness. I now missed my companions; I gave up all hope of saving myself and became almost insensible to all around. Whilst in this situation I felt some water falling on my head, and knowing by that there must be some opening about, I searched for it but the sea water having got in my eyes it was some time before I could find it. I looked up, but could see nothing for some time; at length I fancied I could distinguish several small glittering objects; all at once I came to the conclusion that it must be the sky that I could see, so that it must be the skylight that was above my head; I tried to reach it, and managed to grasp the woodwork, but I was so weak from my recent illness that I dropped down.

I again clambered up to it, and was just getting into the framework when some person from behind put his arms around my body and pulled me down again – this was enough to dishearten me; just at that instant I felt something under my feet, and found it to be a cask, which rose me up to the table which was already floating with a few of the passengers and the captain upon it. The place where I now found myself was a kind of loft between the after-cabin and the poop-deck; it was chiefly used as a depository for the use of the cabin passengers. I sat for some time upon the floating table, with nothing on me but a blue checked shirt, and the water washing over me all night. The captain was standing just before me, with his head out of the broken skylight. I learned that the vessel had broken into three pieces, and we were floating about on the after-part of the wreck. I heard poor G------ calling out to me for about twenty minutes; I answered him, and told him which way to come, but it seems he was jammed with broken timbers, and the water rising gradually to his mouth gave the poor fellow a lingering death. It must have been about eleven o'clock when the vessel first struck, and it was not until about half past six the next morning that we got of the wreck. The place where we were was strewn with broken fragments of the wreck, which kept floating about inside the cabin maiming a great many of us. The deck above our heads was bending like a sheet of paper and threatening to fall and crush us every instant.

III. Respite and return

At length the long-wished-for morning came, and presented to us such an awful scene that no imagination could depict. As daylight broke, I began to distinguish the objects around me. I was sitting upon a pile of broken timbers, and just at my feet lay a poor fellow half buried in the rubbish, and a little further on lay another; I was in the act of pulling off some of the timber, thinking they might only have been stunned, when one of the sailors called out to leave them alone. Groups of half-naked women and men were sitting about; half dead with cold and fright. We could hear some persons above us on the deck, and I got up through the broken skylight upon the deck above.

Here a scene presented itself more horrible than I have the power to describe. The vessel had broken up into three pieces, the after-part, which we were standing on, had floated in towards the shore, the fore-castle was standing in a perpendicular position, and numbers of broken timbers were floating about in all directions. The strand was literally strewn with portions of the wreck, and a great number of dead bodies, which had been washed up. The land lay all round. On looking about I recognised one of my companions; he was standing on the deck, and seemed to have suffered a great deal from the sea washing over him; upon seeing me he put out his hand and asked me where the others were; I told him I did not know what had become of them. Just then I saw the captain standing against us; he was very much bruised, and turning round to me, asked if I was the lad that he had shook hands with on the previous night.

The mizzen-mast had fallen towards the shore, and being held fast by the shrouds, formed a bridge between the wreck and the shallow water. The wreck had been observed from the island almost as soon as day broke, and in the first instance about six Barra[5] men came down to the shore to render all the assistance in their power. By the help of the islanders a rope was attached from the mizzen-mast to the shore, a cart was then backed up to the end of the mast and by that means the females got ashore.

I walked along the mast and then dropped into the water, which was not more than up to my waist then waded ashore. The island where we now found ourselves was ascertained to be Barra head, on Barra island[6], the southernmost of the Hebrides.

The Ragged School Boy

On landing, I had nothing more than my shirt on, and I felt so weak that I could hardly walk. The survivors repaired to a farm, the only one on the island, where we were hospitably received; but the inhabitants of the island being a poor class, and not having too much of the good things of this life, we fared but indifferently. I repaired to a stable, and the farm servants having lit some fire, and there being an abundance of clean straw, we made ourselves as comfortable as our circumstances and situation would permit. Here I rather incautiously put my feet to close to the fire, so that when I went to put my foot to the ground it caused me the greatest pain.

While staying in these quarters we had to make a close acquaintance with some of the inhabitants of these regions, such as pigs and ducks, and small geese.

At length I removed from the vicinity of these acquaintances. My foot, which had been hurt in the wreck had now become so bad that I was obliged to keep my bed, and stood a good chance of being well-nigh starved, so that I was obliged to make excursions to the kitchen on a sort of foraging expedition, and retire again upon the approach of any hostile party.

The island upon which we were cast was about three quarters of a mile in width and about one mile in length, and surrounded on all sides by other small islands; the nearest town lay about ten miles distant. The survivors when mustered amounted to 102, including passengers and seamen, out of these there were 8 cabin passengers[7], 61 steerage, and 33 of the crew showing that the loss of life must have been at least 350. We lost nine of our party.

Capacious pits were dug for the dead, who were buried in exactly the same state as they were washed up from the wreck.

We stopped on the island about a fortnight. The captain hired some small-fishing boats to take us over to the mainland, but the boat I was in was driven out of its course, we had to put in at Bracadale Bay, Isle of Skye[8], where we arrived, after having been two nights and two days from the time we left Barra. The boat in which we sailed lost all her canvas, and it was unsafe to venture out to sea again in her. We therefore set off the same day to Portree, where we arrived the same night, wet and foot sore; but here we met with a much better reception than we had expected; the inhabitants of Portree did all that was laid in their power.

A subscription was got up the next day in the Kirk, and we were taken to an hotel, where we stayed till the boat arrived to take us on to Glasgow; we left Portree on the 18th of October, and sailed by the steam-packet Chevalier and landed on the 19th.

I was now obliged to go to the infirmary on account of my foot; I stopped here about a week. My foot having got better I left Glasgow on the 26th, and arrived in Liverpool the next day; the following day I went to the owners, to receive any information that they might be able to give me of my companion who had been saved with me from the wreck, and who had sailed from Barra one day before me. I expected he would have reached Liverpool at least a week before me; but what was my surprise when the owners told me they had neither seen nor heard anything of him, nor have we gleaned any tidings of the poor fellow yet.[9] The owners gave me the money to defray my expenses, and I started the following day for London where I am now staying, at the school in Bloomsbury. Since my return I have been enabled by a few kind friends, to procure a passage to Australia, and like Robinson Crusoe am about to set out again in the wide world to try my fortune, trusting that by the goodness of God and my own exertions, I may yet live to bless the day I first entered a ragged school.

....

Many would have thought this poor son of poverty and trouble had had enough of the sea, to cause him to sit down on British T*erra Firma* rather than again brave the dangers of the deep. He, however, thinks otherwise. He has sought help again of the committee, which, with the assistance of a lady in Cheltenham, has been afforded, so as to secure a passage for him to Victoria, He has sailed a few weeks since for Melbourne, at which place he has a sister, full well able to sympathise with such a brother, as in going out she was also wrecked, and escaped only with her life. There is reason to hope, that the awful scenes witnessed by this youth, have made a deep, and salutary impression upon his mind, which, with God's blessing, may result in a change of heart and life.

[N.B. Having myself seen this lad after his shipwreck, and asked him some questions when he came before the committee of the

Ragged School Union for a passage to Australia, I wish to add a remark or two to his very well written and interesting narrative, that may give pleasure to all supporters of ragged schools.

It is well known that the Bible is made the foundation of all our teaching, and our boys taught to make its truths the foundation of all their actions. I was myself present when Bibles were given those very boys on their leaving us, and had the melancholy pleasure of commending them to God on their departure, and of impressing on them the duty and advantage of reading God's word every day, under every difficulty and in every danger. I was delighted to find, on questioning the lad Walters, that he and his companions in the "Annie Jane" had not, even amidst such dangers as he describes, omitted to read their Bible, and that they were found by the captain several times reading the scripture to each other before the awful wreck occurred. It is very encouraging to hear this, and I am quite sure all our friends will be pleased to know the fact.

W.Locke, Hon. Secretary.]

About the Ragged Schools:

In April 1844, an attempt was made to unify the ragged schools; the Ragged School Union was formeds with the objective of establishing '*Schools expressly for that destitute and depraved class; in the very localities, courts, and alleys where they abound*'. By the 1860s it is estimated that some 25,000 pupils were attending ragged schools.

In 1847 emigration to the colonies for improved scholars of ragged schools began, and by 1853 more than 400 students of both sexes had been sent to different parts of the world from London ragged schools alone. The Ragged School Committee had engaged passage for small groups of children in almost eighty different ships. Some were sent to Australia, but with the gold rush of 1851, Australia had fallen slightly out of favour, with a fear for the moral welfare of immigrants and a sudden increase in the price of tickets. So Canada was the destination of choice for a short period. It was quite common for the ragged school emigrants to repay the cost of their passage out of their first employment. They were not just abandoned by the Ragged School Union: communication was encouraged, at least for the first period, while the child emigrants were settling down in their new environment.

Up to 1854 the worst accident that had been reported was a broken arm among a group of boys entertaining themselves playing leapfrog aboard a ship.

The boys taking passage on the Annie Jane were: five boys from St Giles and St George School, Bloomsbury; two boys from Kentish Town School, 14 Ferdinand Place; two boys from Richmond Street School, Maida Hill; two boys from Grotto Passage School, 2 High St., Marylebone.

Of the 11 boys, only two survived.

---

1. The appalling conditions that emigrants experienced in Liverpool became a matter of public concern. An emigration depot at Birkenhead was opened in 1852 for British emigrants. It was not luxurious but did provide warm meals, shelter and a safe haven for emigrants.

2. The land sighted would have been St Kilda.

3. Larboard was the old term for Port, or left-hand, side of a vessel.

4. Feeling young today? It's all relative: the cook was only 38 years old.

5. They would probably have been Barra men; Vatersay was cleared of its inhabitants around 1850.

6. Robert makes a mistake here: the ship had actually come ashore on the West Beach of the island of Vatersay.

7. Only four cabin passengers survived.

8. They had sailed for Tobermory on the island of Mull.

9. The missing boy, John Grogan, eventually turned up: he had been kept in a Liverpool hospital for three months with a fever. When released he had to walk all the way from Liverpool to London, arriving at the school he had left in a wretched and pitiable condition.

9

Le Naufrage de l'Annie Jane

The original manuscript was written in French by survivor Marc Ami in 1856, and it was published in book form in Montreal in 1891.

....

**The Shipwreck of
the "Annie Jane"**
An account of the story of
the French-Canadian missionaries
by
Marc Ami, Pastor
Manchester, New Hampshire
Publisher: Le Fidèle Messager
1891
The printing of this first edition is limited to 100 copies

Le Naufrage de l'Annie Jane

Foreword

On the 20th June 1890 the pastor, Mr Joseph Provost, from Springfield (Mass.), described in his magnificent address on St Helen's Island, at the great picnic of the French-Canadian protestants, the sad event which is the subject of the pages that you are about to read:

The period which stretches from 1850 to 1860 is noted for the great success of the French-Canadian Missionary Society. Its sphere of activity grew. The pastor Mr Jean Vernier went to Europe with the aim of bringing over new workers. There took place one of the saddest events that we have on record. Mr Vernier, after having persuaded Mr Kempf, Mr Van Buren, Mr Marc Ami and Mr J. Cornu to come to Canada, left with these worthy missionaries on a sailing ship called the "Annie Jane". This was in the month of August (1853).

The first days of the crossing were favourable and they sailed full of hope. But soon the sea became rough and on the night of the 28th–29th September, the ship, stripped of its rigging, surrendered to the fury of the torrents, breaking on the rocks. It is said that Mr Vernier came to his final hour in perfect peace. He motivated his brothers in despair, pointing out heaven as a meeting place. Such was the sacred and intimate life of a heart who loves, rising above the wild elements to know the hand of God. Mr Kempf, his wife and their two children stayed calm when faced with their tragic end. The next day, they found their bodies on the shores of the island of Vatersay, the land next to the shipwreck. The body of Mr Vernier and those of his unfortunate companions were buried in the midst of a solemn sadness. In losing Mr Vernier, the mission was deprived of a true servant: passionate, generous and truly devoted.

On the 2nd May 1856, Mr Marc Ami, then a teacher at Belle-Rivière, a province of Quebec, and one of the eyewitnesses of the terrible disaster, finished writing down the details of the shipwreck of the 'Annie Jane'. For thirty-five years, the manuscript lay forgotten amongst the documents of Mr Ami. Today, giving in to the requests of his friends, he read it publicly, counting on the indulgence of his listeners.

We were persuaded that this little booklet will be one of the most interesting documents on the history of French Protestantism in America.

Mr Marc Ami is today the head of a French evangelical mission in Haverhill, Mass.

J.A. Derome
St-Anne, Ill., 30th July 1891

The Wreck of the 'Annie Jane'

Chapter 1: The Departure

In March 1853, Mr Jean Vernier, pastor, and member of the French-Canadian Missionary Society of Montreal, left Pointe-aux-Trembles, which is near to Montreal, with the aim of going to find new missionaries in Europe.

He arrived in Glay in France in the month of June of the same year. This village was where, through the efforts of Mr Jaquet, a devoted man full of faith and fervour, an organisation had been founded to develop Christian teachers, evangelists and bible distributers, located in the area of Doubs in the east of France. Mr Vernier himself had been brought up in this institution and had spent many years there. It was there that he had experienced the peace of the Lord and resolved to devote himself to the ministry. He went to finish his studies in Geneva with this intention and it was there in that city that a pastor called Mr J.E. Tanner of the French-Canadian Missionary Society had engaged his services twelve years previously (1844). Mr Vernier was a native of Glay and visited the village of Meslières, where his parents, two sisters and other family members still lived, before his departure for Canada.

In coming to Glay, Mr Vernier hoped to find some people in the Institute willing to devote themselves to the work of the mission: his expectations were not disappointed. He offered me the position of teacher at the school of Pointe-aux-Trembles, and to Mr Lammertz Van Buren, a man from Holland who had come to Glay to learn French, that of missionary. Others had been about to join us but found themselves prevented from doing so by circumstance. After having spent some time at Glay, both to visit his parents as well as to inform us about our future work, Mr Vernier left for Geneva in order to find more labourers, if possible, for the work of God by means of the town's evangelical society. He needed pastors and missionaries. During his trip to Neûchatel, he persuaded Mr Kempf, who was married and father to two children, and Mr Schaffter, from Berne, to come to Canada. Mr Schaffter, however, would not leave until later on.

Time was going on and the moment of the departure drew near. Mr Vernier let us know that we all had to go to London for the 15th August. After a visit to Geneva, my home town, and after saying goodbye to my parents and my friends, I returned to Glay where Mr Cornu, one of the recruits from the Geneva evangelical society, came to find me and we both went to London together. Mr Cornu was accompanied by a young man named Häberli, I think, whom he had been put in charge of taking with him to America. On the set day, we were reunited in the great English metropolis and spent five days there visiting its main attractions, after which we left for Liverpool.

The vessel on which we would be making the voyage was magnificent – new, sturdy, triple-masted and, we were assured, an excellent sailing ship. She was called the 'Annie Jane'.

On the 26th August, 1853, we set sail for Quebec. The wind was favourable, the sky was clear, and everything breathed life and joy.

Under such circumstances, we thought we would have a wonderful and pleasant crossing. The steam boat which towed us into the open sea left us at night and we counted on an enjoyable journey.

Chapter Two: Setbacks and Premonitions.

We made rapid progress when, on the morning of the 28th (August), we were alarmed to hear terrible cracking sounds. We went up to the deck and noticed that sadly the three masts of the vessel had been broken by a sudden gust of wind. The captain, seeing the impossibility of continuing the journey with a ship in the state in which we found ours, resolved to return to Liverpool. We were then in the North Channel and a good wind favoured our plan to return, sailing along the west coast of Ireland to return via the south. On the 1st of September, we were in view of Holyhead and on a telegram from the Captain, a steamboat was sent to take us to Liverpool. On the night of the 2nd September, we dropped anchor in front of the city and on the following day we made our entry to the docks.

Mr Vernier, Mr Van Buren and I went straightaway to the owners of the vessel to reclaim the £70 sterling that we had paid for our crossing.

Despite all our efforts, it was impossible to get anything back. Our situation was a most difficult one. What to do? We would have either to lose this sum by going on another ship or wait until the 'Annie Jane' could set sail. In the first case, how to find the money? In the second scenario, would we be safe on the 'Annie Jane'?

The owners of the ship showed so much interest in providing liberally for all our expenditures while they were repairing the damages, and assured us with such certainty that it would be in a better state to go back to sea, that we could only do as they told us. There were other reasons besides, which supported their arguments, and here is the main one. We would have on board Captain Rose and his wife as passengers. An experienced sailor of 53 years of journeys and hardships, he had also decided to take the same vessel again, even though he had found a free place on a steamship. He said to us that having seen the way in which they were repairing the ship's damage, and also that the cargo, consisting of materials for the construction of a railway, had been better arranged than before, he thought that we could safely entrust ourselves to the 'Annie Jane'.

However, despite the care taken and the encouragements from Mr Mason, our Captain, Mr Vernier fell several times into a solemn melancholic state remembering his wife and children whom he had left in Canada. Nothing could be done to comfort him at such times because it seemed to him that he would never see them again – at least on this earth – which unfortunately would become only too true.

We spent our time admiring the attractions of the town and that of its magnificent harbour. I will not try to describe the places which we visited. I could only do so in an imperfect way and I would stretch out my story unnecessarily.

Every day we went to the quay to see how the repairs to the

vessel were moving forward. They were done so quickly that, on the 9th September, we had to return on board the ship. We were brokenhearted at the idea of leaving dry land, and faced with the dangers that were present at this time of year on a trip to America. But once on board, we forgot these sad thoughts in the thought of the crossing, which soon quickly unfolded before our eyes to distract us.

Our course was the same as the first time. The sea was calm, and a nice little breeze from the southeast favoured our progress and we went ahead with full sails. Everyone seemed happy, except those whom seasickness affected. We were 430 people in total, including steerage. The passengers of the tweendeck were made up of Irish and Scottish people, going to Canada to work on the construction of a railway.

On the Sunday morning, 12th September, the wind rose violently, breaking the mast at the bow, a part of the mainmast and the bowsprit. We were precisely at the same place where the first accident of this type had happened. The passengers, worried about continuing their journey in these dreadful conditions, all got together and begged the Captain to go back. They would prefer, they said, to lose the price of their passage rather than continuing the journey in a vessel which seemed destined to make them suffer and perhaps kill them. The Captain was inflexible and I thought at one point that a revolt might break out. Many passengers spoke of seizing the Captain and of directing the boat to Liverpool. Mr Mason, recovering his composure, tried hard to prove to us that there was no danger of continuing the voyage in this way. He ordered the sailors to repair the damage and to replace the masts and the broken yardarms with the spare masts and yardarms that we had on board. The crisis passed agreeably to general satisfaction because the Captain, pistol in hand, had brought handcuffs for the mutineers. The wind lost its strength and changed direction; the clouds disappeared, the radiant sun came out and spread calm and happiness in all our hearts. Our crew, which was made up of fifteen English sailors and of some French-Canadians, had soon repaired the damage to the 'Annie Jane'. All the sails were unfurled and we advanced with a speed of 11 knots an hour.

Chapter 3: The Storm

New disasters awaited and they lost no time in befalling us. From the next day, the 13th September, the wind turned to the west and blew in the same direction for eight days. It was the time of the equinox, a time when the winds are very strong and changeable. It was then that we saw the rock of Kilda, located at a great distance to the north of the Faroe Isles. The reader can understand our amazement at seeing ourselves follow a course so diametrically opposed to that which would take us to our destination! But what could men, or even the most skilled sailor, do against adverse winds? The Captain, disappointed by such a terrible setback, was not disheartened and we saw by his bravery and kindnesses towards us that he was disposed to do everything in his power to get us through this difficult situation. As he had become very close to Mr Vernier, the latter told us his plan. The Captain wanted to direct us towards the North in order to encounter a more favourable wind that would take us directly to the Gulf of Saint Laurence.

When we were not ill, we spent our time in various ways, and especially in meditation and in singing, amongst other things. The Captain often invited us to sing our French hymns, even though he did not understand a word. We can only praise him for his conduct in every respect. Everything was done on board with speed and order, and he was strict with regard to discipline. Captain Rose helped his companion and colleague in his operations; one or the other was always on the deck, watching over the sailors and observing the course of the vessel. Small incidents sometimes came to break up the monotony of the journey and gave us a diversion from our normal activities. Mr and Mrs Rose were excellent Christians; they often took part in our religious practices, which always gave us pleasure.

I liked to go up to the deck with our dear brother Vernier to admire the amazing works of the Lord and to think about the words of the Psalmist: "The heavens declare the glory of God; the skies proclaim the work of his hands." We liked to follow by eye the movements of some of the mysterious beings who, by the thousand, sailed to and fro across and filled up the depths of the ocean. Sometimes a pod of dolphins played around the ship, diving, resurfacing, diving again, breathing out with force and seeming to try to race us. It also pleased me to help the sailors, depending on the strength of my resources, which made my body feel better and restored my spirits.

On the 23rd we reached 20 degrees West longitude and 60 degrees North latitude, when a fierce westerly wind picked up all of a sudden and started to make the waves rise. It doubled in strength in a short period of time and we saw all the signs of a terrible storm. The captain brailed in the sails and secured the tiller firmly, as the men given the task of taking care of it could not hold it any longer because of the force of the waves. We were therefore ready to suffer this new assault when the night came and covered us in its shadows. It was not without worry that we went to sleep; after praying to God to save us from misfortune, we were calmer. We heard the whistling of the wind through the rigging and the rolling of the ship was very strong. Many of our friends suffered terribly from seasickness, the kind that even sleep could not conquer. The next day, the storm was at least as strong as the night before, even if it had not doubled in fury. Everyone was anxious; the waves, resembling mountains, came crashing down on the ship and covered it entirely. It was like a frail craft on a lake in torment. I went up on deck to have a look at this brand-new spectacle before me, spectacular and terrible at the same time. I had to make myself hang on with all my might to what I found in front of my hands, to not be thrown into the abyss. The waves which broke on the bow threatened to sink us, as the ship filled up with water. The Captain had placed men on the pumps, and for as long as the storm went on we had to make them work with the help of the passengers. No one dared to go up on the deck; such recklessness would have been paid for with a life. To protect us from the water entering the cabins by the windows of the deck, the captain had placed a piece of strong oilcloth on which he had placed some planks. We could not help being made afraid by the sinister sound that the waves made when breaking against the sides of the vessel. All the members of the Kempf family and Mr Van Buren were ill and nothing could be done to help their sickness. Because of the storm, it was impossible even to light a fire in the kitchen. For three days, we were thus tossed around by the torrents; the sailors could only remain idle and, as for us, we were forced to remain in our cabins or in the sitting room to obey the orders of the captain.

These three days seemed like three centuries to us. We passed them praying, reading the word of God and comforting each other. The nights seemed even longer because we could not sleep. All that we could do was to hang on to our beds to avoid being thrown from one side of our cabins to the other. Finally, during the night of the 26th September, calm was restored and we were happy to be able to go up on the deck.

But how astonished we were! What a sorry sight appeared before our eyes. The ship was more or less in distress. The masts were broken at the height of the first topsail, the rigging was fluttering at the will of the winds, a single sail in tatters, a part of the tiller broken, the compass and one of the rowing boats swept away by a blow from the sea – these are some of the damages of this awful storm. As much as it is beautiful, and I have to say majestic, to see a ship in full sails, how sad it was to see one in the state of ours. Everyone privately felt that there was no chance of being saved. Far from dry land, without anything around to gain perspective apart from the immense ocean and the expanse of the sky, suspended, so to speak, above an unfathomable abyss from which we were separated only by a plank, we were plagued by such sombre thoughts that would make the bravest man weep. Under such circumstances, even an atheist is aware of his great frailty before the mysterious power which he denies the existence of, before this power which, alone, can make the waves die down and be obedient in an instant. Who could not, in these solemn moments, admit to his powerlessness; not find the hand of God, whose decrees are too wise to be understood by men? If in these hours of anguish, the soul of the unbeliever is moved at the thought of death that is ahead of him, the Christian, on the other hand, is happy to trust in the Saviour, even if the ocean must serve as his tomb. That is when the believer understands how important it is not *"to make flesh his arm"* nor to count on his own merits. That's when his heart lets out a cry which reaches the throne of His mercy: *"Oh God, be good towards me, great sinner that I am."*

Chapter 4: Moments of Respite

I return to my story. The sky was magnificent; there was not the least bit of cloud as far as the eye could see. Our two captains started working out the distance separating us from our destination with the help of their instruments. They soon told us that we were 500 miles off-course and that we could not be too far from the islands surrounding Scotland.

It was impossible for us to continue our journey and, for the second time, we set course for Liverpool. Otherwise certain death awaited us. The wind was favourable and the Captain directed the path of the ship towards the south-east to the great pleasure of everyone. Saying that our sick friends suffered during the preceding days is an understatement. Plagued by storms which gave them seasickness, unable to eat anything, they were so thin and weakened they looked like ghosts. We had to carry Mr and Mrs Kempf to the deck to allow them to breathe clean and invigorating air and improve their weakened state. But after an hour they had to go down to their cabins as they were so exhausted. As for Mr Cornu, Mr Vernier and myself, we suffered little to no seasickness and were able to stay on deck.

The Captain had repaired the vessel as well as he could; but we had only three sails at our disposal. In spite of this, we sped along quite rapidly thanks to a favourable wind. On the 27th September, we were surrounded by a thick fog that shielded us even from the light of the sun. The weather was cold and we stayed in our cabins.

The 28th arrived – a terrible and memorable day for us all. The fog had still not cleared. The Captain appeared to be profoundly distressed but we could not have known the reason for it. Towards 2.00 p.m. in the afternoon, the sea was calm; a westerly wind rose and made the fog around us disappear. Looking towards the east, I discovered, somewhat with a struggle, something that looked like a mountain. I ran straight away to alert the Captain, who, with his telescope, saw indeed a mountain which he said was the Isle of Barra, a part of the Hebridean isles. We were happy to see land, which we had lost sight of for nineteen days. We felt as though we had already arrived in port. A vain illusion! Everyone shared their hopes and thoughts with their friends – an extraordinary restlessness gained hold on the deck. Everyone seemed happy, with the exception of the Captain who, leaning on the mast of the topgallant yard, examined the land often, then spoke to Captain Rose and seemed to be in a mortal anguish.

Le Naufrage de l'Annie Jane

I even once saw him shed tears. After this brave sailor spoke to us, we could see during the night the light of the Barra Head lighthouse, the last island in the Hebrides. The wind grew violent and we felt worried at seeing ourselves rapidly getting closer to land.

Towards seven o'clock at night, we made out the lighthouse and we saw with trepidation that we were heading for dangerous reefs. This isle of Barra Head, as we were told by the Captain, is surrounded by rocks and breakers on which we would find a certain death. The Captain was tortured by the most incredible anxiety. All the sails were deployed to try to reach the open sea as quickly as possible. But the high seas and heavy cargo of the vessel were two tremendous obstacles to our plan. Danger became imminent. We went down to our cabins to prepare ourselves for the disaster that seemed inevitable.

Mr Kempf, having learnt of the danger which threatened us, and finding himself too weakened by the sickness that he had suffered, fainted, and it was only with a lot of effort that we helped him recover the use of his senses.

All of a sudden, looking over at the sitting room compass, I saw that the direction of the vessel was no longer the same and we were now heading towards the North. I said this straight away to Mr Vernier and, on climbing up on deck, we made out that the lighthouse towards which we had been heading was now at the stern of the vessel.

Relieved by this change, we thanked God for what he had done to help the efforts of the Captain. The Captain, who had performed a master stroke, assured us that all would be all right and that we could go and sleep in peace.

If we had only been one mile further away, we could have passed without danger the last island in Scotland.

The wind was still very strong and the tide very high. In spite of this, we lay down to sleep on seeing the serenity that had come over the Captain's face.

Everything soon became calm around us. In spite of the rolling of the vessel, tiredness and exhaustion made us fall into a deep sleep. The Captains stayed on the deck; Mr Vernier slept in the sitting room and the most complete feeling of safety overcame our worries. But what a terrible awakening awaited us. Who could have known or even imagined?

Chapter 5: The Shipwreck

Towards midnight, a sinister noise could be heard. Sad cries came to my ears and at the same moment Monsieur Vernier appeared before us, telling us in a voice of the most profound sadness: *"Get up my friends, we are in great danger. We are crossing a place filled with reefs."*

These terrible words had soon driven sleep far from us by showing us the horror of our situation. We dressed quickly and I don't know what made me think to dress myself warmly. I put on three sets of clothing and, putting on my hat with care, I went up with Mr Vernier to the deck to understand the situation. I could not believe what my eyes were seeing as it was so awful. The waves crashed on the deck of the vessel at every moment; the night was darker and we were amongst high rocks against which the sea broke with an incredible violence and a roaring which filled us with fear.

Everything was thrown into confusion. The Captain, alone, was calm in the middle of this general upheaval, giving orders to the sailors. The sailors, having to hold on tight to anything that they found to hand to not be thrown into the sea, could not easily obey him. The violence of the waves at the bow threatened to throw the anchor overboard. The lifeboats, untied on the orders of the Captain, which were our last hope of salvation, were swept away by the waves.

We were thought to be between the isles of Barra and Vatersay, in a narrow passage which separated the two. But battered by the storm, the vessel soon found itself in a bay spiked with reefs.

A silence of some seconds followed the crash. It was time for the peak of the crisis. All of a sudden, piercing cries were let out on all sides. We had hit the rocks. From then on, every hope of salvation was out of the question. We were resigned to die, far from those so dear to our hearts, in a deserted place, and in the middle of the struggles and sufferings of an awful shipwreck.

Numb with cold and literally soaked to the bone, I started to lose the strength to hang on to the vessel and I returned to the cabins. I waited for death at every moment. I placed my soul between the hands of Him who had saved me through his death. In the sitting room, I found the Kempf family and Mrs Rose sitting on the sofa, calm and praying to God, even though their faces betrayed the suffering of their hearts. Our position stayed the same. The creakings of the ship made it sound each moment as though it was hitting the rocks and these violent jolts made us search for a handhold to avoid falling flat on our backs. Mr Vernier was not with us. I begged the Captain, who was standing at the top of the stair, to tell him to come and join us, because, at this solemn hour, we wished to be all together to pray, to encourage each other and die together. Our dear brother Vernier soon came to us; he was sad and silent. He seemed to pray constantly and deep sighs came from his breathless chest. What was the reason for this? It was the same reason which had filled him with sadness when we had returned to Liverpool. He had left in Canada a much-loved wife, five dear children, and sisters to whom he was dearly attached. In France was his elderly mother who would be coming to join him in Canada the following spring. And his heart, broken at the terrible thought of separation, went towards God, towards the Father of orphans whom he was entrusting with his family so that he would take care of them and combat the emptiness that the departure of this Christian was going to create in his loved ones.

We were all together in the cabin of Captain Rose. The nephew of the Captain, and a young man who served as interpreters for us, joined us. There, kneeling before God, in the presence of whom we would soon be appearing, we took up passionate prayers towards the throne of His grace. Strengthened by this outpouring of our broken hearts, and feeling that our good heavenly Father had heard and answered us, we felt stronger. I saw, however, that there was still a tough battle going on in the soul of our beloved brother Vernier. Taking a lamp, and accompanied by Mr Van Buren, he went to kneel in our cabin to invoke God again. I joined them, and our dear brother poured out his pain into the bosom of our Saviour. He prayed for his wife, his children and his parents; and the extent with which he commended them to God, with such fervour, filled him with true love. His forehead became serene and his face beamed. When he had finished praying, he felt happy to be going to join his Saviour, who had died for him and to the service of whom he had devoted his life.

Then terrible cries rang out on all sides. We saw a group of people throw themselves into the sitting room, crying, weeping, and moaning. It was the passengers from the tweendeck who, seeing that all was finished for them down below, had pushed in the connecting door to the cabins, and came close to us, begging for help. Poor people! They were so panic-stricken by the approach of their death, that they did not know what to do. The women, the young half-clothed girls, with tired eyes, hair dishevelled, begged the men to give them assistance, which they could not give them. They themselves, ruled by fear, joined the cries of those of the women who were hysterical.

While we were returning to the cabin of Mr Rose, Mr Cornu, who was very cold, took refuge in bed. We each took a seat, and on looking from one to another, we dissolved into tears, we said our last goodbyes on this earth, and we arranged to meet in the heavenly homeland, at the feet of the throne of Jesus.

When I think even now of this sad moment, my heart breaks. Because it reminds me that a few moments later, these dear friends were no more than cold dead bodies, thrown on the shore by the last of the gusts of the storm.

Chapter 6: The Disaster

While we were giving each other mutual encouragement, and while the fervent prayers lifted our hearts towards the Lord, a strange turmoil prevailed in the sitting room. Where had it come from? Why such a contrast? Why were we calmer at this solemn hour that the panic-stricken masses whose tortured cries we heard? Were we less exposed than them to danger? Did we have a stronger hope of escaping death? Not in the least. Where had this behaviour come from then which was so different from theirs? Every child of God, every Christian, will understand this easily. In our cabin, there were men, mortal like the others it is true, but whose hearts were with God. They believed in the saviour Jesus Christ, whose blood had been spilled for them, and their belief was unshakeable. They knew that beyond this life, after the sufferings and anguish, a glorious life awaited them: they would go towards the heavenly Father.

But the passengers in the sitting room, didn't they have the same belief? Only God knows. However, we know the fruit of the tree; and, seeing those there, before the death that awaited them at the bottom of the depths of the ocean, feeling full of terror and completely lost, one could be entitled to say that they wanted to drive away, by their moaning, and I could almost say, their sorrowful cries, the hideous ghost of 'the king of terrors' who clasps them already in his icy grip. If they had placed their trust in Jesus Christ, they would have accepted death as being the path of suffering to the happiness and peace of the comfort of God.

I find myself moving away again from my tale, but doesn't the terrible situation in which we found ourselves justify some reflections on the duties of man to his Creator? Only those who have seen, as I have, death so close, can understand me.

We were still in the cabin when Mr Van Buren pointed out that water was coming in rapidly. The ship was strongly angled on its side and the water was seeping into the inside by the cracks in the floor; which made us think that we would go under. The muffled clamours coming from the tweendeck below us warned of the danger which threatened us. At the same moment, an enormous swell opened the side of the boat and the waves entered with a fury. We climbed onto trunks which we found there, in order to prolong our existence for a few more moments. A terrible cracking sound was heard next, the water rose and soon covered us: the shipwreck had struck.

Plunged into profound darkness, buried under water, I could not breathe, and I believed that we were all done for. Oh joy! The water level dropped by a couple of inches and I breathed ecstatically. I called out for Mr Van Buren and Mr Vernier: no response. Weak moans could be heard around me. I recognised at my feet, the voice of the two children of Mr Kempf saying:

Father... fath... fath... we are... going... towards... Jesus!...

Poor children! I couldn't give them any help, being like a prisoner myself: I felt my arms squeezed together without being able to understand the reason for it. All that I remember is that when the water came into the ship, I naturally sought to throw myself above the torrents, and put my hand on the door. My other arm found itself in one of the handy openings in the cabin partitions which let the light enter from the sitting room. Later on, I discovered that the fallen mast of the stern had covered the deck with debris, and it was this which kept me prisoner. After some seconds, the water rose again and covered me for a second time. Having been able to breathe in between, I stayed under water without feeling as though I was suffocating. I had already swallowed a considerable quantity of water when I managed to put my head above the waves and avoided a swift death. Around 15 minutes passed in this way. Everything was silent around me. Those who had escaped the raging elements were found on the deck: the others were in the afterlife. I would have stayed in that same place until someone had come to help me, if a wave had not come to give a violent jolt to the ship and freed me from my perilous position. I was thrown into the cabin of Captain Mason. But thanks to God and to some superhuman efforts, I found myself on a solid object and high enough to be able to breathe freely.

I could not say how long I stayed there. I was extremely weak, and my thoughts became confused. Perhaps I would die at this moment, and again I prayed for the last time, that God Almighty would receive me in his beautiful heaven, when I saw a faint light as I looked ahead. I came to as soon as it came in the window of the deck and I thought that it was a means which God had given me to come out of the tomb where I had been buried alive.

I dragged myself to the bottom of the window, putting my hand sometimes upon a dead body, sometimes on the debris which filled the sitting room and which left little space between me and the ceiling. By means of a barrel, I climbed onto the deck; there, the view, albeit different, was not in the least bit less horrible. The night was still very dark; the wind blew strongly, and the foaming waves constantly swept away the debris of the ship. In spite of the profound darkness, I could see where we were quite well. A little distance from the place where those who had escaped the shipwreck were assembled, I could see the tip of the bow of the vessel buried in the sea; the part on which we were on, a length of about fifteen feet, was almost covered in water and very tilted. Huddled together to warm themselves and to protect themselves from the waves which crashed constantly on them, the survivors thanked God for having saved them.

The weather was cold and damp. Almost frozen and wet to the bone, weakened by misery, I tried to place myself in the middle of the group, but I could not get there. I looked also for Mr Vernier and my other journey companions, but without success. I thought them all dead. Against the biting cold, I was at least less pitiful than many of the others, having taken care to dress myself warmly. Some of the young women, semi-clothed, trembled at my sides. I took my jacket and bid them use it as a bit of shelter in order to protect them, if not from the cold, at least against the fury of the waves. The cold became so intense that I saw many fall into a deadly paralysis, sleeping on the deck and soon dying at our feet. During this awful night, seven of our companions died this way. Our hearts were breaking, but what could we do for them? We had tried rubbing them vigorously, nothing could be done to take them out of their stupor, a sinister precursor to death. From time to time, we let out loud shouts in the hope of being heard by the inhabitants of the island. For every response, we heard only the whistling of the wind and the heavy moaning of the ocean in a rage, from which the waves erupted with violence. With no means of reaching the shore, we were forced to spend the night in this way.

Oh! How long were these unhappy hours! What sombre thoughts filled our souls at that time! Floating between hope and fear, we could only pray that God would snatch us from death. We did not even know if the fate of our unfortunate companions would not also be reserved for us. Our existence came down to so little: to some badly held together boards that a blow from the sea could break, sending us to the bottom of the sea.

Chapter 7: After the Shipwreck

Towards three o' clock in the morning (29th September) the wind grew less violent; the sky started to clear, and we made out some stars in the firmament; the waves died down, little by little; and we felt hope reborn in our hearts. Finally, day came; how beautiful the twilight appeared to us that morning. Oh, how happy we were to greet the budding dawn, a precursor of a light that we had thought we would never see again. The objects surrounding us then became visible. What we had taken for rocks in front of the ship were only sand banks, covered in wreckage, sad signs of our misfortune. On the shore we could not see a single human being.

Soon the sun came up over the horizon, radiant as on a festival day, and its rays gave our bodies the heat which they were so needing. Our group went off in different directions and I saw Mr Van Buren. Beside myself with joy, I threw myself on his neck and we hugged tearfully. *"Where is Mr Vernier?"* followed as our mutual next question. Our answer, for both of us, was negative. We had not seen him. Mr Van Buren then told me about the way in which God had also snatched him from death.

"When the water came into the vessel", he told me, *"I was thrown out of the cabin onto the sitting room table. As there was only a small space between the ceiling and the table, and as I could not stay standing, I felt with my hands to the left and the right and I found the window of the deck. I broke the bars of it with the help of some people; I climbed out first onto the deck and I helped the others climb out after me. Like you, I spent the whole night there"*.

After I had also told him about the way in which I had been saved, we saw Captain Mason and many others coming out of the cabins. Neither Mr Vernier nor our other friends were visible, and the Captain did not know anything more than us on the subject. All of a sudden, we saw some men on the shore. A cry of joy left the vessel, and we motioned to them to come to our help. They seemed not to understand us. We noticed then that quite a great distance separated us from them, and we saw that the tide was falling. With the aid of a rod, a sailor found that there was only five feet of water around the vessel. Another climbed up the length of the poopmast of which one end rested on the deck and the other end had fallen near the land, attaching a strong rope to it. One of the ends of this rope was solidly attached to the shore: we were saved.

I went down with Mr Van Buren to see if any of our group could not be found in the cabins. On entering our cabin, we saw Mr Cornu busy changing clothes. We had thought him dead, having been left sleeping in his bed. Finding himself in the upper alcove, he had escaped death. If we had stayed in this cabin, not one of us would have perished. But the will of God was not our will and his thoughts were not our thoughts. Our friends, the Kempfs, had left the world for a better life. Mr Vernier also had gone to rejoin his Saviour, to whom he had dedicated his life in service.

Our belongings were almost all dry. The Captain brought his things on land and those of ourselves. I wanted to lock my trunk – a small detail for which we will see the reason soon – but the pain which I felt in my left arm stopped me. We left then to go and warm ourselves in neighbouring houses, having given our things to a young Mr Taylor, our cabin steward and also our interpreter. Mr Cornu stayed with the sailors to help them to find the bodies and especially those of our friends. As soon as we were on the shore, a joyful feeling and inexpressible gratitude towards God filled our hearts. It is difficult to explain what we experienced after having escaped from such a great danger. Never will I forget the feeling of this moment.

The house towards which we were directed was situated a mile from the shore and hidden by a mountain. A great fire had been made and we approached it with joy. Some moments later, we were delighted to feel a sweet heat around our limbs numb with the cold, and soon we rested from our tiredness. Towards midday, we returned to the vessel: the high sea, however, stopped us from getting onto it.

Chapter 8: Scenes of bereavement

Searching then for the bodies of our friends amongst the numerous victims of the shipwreck, we firstly saw only those of the two children of Mr Kempf. In the evening, Captain Mason, the Second Mate, some other passengers, and myself, had an excellent bedroom in the house where we had already been welcomed. The steerage passengers were staying near this house. The Captain took care of us as well as he looked after himself. He was very distressed by our misfortune and especially by the death of Mr Vernier, to whom he had been very attached.

The next day, which was a Friday, the Captain let us know that in the early hours of the morning he had found the body of Mr Vernier. He had brought back his watch, showing it to the friends of the deceased. After lunch we returned to the shore to see the mortal remains of our brother. He was dressed in the same clothing that he wore on the day of the shipwreck, except for his coat, which had been torn. There was not a bruise or wound on his body, which was red in colour and very swollen. I transported him to the middle of the island and, on the order of the Captain, the carpenters made a coffin in which we laid his mortal remains.

I went back to the vessel with Mr Cornu to bring back our belongings. Upon lifting my suitcase, I found it to be too light and on opening it I saw that someone had stolen all my belongings. What an unfortunate turn of events! It was not possible to change clothes, and the same had been done to Mr Cornu. The Captain made enquiries which were just about fruitless. The rest of the day was spent in the house. I busied myself writing to some friends on the details of our disaster, because the postman would come that night. The minister on the Isle of Barra, Mr Beatson, came to visit us and promised to return the next day for the funeral of Mr Vernier. We had also found the bodies of our other brethren, including Mr and Mrs Rose. They were placed side by side in the coffins and buried in a common grave on the shore. Our hearts were sad to see the unfortunate people whom we laid in the grave to await the glorious day of the resurrection.

On Saturday 1st October 1853, Mr Beatson came to our house, as promised, and at four o' clock in the afternoon we accompanied the body of Mr Vernier to his final resting place. More than 60 people attended the service. The minister gave a most touching sermon – speaking of the terrible tragedy, he brought tears to the eyes of more than one listener.

No other incident worth mentioning happened to us during the 15 days that we spent on the Isle of Vatersay. Mr Beatson invited us to come to his house in order to distract ourselves and to rest a little. We often thought about our unlucky companions on the journey who had been so abruptly taken away by death, and we would have been happy to see them with us still. These ordeals, which God had wanted to us to get through, had weakened our health. During the first eight nights of our stay on the island, we could not sleep a wink. We were plagued by awful nightmares which brought back scenes from the shipwreck, and took away our rest. Mr Van Buren, especially, was very weak; his health had never been very good and the suffering which he had experienced on the sea had exhausted his strength. I myself was stricken by terrible headaches and stomach pains.

Soon a convoy of two vessels loaded with passengers from the 'Annie Jane' were leaving for Glasgow. They went first of all to Tobermory, a small town located thirty miles from Vatersay, and from there, boarded a steamer to Glasgow.

Chapter 9. Departure for Glasgow

Our turn soon arrived. We could not have been more than 32 people shipwrecked on the island, including the captain, the doctor and the cook, who stayed behind to take care of our belongings. The schooner which had to take us to Tobermory was the last to set sail, and we had to say goodbye to the Captain and our hosts. The journey should have been short, but in the absence of wind, we only did 8 miles on the first day. Night came and we slept on our trunks – the schooner was intended to be used only for the transportation of goods and did not have cabins. The next day, we had a favourable breeze and we were a short distance from Tobermory when a sudden gust of wind tore the sails, which were old. Seeing that it was impossible to fight against the wind and the waves, the Captain decided to direct us towards a bay on the island of Canna, a very safe place, he said, and which he knew very well, in order to spend the night there. Night came upon us before we could put this plan into action. We were in the middle of rocks; a thick darkness surrounded us and the rain fell in torrents. However, thanks to the courage of the Captain and the dexterity of the sailors, we overcame the danger. It was very difficult to direct the boat and, sometimes, we were so close to the rocks that we could have touched them by hand. At one point I feared another shipwreck. Many of the sailors of our shipwrecked vessel told me later on that they had been more afraid than on the 'Annie Jane'. Finally, thanks to God, we came out of this impasse to direct ourselves towards the isle of North Uist. The weather becoming more favourable, we headed for the Isle of Skye. The next morning, we put down anchor: we were finally in a safe place, and we settled down to sleep. A pointless attempt! Hunger, tiredness, and our irritated nerves made sleep impossible. The following day, the Captain and some other people took the rowing boat and went ashore. We were in the bay of Bracadale. They did not return until around four o' clock in the afternoon. We had eaten nothing since the departure; thinking that the journey would take a few hours, we hadn't brought supplies with us. In the evening, a good meal was served to us in the houses which neighboured the shore. The minister of the area, amongst others, came to see us and provided liberally for our needs. They gave us carts to carry our things, and also the sick or wounded passengers, to Portree, which was around 24 miles away. Under the direction of a guide, we left at four o' clock in the afternoon, ignoring the tiredness which overwhelmed us. We had to walk to cross the fields, the valleys, the marshes, and climb the mountains. The rain surprised us on the way, and had soon penetrated our clothes. We hurried our journey in the middle of the most profound darkness. The pretty groves of trees, the beautiful country houses, told us we were approaching a town. At midnight we were at a hotel, exhausted with tiredness and happy to experience a peaceful sleep, after having given thanks to God for his amazing protection. The next day, which was a Sunday, we received many visitors and became the objects of a thousand thoughtful gestures, and numerous questions were asked as to the circumstances surrounding our shipwreck. Already, many unfavourable rumours had been spread as to the behaviour of Captain Mason. Some people said he was responsible for our misfortune. But we knew he was innocent and we made sure to exonerate him from all blame, and quieten the slanderers.

Chapter 10: Mr Necker from Saussure

In the town of Portree, at that time, there was a respectable old gentleman, originally from Geneva. Tired of the madding crowd, and enjoying a large fortune, he had come to spend the rest of his days in a magnificent residence in Portree, in which he had lived for fourteen years. He was Mr Necker from Saussure, well-known from his work on the geology of Vaud. Having heard talk of our shipwreck, and learning that some of his compatriots were amongst the victims of the disaster, he came on Monday to our hotel, and showed us the great pleasure he had in seeing us. He joined us in the sitting room and we were served an excellent dinner, during which we talked about the accident which had brought us to the town, and of our far-away homeland. Touched by our misfortunes, our new friend took a great interest in us, and offered us his services. The young man whom Mr Cornu had brought with him was with us. He had been reduced to begging, and we made the most of the generosity of Mr Necker in asking him to take an interest in this unfortunate man. But this aristocratic old gentleman also insisted that we tell him also about what we were needing: *"Come"*, he said to Mr Van Buren, who was the eldest of us, *"and I will open a little account at my bank for you"*.

After a few moments, Mr Van Buren, pale and his eyes filled with tears, came back into the sitting room: *"Dear friends"*, he cried out, *"Oh how God is good! How many times have we known his goodness. We have entrusted in Him. See if he has misled us!"* And, on saying this, he placed on the table his purse filled with gold coins. We couldn't get over our astonishment as we talked about the munificence of Mr Necker. We who just before didn't have a penny, now were the holders of two hundred and fifty dollars.

Mr Necker, himself, soon arrived but would not allow us to thank him. *"It is not worth the trouble"*, he said. *"If this small sum is not enough for your immediate needs, say so. Furthermore, you will not share food and rooms with the other passengers. Ask for all that you desire, and I will see to the expenses. And when you go to Glasgow, take the First Class cabins: I will see to everything."*

And he kept his word. The manager of the hotel, who had been recommended to us by Mr Necker, was very polite towards us and anticipated all our desires.

It was with joy that we poured out our hearts before God. We could say with Job: *"The Lord giveth; the Lord taketh away; Blessed be the name of the Lord!"* At this time, we found ourselves in abundance. It was also a remarkable coincidence that we had met a man so generous and devoted to his compatriots.

During the three days that we spend in Portree, we were able to visit this pretty little town at our leisure. It is built in a most picturesque location, at the bottom of a little bay, and surrounded by two hills topped by magnificent terraces, and lined with charming groves. Portree is sprinkled with splendid detached houses, and sites as magnificent as they are varied. The inhabitants of the town were hospitable, pleasant and polite. It was there, in this small obscure town, that we found even more native Scottish people with warm hearts, and with courteous manners, and whose politeness was proverbial. But I return to my story.

Chapter 11: Meeting with Mr James Court

Three days after our arrival in Portree, the hotel manager came to tell us that the steamer had arrived and would soon be leaving. So our trunks were taken to the quay, and after lunch, we went on board the vessel. We were in a bit of an awkward situation, not being able to speak English, but we had up until then found friends everywhere, and we trusted in our stars, despite our setbacks. There was a gentleman on board who we had met the day before, Doctor Hill. He knew enough French, and having been made aware of our embarrassing situation, he soon took our belongings on deck, and we went down to the sitting room with him. During the journey, we met lots of very pleasant people who seemed very willing to help us.

We sailed gazing at the magnificent panorama for the two days that the journey lasted. The islands, covered in thick forests and beautiful castles, presented themselves before our eyes while the enormous masses of rocks with a savage appearance reminded us of my dear Swiss mountains, of which people often said:

In this country beats the hearts of free men, free like the rocks of our mountains which no man can climb.

We finally arrived in Glasgow, and everyone got ready to go home. But for us, what were we going to do? Where would we go? We did not know anything. One of the officers of the 'Annie Jane' went to get information for us. We waited; no one came. Finally, we saw the nice Doctor Hill coming back, who told us that we were to go to the house of a friend of our French missionary group, Mr Young, who would send a telegram to Mr James Court – (one of the pioneers of French Evangelism in Canada. J. A. D.) – from Montreal, who was in Edinburgh for a few days. Mr Van Buren went with the doctor, and returned to tell us that he wanted to send us to one of the best hotels in Glasgow, which was beyond our poor resources. As we were talking about this together, a young man came to tell us to go to the Regent Hotel in Glasgow, and that, thanks to friends, everything was ready for our arrival. We went there happily, and after a few minutes, we saw Mr Court arrive. After having responded to his touching questions about our misfortunes, he prayed to God with us, and left for Edinburgh again, promising us that he would return the next day. Our first thought was to equip ourselves with appropriate clothing and shoes, in order to be able to present ourselves before our friends in an appropriate manner. Mr Court returned on Saturday, and on Sunday we had the pleasure of taking communion together in the Scottish church of Dr Arnott. After having visited several friends, Mr Court inquired about our future plans. What were we going to do? To go to Canada or return to our home country? The answer was not very easy.

The doctor, under the care of whom Mr Van Buren had been placed in Glasgow, told us that our brother would not be able to undertake the ocean crossing. It would be necessary for him to return to his home to rebuild his health, which had been weakened by so much suffering. Mr Cornu resolved to go to Canada. As for me, I wished to go there also, but I was hesitant. At the time of my departure, people had said to me not to undertake the journey without knowing the will of God. If his will was that I stay in my homeland, he would know to bring me back to it. It was therefore natural for me to make this reasoning: *"Here are two times that I have left Liverpool and I have come back to it a third time. Is this not a sign that I shouldn't go any further?"* On the other hand, I said to myself: *"If God had saved me from the shipwreck, is it not so that I will be more devoted to him with even more fervour?"* I had to put off my answer until later on, not being able to disentangle my thoughts on the subject.

The next morning, we left for Liverpool, where we arrived in a short time. Mr Court kept a place on the steamer 'America' for Mr Cornu and told me that he would wait for my answer until the next day, the leaving day. On Tuesday, after the worship, Mr Court asked me what I was going to do. I had prayed to God to guide me, and I responded: *"I will go to Canada."* He seemed happy, kept another place for me, and left with Mr Van Buren. During the time that we were in Liverpool, Mr Cornu and I visited some acquaintances, amongst others the wife of Captain Mason whose house we stayed in for a part of the time.

We made the necessary purchases, and on the 29th October 1853, just one month after the shipwreck of the 'Annie Jane', we left on the 'America'.

As nothing remarkable happened to us during the crossing, I will not speak about this journey. Except for adverse winds and a couple of storms – things which we had become used to – the journey was pleasant and quick. I suffered a lot from headaches and stomach aches; the good food and tender care of my friends relieved me greatly. We had the pleasure of making the acquaintance of

Kirk pastors, from Boston, Irvine, and Toronto. They proved to be charming companions, and they were very useful to us when we set foot on American soil, after fourteen days of sailing. Our hearts were pounding at the sight of this land, the aim of our journey. How happy we would have been to be able to bring Mr Vernier with us! We would have at least wanted to take back his mortal remains to his grief-stricken family. But it was not to be; he slept in a faraway land. The only hope remaining of seeing him again, for his family and friends, was in a better land.

Epilogue

Monday 14th November, we left Boston and on the morning of the 15th we were in Montreal. After the obligatory social calls, a friend drove us to the schools of Pointe-aux-Trembles, near to Montreal, where we were received with the greatest warmth by our brethren who, while rejoicing at our arrival, could not stop themselves from crying at the death of Mr Vernier. When leaving Liverpool for the first time we were eight friends together and two alone had reached their destination.

This story, which I have written for myself and for some other people who wished to know the details of our journey, has not been done in an elegant style. It is only a simple tale of sad ordeals which God allowed us to survive.

He is the comforter of those who have been so tested! He gives us more love, and we have more trust in him who saved us from death in the middle of the deep waters of the ocean, while on all sides people said a last farewell. This is the ardent wish of the person who wrote these lines: *"Praise the Lord, O my soul! Do not forget all of his kind deeds."*

Marc Ami,
Teacher
Belle-Rivière, Lower Canada,
2nd May 1856

Appendices

The Manchester Guardian (England) on the 12th October 1853, gave us a long and heart-rending description of the shipwreck of the 'Annie Jane'. We reproduce it here*:

We fulfil a hard task in breaking the news to our readers of one of the most appalling shipwrecks which has ever taken place on the Scottish coast, and which claimed the lives of more than 400 human beings. The 'Annie Jane', captained by W. Mason, a ship of 1294 tonnes, bound for Quebec, had set sail last September on the 9th, having a great number of passengers and cargo made up of a great quantity of iron, intended for the construction of a railway in Canada. The list of registered passenger places grew to more than 400, without counting a considerable number of children. The crew numbered 45 men, including the Captain and the officers.

The majority of the cabin passengers were French-Canadian**. After a few days of favourable sailing, the ship was attacked by a storm. The ship was badly loaded, the cargo extremely heavy, and the rolling of the vessel became alarming. The havoc was such that the Captain decided finally to return to Liverpool. But the 'Annie Jane' could not reach the port. Driven by the storm, the ship was wrecked on the coast of one of the Hebridean isles and only two hundred people escaped death.

* In this article, there are some numerical errors, as often happens in badly investigated newspaper reports. The figures which I give after the lists are correct – M.A.

** Not French-Canadian, but Swiss – M.A.

<u>Letter from Mr Jean Cornu</u>

...At midnight, we heard again the voice of the Captain and the noise of the sailors on deck. Our brother Vernier understood immediately that the danger was far from past. We had barely gotten ourselves up, when we felt stronger tremors than before. Our vessel was still halted and aground on the rocks, at the bottom of a little bay in front of the isle of Vatersay, Barra. Everyone waited in silence; the sort served for God Almighty himself. I was constantly in prayer. I climbed up to the deck. The sea had covered the ship in the meanwhile and it was necessary to cling on strongly to avoid being carried away. The sailors who were at my sides shouted in despair. I told them to confide in God. We were one hundred feet from land and such was our misfortune that no means of rescue could be put into use. The rowing boats remained stationary until, broken away by the waters, they were thrown in pieces on the shore. We had no light and no way of drawing attention to ourselves. With nothing to be done, I went back down to the cabins. Very soon, cracking sounds were heard and cries of distress came to us from the tweendeck. Several passengers took refuge in our cabins. They were in the most sorry state. My friends sought refuge in a cabin of an old sailor who had 53 years of service. The cracking noises started again; these were the last. I realised that our ship was breaking – then I felt it sink into the ocean. My bed collapsed; everywhere around me were cries of anguish: I was in complete darkness. I waited for certain death. I forgave all those who had injured me. I commended my parents to the benevolent watch of God and gave my soul to him. But then he gave me a deliverance that I had not hoped for.

At the moment when I thought the partitions were ready to break, God gave me the thought to make an incredible effort to free myself from the water and the dead bodies which crowded the cabin. I escaped on deck by a window. I found many people there. I saw that the ship was broken into three parts. The part we were on had surfaced above the waves. It was almost two o'clock at night. Around three hundred human beings had lost their lives. Thanks to the ebbing tide, we could get to land by sliding along the length of the mast. My first thought was to give thanks to God.

We heard the young Kempf boy, twelve years of age, crying out at the moment of death: *"Father! Father! We are dying! We are going towards the Good Lord!"*

<u>Letter from Mr L. Van Buren:</u>

Dordrecht, November 1853

...Towards 2.30 am, Mr Vernier asked us to get up, saying that we were in great danger. I took my coat and went up on deck. I was convinced that our final hour was near. The ship, pushed by a terrible gale, covered in water, surrounded by a dark night, was close to breaking on the rocks. The Captain did everything possible to turn around the ship and save the passengers. The order was given to direct us into a bay off the Isle of Vatersay... soon after, the ship hit against the rocks.

The cries of despair from the passengers who were in the tweendeck were terrible. We were on the deck. Wet, cold through and shivering, we held on strongly to the ropes to avoid being thrown into the sea. Seeing that all hope of salvation was vanishing, we returned to our cabin. There, I found Mr Kempf, his wife, and his two children, sitting on the sofa with the wife of Captain Rose, a noble and pious Christian. Soon after, a strong jolt threw them all from the sofa in the middle of the bedroom, and at the same time, a surge of water filled part of the cabin. Mr Ami and Mr Vernier were still on deck, but they came back down to us, as well as Captain Rose. The latter took his wife by her hand and invited us to follow him to his cabin in order to unite ourselves in prayer. Mr Vernier fell to his knees and asked God to give us peace and hope of salvation, to pardon us from all the bad things we had done during our lives, to give us the spirit to submit in order to be able to gaze on Him in whom we believed. This prayer finished, he took me by the hand and followed me into our cabin where we prayed again for his wife and their children. Next, we returned to the cabin of Captain Rose, everyone with a candle in hand.

During this time, the ship had not stopped breaking on the rocks and the walls of the cabin were separating, which I pointed out to Mr Vernier.

The little Kempf girl, ten years old, said then to her brother: *"In a little while, we will be with Jesus... the ship is going to sink."*

At the same moment, Captain Mason came in and declared before God that he was innocent of everyone's death. He had barely spoken these words when the ship broke into three pieces. Next, the part between the first and last mast sank to the bottom. At the same time, what was underfoot also broke, killing the passengers of the tweendeck.

As soon as the structure broke, water entered with force into the cabin and covered everything, putting out the lights and stopping us from breathing. Fortunately, the water soon went down and allowed me to see, for the last time, those around me. The little Kempf girl was between me and the safe, on which I had placed myself; but a second wave knocked her over again and pushed me into the dining room. Ami, who found himself against the partition of Captain Mason's cabin, was pushed through the wall of the cabin and with a third wave, found himself in the same bedroom as myself. At this point, there was no longer a cabin: everything was upside down; the bedroom was filled with all sorts of objects and dead bodies, which we stepped over. After the third wave, I found myself on a table and under the windows, of which the windowpanes were broken, but the wooden frame was still whole and stopped anyone getting out. I broke it by hand and helped those who were before me. Next, I also went outside. I grabbed the tiller and I saw more than one hundred people on this tiny bit of the deck, holding each other. It was a little more than three o'clock at that time. There were neither moon nor stars visible, the sea covered us at every moment, and the North wind froze us and killed many people on the deck, so that I had three dead at my feet. It was in this state that we remained until six o'clock. Then the inhabitants of the island came to our aid. They cried to us to throw a rope. A sailor went forward on a mast and threw a rope to the inhabitants who went into the water to get it. We slid along one after the other on the mast and from there, we took the rope in the water, and we were able to get to land.

Mr Vernier was buried in Vatersay by the minister of the Isle of Barra. Mr Kempf and his son were in the same coffin, and his wife and their daughter in another.

Jean Vernier
(1822–1853)

In the number of shipwreck survivors who escaped death during the disaster of the 'Annie Jane', were Marc Ami, Frederic Lammertz van Buren and Jean Cornu. These three brethren who had solemnly promised to help with the French-Canadian missionary, were not left discouraged by the tragedy. On the return to Liverpool, they embarked again on another vessel and arrived in Canada on the 15th November 1853. Of these three brave workers, two are no longer living. Only the pastor Ami is still at work, full of energy, in spite of the weight of a forty-year struggle.

Marc Ami

Fred L. Van Buren
1824–1888

Jean F. Cornu
1823–1891

....

About the French Protestant Missionary Society.

What were a group of eight French-speaking protestant evangelical Europeans doing taking passage aboard the 'Annie Jane' en route to Quebec? Lower Canada was generally perceived as a conservative Roman Catholic community.

In 1839, with the help of missionaries and British protestant organisations, the French-Canadian Missionary Society was established to teach Roman Catholic French-speaking Canadians about the great doctrines of the reformed faith.[1] The Society was ecumenical: Presbyterians, Baptists, Congregationalists and Anglicans together founded the Society to spread Christ's gospel in French to all the inhabitants of Canada, including indigenous tribes.

This represents one of the most extensive Protestant efforts to evangelise the French-speaking population of North America.

This evangelical movement had begun far away in Europe. In 1834 a party of four Swiss nationals from Lausanne landed in New York. Within a short period of time they had travelled up the Hudson River, and approached the fertile valley of the St Lawrence River where the first French settlers had established homes and towns. Until the loss of Quebec to the British in 1759 they had been protected from foreign interference, geographically and culturally isolated from other North American and European influences. Roman Catholicism was deeply entwined in the culture and the lifestyle of the inhabitants of the region.

In 1836 began one of the most troubled periods in Quebec's

history. There was a wheat crop failure followed by a major financial collapse in 1837, causing major social discontent amongst the French-speaking population, increasingly disenfranchised by large numbers of British immigrants arriving every year. Another major factor was that the aggressive British commercial class were buying up vast tracts of land and were almost totally in control of the local economy and commercial activity.

A group called *Les Patriotes* was formed, led by a French-Canadian called Louis-Joseph Papineau. In 1837 there began a rebellion. Armed uprisings began in many communities and there was fighting in the streets of Montreal. The legislative assembly was dismissed and the constitution suspended. Papineau led a committee that organized a boycott of all British goods to Lower Canada. The *Patriotes*, very often poorly organized, took up arms against the British army; the dissent was quickly suppressed, villages were burned to the ground and people were made homeless just as winter was setting in. Papineau was forced into exile: when a warrant was issued for his arrest as well as all the other leaders of the *Patriotes*, on 25th November 1837 he crossed the border into the United States, where he received a guarded welcome. The whole of Quebec was left in chaos with feelings of dissatisfaction just below the surface in working class areas of Montreal, and in all the small outlying communities[2].

As the dissent grew, the Roman Catholic Church fell out of step with the local population, primarily because of a split between Les *Patriotes* and the Catholic clergy. The Roman Catholic Church and clergy up to that period had always supported a separate French-Canadian identity.

Papineau began to make anti-Church and anti-clerical statements, and even more radically proposed the abolition of the tithe system which was mandatory for the French-speaking population. The rift between Church and population widened. During the summer of 1837 Monsignor Lartigue, Bishop of Montreal, requested his priests not to give absolution to the seditionists. This led to over a thousand *Patriotes* demonstrating in front of the Cathedral, and caused the Bishop to issue a proclamation demanding civil obedience.

The Bishop caused so much public outrage with those measures that he prepared to flee if necessary to the safety of Quebec City.

The Bishop of Quebec took a similar stance against the popular uprising.

This schism within the established Church created conditions that assisted Protestant missionaries in proclaiming and expanding their congregations with a new spirit of openness and tolerance among the local population. Civil disturbance continued into 1838 when another rebellion broke out. This was even more brutally suppressed: villages were again pillaged and burned. Almost 1000 people were arrested, 60 were deported, and 12 were hanged.

The Roman Catholic Church's stand against the armed insurrection had embittered many insurgents and their alienation became complete when they were excommunicated.

Les Patriotes and their cause enjoyed wide support throughout the country, and the Church's opposition to them drove disillusioned French-speaking Canadians in many communities into providing eager welcome to Bible Society *colporteurs* (Bible distributers) and itinerant protestant preachers.

Many Protestants were eager to capitalize on this opportunity. In February 1839, under the guidance of James Thomson, agent for the Montréal auxiliary of the British and Foreign Bible Society, an interdenominational group of twelve like-minded people gathered to consider all options. This led on 8th April 1839 to the formation of the French-Canadian Missionary Society (FCMS). In the words of its constitution the society's exclusive object was to provide means for the preaching and disseminating the Gospel of Christ among the inhabitants of Canada, using the French language.

At the core of the Society's motivation was the overthrow of Catholicism and its replacement with evangelical Protestantism. The infant FCMS concluded that their need to find suitable missionary candidates would be best achieved by recruiting in Europe.

In 1846, as part of their outreach activity, an institute was established at Pointe-Aux-Trembles, about ten miles downriver from Montreal. The aim of this institute was to compete with the Roman Catholic Church in education, so that pupils would be exposed to those religious influences which might give a new direction to their lives.

Pastor Jean Vernier, who was originally from Blamont, part of Herimoncourt (Doubs) in France, arrived with his wife Lydie, a

Swiss national, in Canada around 1843. He took up his post as a teacher in Pointe-Aux-Trembles Institute and they had six children between 1843 and 1852, one of whom died in infancy. They were Paul in 1843, Henri in 1846, Pauline Lydie in 1847, Sara in 1849, Suzanne in 1851 (died 1852) and lastly Paul Louis Samuel in 1852.

In March 1853 Jean Vernier was tasked with recruiting new workers for the mission field. He made a journey to France and Switzerland, having achieved that purpose, and was returning to Canada with his new recruits when tragedy struck.

The Greenock Advertiser of 27th December 1853 carries an appeal:

> **French-Canadian Missionary Society** – In September last, the Rev J.Vernier together with the missionaries engaged by him in Switzerland for the above society, while on the way to Quebec, were wrecked in the 'Annie Jane' off the island of Barra.
>
> M. Vernier was drowned along with two of his company and two children. M.Vernier whose age was about thirty years had been a teacher in the Pointe Trembles Institute for ten years. His piety and earnest zeal rendered him a valuable labourer in the Canadian vineyard, his loss the society will not easily get supplied. M. Vernier has left an aged mother, a young widow and five children under twelve years of age totally un-provided for. The friends of the mission here and in other parts of Scotland, desirous of helping the widow to support her family, are taking means of enlisting the sympathy of the Christian public on their behalf, and an announcement elsewhere gives the names of gentlemen who have kindly undertaken the duty here.

On another page in the same newspaper:

French-Canadian Missionary Society

> Donations for the widow and family of the late Rev J.Vernier who was drowned in the wreck of the 'Annie Jane' will be received by the collectors when making their call for the annual subscriptions for the above

society, early in January, by the Rev J.J Bonar , secretary; Mr M'kelvie, stationer, Hamilton Street; or by the treasurer George Hinmers, 5 Cathcart Square Greenock.

---

1. people.bethel.edu/~gscorgie/articles/fcms.doc

2. Notes taken from https://www.collections canada.gc.ca/confederation/023001-2200-e.html

Le Naufrage de l'Annie Jane

Le Naufrage de l'Annie Jane images
Digitizing sponsor: University of Ottawa. Contributor: Canadiana.org.
https://archive.org/details/cihm_08085

"Le 26 août 1853, nous mimes à la voile pour Québec."
"On the 26th August 1853, we set sail for Quebec."

" Une bonne petite brise du sud-est favorisait notre marche, et nous avancions à pleines voiles."
"A nice little breeze from the southeast favoured our path and we went ahead with full sails."

Le Naufrage de l'Annie Jane

"Pendant trois jours, nous fûmes ainsi ballottés par les flots."
"For three days, we were thus tossed around by the torrents."

"Vers sept heures du soir, nous aperçûmes le phare de Barra Head."
"Towards seven o'clock at night, we made out the lighthouse at Barra Head."

Le Naufrage de l'Annie Jane

"Au même instant une lame énorme ouvrit le flanc du vaisseau."
"At the same moment, an enormous swell opened the side of the boat and the waves entered with a fury."

Le' Naufrage de l'Annie Jane.
"The Shipwreck of the Annie Jane."

143

Jean Vernier (1822-1853)

Marc Ami in 1891 aged 57

GIRLS' SCHOOL, POINTE-AUX-TREMBLES.

POINTE-AUX-TREMBLES.

FCMS schools
Girls' school, Pointe Aux Trembles.
Main School Pointe Aux Trembles, built in 1846.

Taken from Annual Reports of the French Canadian Missionary Society.

10

The Beechey Inquiry and Recommendations

The survivors and the relations of those who died did not waste any time looking for some form of justice. In October, they mistakenly sent a memorial, a statement of facts, what we nowadays would call a petition, to Lord Palmerston, Her Majesty's Secretary of State for the Home Department. He redirected it to the Board of Trade. It begins:

> The humble memorial of Donald Fraser, joiner Aberdeen, and others, part of the survivors of the passengers of the "Annie Jane" of Liverpool and John Mitchell, Engineer in Glasgow, and other friends and relations of the said passengers, resident in Glasgow...

It then details the circumstances and failings of the first voyage, the inadequacy of the inspection by the emigration agent in Liverpool, the subsequent failure to act on the complaints of the passengers and the catastrophe of the second voyage and the needless loss of life. It finishes:

The Beechey Inquiry and Recommendations

Your Memorialists, some of whom are survivors from the wreck, and others are the relations and friends of the shipwrecked passengers, while deeply deploring this melancholy catastrophe, cannot but think that the circumstances exhibit a disgraceful recklessness for the lives of the passengers on the part of those interested in the management of the ship, while they cannot but complain that her Majesty's Emigration agent manifested but little interest for the welfare of the unfortunate passengers on board; and they feel assured that your Lordship, on taking into consideration the foregoing facts, which the memorialists are ready to prove, will not hesitate to order such an inquiry to be made into the circumstances as will necessarily bring out on whom the responsibility rests for the sacrifice of so large a number of human lives.

The Memorialists therefore humbly pray that your Lordship may be pleased to issue a Commission for a searching inquiry to be made into the facts connected with the loss of the "Annie Jane" and to report the same to your Lordship with the view of your Lordship directing such further steps to be taken in the matter as may be necessary for the vindication of the ends of justice, or to do otherwise in the circumstances as your lordship may seem fit.

John Gibb	John Murray	Donald Frazer, survivor
John Campbell	Charles Smith	William Frazer, survivor
James Pratire	John Mitchell	James Rodger, survivor
George Murray	George Hossack	Abraham Brooks, survivor
Daniel Graham	Adam Kerr	Angus Mathieson, survivor
James Campbell	Agnes McClements	George Lennox, survivor
John Laing	Christina her X mark Wood	Charles Smith, survivor
Alexander Kerr	David Campbell	William Ross

The Beechey Inquiry and Recommendations

On 1st November 1853, just over one month after the event, with a speed and efficiency we can only marvel at today, Royal Navy Captain Frederick William Beechey opened an official inquiry, *Into the causes and circumstances attending the loss of the "Annie Jane", a vessel employed in the conveyance of passengers.*

This was one of the first times that the shipwreck of an emigrant ship was thought fit subject for a judicial investigation and there is little doubt that were it not for pressure from the press and the public it would not have taken place at all, for all that newspaper reporters were not allowed access to the proceedings. 23 witnesses in total were called, beginning with the owner, then the emigration officers, the stevedore who supervised loading the ship on both occasions, various members of the crew, and passengers, beginning with William Hendrie, who did have his day in court.

None of the French-Canadians sailors was called: they had been sent with haste home to Canada, their passages paid to New York by persons unknown.

William Hendrie had been summoned from Glasgow to give evidence. While on the stand he handed in witness statements from others: George and John Taylor, and Alexander Kerr. He revealed that they were still resident in Liverpool and had never left after the first voyage of the 'Annie Jane'. They were all then called as witnesses and asked questions about the first voyage. Abraham Brooks, Angus Mathieson and Donald Fraser were the only steerage passengers asked to give evidence about the second voyage. Captain Beechey seemed to focus on the loading of the ship, the storage and positioning of the iron cargo, the inadequacy of the French-Canadian sailors and the language difficulties. These subjects came up time and time again.

James Taylor, second steward and a fluent French speaker, was asked:

You came over with the Canadian crew, could these Canadians speak English? *No, not the half of them: only six. One or two of them could speak a little English; and there are two of them that are dead now that could speak the best English.*

Could they understand the orders they were given? *No, not the half. There was a great complaint against the sailors: they treated*

The Beechey Inquiry and Recommendations

them very badly, and I told the captain and the mate that I would not wish to see a sharper crew than they were, with their own countrymen.

With their own captain – a French captain? *Yes; and it was as smart a crew as you would wish to see.*

All the witnesses had been heard by 4th November. One important witness was missing: proceedings were delayed until Captain Mason returned from Vatersay. It was 14th December by the time he gave his evidence. He was on the witness stand over two days with a rest day in-between. Captain Mason completed his evidence on 16th December, yet he was asked only 52 questions. There is no doubt Beechey was remarkably gentle with him. As a contrast, Thomas Markham, the Second Mate, was asked 278 questions in one gruelling session, William Moore, sailmaker, 157 questions and then recalled later for another 52 questions.

When Captain Mason's evidence was completed, his testimony was then signed and witnessed by Thomas Gray[1], an employee of the Board of Trade. Captain Mason then handed over several documents signed by different parties, giving glowing testimonies about his character and temperament during the voyage.

As cabin passengers on board of the "Annie Jane" we make the following declaration regarding the conduct of the Captain, which has been grossly slandered. We hereby declare that all that has been published in the papers against Captain Mason's conduct is false. Being more frequently in his company than the steerage passengers, we have but to praise him for his conduct towards us, and he always behaved very kindly to all the passengers. We were full of confidence in his ability, seeing that he discharged his duties conscientiously, and with perfect presence of mind. As regards what has been said of his conduct on the day of the wreck it is a calumny. Never, we may say it before God, we saw him behaving more courageously and attending better to his duties. From the moment we sighted the land he was almost constantly on deck, and when obliged to rest Captain Rose took his place; both made frequent observations to know our position.

> We may certify that Captain Mason did all in his power, at the risk of his own life, to save as many passengers as possible; he was cool in the danger, commanding to the last moment, and the misfortune cannot be attributed either to the ship, which was new and strongly built, nor in the way it was manned, but only to the succession of bad weather we experienced. Signed F. Lammerts Van Buren, J. Francois Cornu, Marc Ami.
>
> *Liverpool 25th October 1853.*

They failed to mention that they were all in Liverpool, staying in Captain Mason's home, at the time.

Another letter followed from John Morgan, the other cabin passenger, more guarded but still praising Captain Mason for being of sober disposition. The next was from Thomas Holderness:

> **Captain William Mason**
>
> Dear Sir – In accordance with your request we certify below the time you have been in our service as master of ships, but I cannot, without sending to Hull, find out how long you have served in that employ as a mate; all those accounts are kept in Hull. 1842 as master of the "Good Intent" about 680 tons, and afterwards in the following ships all of larger tonnage; "Bolton Abbey", "Warren Hastings", "Lady Constable", "Hercyna" and "Annie Jane", making a continuous service of between eleven and twelve years; and your conduct has been such as to meet our approbation on all points, and with the underwriters you are well and favourably known.
>
> Your most obedient servants, Holderness and Chilton
>
> *Liverpool 12th December 1853*

Beechey closed the inquiry in Liverpool and returned to London. His report was complete on 30th December and presented to the Board of Trade. Its publication and release to the press was delayed until February 1854, prompting an impatient William Hendrie to

The Beechey Inquiry and Recommendations

write another letter to the press dated 24th January:

> Sir, – Having seen the question asked what has become of the investigation of the 'Annie Jane', and there is no answer to the question yet, the public are beginning to think it is all a farce, and I think so myself. If a murder had been committed on the Isle of Barra, and only one life lost, there would have been no trouble or expense spared to bring all the witnesses forward to prove the case, and bring the guilty party to justice. Now sir, here is a wholesale loss of life, where about 300 persons perish. What name can you give it, where a captain could stand up and tell about 400 passengers, when his ship was in such a disabled state, *"Quebec or the bottom"* and like a man of honour, he kept his word and sent them to the bottom... And when an investigation took place in Liverpool on such an important case as this, there were only three witnesses sent from Glasgow, when they could have got three times as many, and the three of us who did go to Liverpool were shamefully paid, having received only about 2s a-day, being half what we could have made at our own work. But to show how mean the case was gone about, I got a letter from three of the passengers who were in Liverpool to give to captain Beechey to prove the truth of my statements as published in the newspapers, and captain Beechey wanted to see them, and I went for them, and they lost about half a day each, and asked their pay for lost time, but were told that they could not get any; but the sailmaker, who was a part of two days taken from his work got 5s each time, besides a present from Mr Holderness. ...I hope however, that this case will be taken up by some of the members of the Scottish Rights Association at their first meeting, to show the injustice that Scotchmen get in important cases as this.
>
> It is now nearly three months since the investigation took place, and no more has been heard of it; and as there are some of the witnesses going to emigrate in the Spring, it is surely time something should be done about the matter.

Captain Frederick William Beechey's written judgment ran to over 3500 words: its conclusions follow.

> There can be no doubt that the loss of the "Annie Jane" was occasioned by her taking aboard a cargo of iron, without due care having being observed in its stowage. The improper disposition of the weight caused the vessel to roll and lurch so violently, that she tore away her masts, and strained and leaked throughout... Under these disastrous circumstances she had a crew who, though in appearance were more than ordinarily good, were not sufficient in number for such a vessel, especially at such a season of the year, and besides were composed partly of Canadians who with very few exceptions were afraid to go aloft at sea, and who could not or would not understand the orders they were given. By the agreement[2] there were 41 persons in all, of which 9 were either: mates, stewards, surgeon, cooks, carpenters, leaving only 32 seamen for a vessel of 1294 tons of which 18 were Canadians, the greater part who in the hour of difficulty were nearly useless. It is stated in the evidence, that the refusal of this part of the crew to go aloft was the cause of the loss of the top-mast sail, and by one witness of the mainmast from the impossibility of furling the sail with such part of the crew only as went up.
>
> It would also appear that, after the loss of the fore-top-mast and foreyard, on the 12th of September, there was great delay in getting up jury sails, and that six days elapsed before the vessel could be wore round to return towards an English port, during which time she was driving to the Northward, which I do not think would have happened in a vessel properly manned. But in the absence of the ship's log, and of the chief officer, who was drowned, I am not disposed to attach too much importance to this apparent negligence... The master admits that he threatened to shoot the first man who should attempt to take the ship from him, and it is

The Beechey Inquiry and Recommendations

> evidence that he treated with contempt the memorial of the passengers urging him to return, and that he used the expression "*Quebec or the bottom*"; but all this appears to be done under excitement, and with a secret determination to put the ship round when he could.

He then reproves Mason gently for not informing the passengers of his intention to return to Liverpool, and then softens the verdict, by praising him for his seamanship and judgment, for directing the vessel into Vatersay Bay.

He further states that the water closets should be more substantially built; and in a less exposed position on the deck, for the comfort of the female passengers. He closes with:

> I am fully aware of the difficult nature of the duty the Emigration Officer has to perform; the responsibility of detaining a ship, under such circumstances, when ready for sea, by refusing a clearance for the inefficient performance of particulars is very great; still, this responsibility should be incurred and fully authorised. I suggest that whenever the clearance officer has good reason to suspect the stability of the fittings, or the stowage of the cargo, or even the efficiency of the crew, either from their ignorance of the language or from any other cause, he be directed to refuse a clearance certificate.

The survivors and relatives of the deceased tried to instigate action against the owner of the 'Annie Jane'. Meetings were held in Glasgow, subscriptions raised, but all to no avail. No further action was forthcoming. The press and public interest had moved on to new disasters, of which there were many in those times. In 1853 there were 832 wrecks around the British coastline alone, with at least 989 lives lost. The 'Annie Jane' was by far the worst that year, but coming to the end of the era of sailing ships such disasters were commonplace. A new era of reliability was starting with steamships beginning to take over the emigrant routes.

The survivors got on with their lives; the families of the dead were left to mourn alone.

The Beechey Inquiry and Recommendations

Only one change was made to the law: an order of the Colonial Land and Emigration Commissioners was made in March 1854, by which, after stating that they had under consideration the reports made to them of the loss of the 'Annie Jane' and the 'Tayleur'[3], they directed *'that no ship be permitted to clear out without having an Azimuth compass[4] on board, or with a less crew than four men to every hundreds ton burden, O.M[5]'*. The effect of the order was to increase the number of seamen on board emigrant ships by one half.

When the mainmast that Captain Mason had thought sunk was examined on the beach in Vatersay, the base was described as frayed like a brush. There must have always been some movement, to cause such serious damage in a short space of time. Given the stormy conditions the 'Annie Jane' encountered, it was only a matter of time till it failed with catastrophic results.

---

1. Thomas Gray comes up again in this story in the next chapter.

2. When Captain Beechey mentions 'the agreement', he means the Crew Agreement on which the name of every crew member is written with his register number. My thanks to Anna Murray for its discovery in the National Archives. Beechey states 41 crew members. There are 41 names on the Crew Agreement from 24th August, and then another six join for the second voyage, and have been added to it with a date of 07/09/53. One name is missing, that of James Taylor, second steward, and one name is wrong, that of the surgeon: but his entry states: left the ship 02/09/53. Beechey had been given, and based his conclusions on, the wrong crew list. There was actually a crew of 48 for the second voyage.

3. The 'Tayleur' was a new ship on her first voyage, wrecked on the island of Lambay just outside Dublin Harbour; 378 lives, mostly Irish immigrants, were lost. The disaster was blamed on a faulty compass and foreigners who could not understand the instructions of the Captain, not French-Canadians on this occasion. This time it happened to be Chinese, Spaniards and Germans.

4. An Azimuth compass is one marked with degrees as well as Cardinal points: North, South, East, West.

5. Overall Mass.

11

The Gray Report and the Monument

Another year, another shipwreck...

In the mid-Nineteenth Century the west coast of the Outer Hebrides was strewn with the remains of ships taking the transatlantic route to or from North America and failing to make the crossing. Like a magnet, the Isles of Barra and South Uist seemed to draw them to their reefs and rocks – the list almost endless. After the 'Annie Jane' in 1853, the pattern continued of wrecks and survivors being systematically robbed of everything of value. The wealthy and the establishment were accused of being just as complicit as the lower classes in these crimes, driven by their greed.

Thomas Gray, Chief Clerk of the Board of Trade in London, was sent to investigate conditions in the islands of North Uist and Barra in August 1866, after concerns were raised by members of Lloyd's about the conduct of local officials with regard to wrecks. In response, he wrote a private letter and an excoriating report of the treatment of survivors and the exploitation and salvaging of materials from wrecks. His confidential report begins with a summing up of the first part of the year:

> In the six months ending June 1866 nearly £300,000 worth of property have been washed ashore off the islands on the West coast of Scotland. The islanders look upon this as the special dispensation of a wise providence.[1]

He then moves on to a description of the female sex in Barra, and their attire:

> The people are frightfully dirty at least the women and children are... For clothing the women seem to wear all sorts of odd things. It was a matter of wonder to me at first, where they got their clothes from. They do not appear to wear as a rule clothes of home manufacture of native wool but to have a selection from a most marvellous miscellaneous collection of old clothes. In fact among the women of the villages in Barra, you would see specimens, very faded ragged and worn out it is true, but still specimens of costume that would correspond with any costume from Queen Anne's time downward. The only conclusion I can come to is that they get their clothes from wrecks and that they obtain the fashions of almost all nations. The one drawback is that through being slept on in the ground at night, and getting wet all day, the garment loses its distinctive colour and pattern and all alike seem to be dirty draggled and deplorable.

There follows a description of what he perceived to be a typical Barra woman:

> A robust woman broad in the shoulders, thick necked, large handed, bare legged, with her hair halfway down her back, with a strong voice and a short ragged garment, with little or no covering for her head is the ordinary type of Barra woman.

Shortly after this, he describes the character of the men:

> The people are the Ishmaelites of Scotland. Each man's hand is against his brother, but this only so long as no stranger is in the case. I found as a practical fact that everyone I spoke to had something to tell confidentially about somebody else that would have assured transportation if true and proved. The moment a stranger's name was mentioned then everyone condemned him. They quarrel amongst themselves and live in a state of quiet hostility each watching for the fault of the other, but if a stranger comes to the island to buy or if a ship comes in distress, then they will band together against the intruder. They act on the direction literally "If a stranger comes within your gates take him in" and they do take him in with a vengeance. I have paid as much for the use of a dung cart without springs and the horse without harness, to take me over parts of the islands, as I should pay for the use of a two horse Brougham and man for the same distance. At the wretched inns the charges are higher than at the Waverley's and yet we had to sleep on tables in the tap room, with geese for company.

After dealing with the discomfort of travellers, he changes subject to the exploitation of wrecks: the Mr. Beatson he refers to is the Reverend Henry Beatson, Church of Scotland minister in Barra.

> Great value is attached to the seaweed, this may be understood from the time the wreck of the "Annie Jane" lay in Vatersay, the farmer's people had to walk around her instead of going straight to the place as they were in the habit of doing when she came ashore. In fact they went out of the way some yards and for this, under the head of circuitous route which had to be taken for seaweed, the charge £127. It seemed a favourable opportunity for making a stranger pay for something and was too good to be lost.
> Surface damage is another favourite claim when a wreck comes ashore it may do a little damage, and people passing and re-passing may do a little more, I

say may do. If a wreck were to happen on some parts of our coast on the margins of cultivated fields, damage would be done, but when a wreck happens on granite rocks and is confined to those rocks between high and low water mark no damage can be done to the coast.

In the case of the "Alfareeta" this happened, for the space of about 3 acres patches of grass had been covered with wreck and had faded and patches of bent[2] in a space included in 100 yards had been worn off the sand. A croft of ten acres costs £7 a year. The damage done to the bent could be repaired by half a dozen labourers in two days but £30 was charged for surface damage. In the case of the wreck of the "Annie Jane" which happened in a sandy bay £100 was charged for surface damage... At the wreck of the "Annie Jane" Mr. Beatson gave information to the relatives of the sufferers which led to them asking disagreeable questions about their property that had been appropriated by the inhabitants and some of the magistrates and for this he had his cattle harried and killed, and to save himself from utter ruin the remainder were sold under value to a magistrate who it was later believed had been the person to cause all the mischief to be done to his property.

Mr. Beatson hailed my appearance on the island with delight. He was anxious that something should be done, and he wished to give me information, but he was afraid to be seen with me. He dreaded a repetition of annoyance. He told me that after the wreck of the "Annie Jane" several of the farmers had great quantities of jewellery one a magistrate sent a quantity to Glasgow to be made up, and he gave me the names of several persons who would be able to give information on the subject. The affair happened in 1853 so that it is now too late to re-open it.

A Mr. ------ -------- is one of the persons who is alleged to have obtained possession of so much of the jewellery belonging to the "Annie Jane" there is no evidence against him. I told him amongst other things that I had

The Gray Report and the Monument

pretty good evidence where some of the jewellery went to. He turned very white and it was some time before he gained his self-possession. At the time of the wreck of the "Annie Jane" it was this gentleman who managed the business of his brother in law on the farm the wreck took place and a bill was sent in to the owners that could only be equalled in fiction. Amongst other things equally monstrous was a charge of £364 for cattle scared so that they would not feed, another for drying ropes and for frightening cows £360 and another for cows that slipped their calves and calves lost £420. So that it would appear that all the cattle in the island went to see the wreck, and that all those cows were in the family way and in such a precarious state at one and the same time. That the wreck had such an effect on them as to bring on premature delivery and to cause the offspring to die. This would not be believed in a novel and yet it is a stern fact. The whole amount of the bill was £1736:17 shillings. It was contested and the court gave £156.00. Perhaps the worst feature of all is the way the survivors were treated, they were in many instances pitilessly plundered of what little they had contrived to save and bring ashore. A charge was made of £225:15 shillings for burying the dead. I learnt that the dead were buried in two holes packed like herrings in a barrel. There is no mark not even a rail or bit of wood where these bodies are buried, I should like to see a stone erected to mark where the victims of one of the saddest wrecks of our time lie interred.

Gray then records his impressions of more current events:

To show that they are now no better than they were in 1854. I may mention that at the wreck of the "Bermuda", last year that happened in the depths of winter with the snow thick on the ground. The Captain's wife had her garments taken off her back and his children had their shoes taken off their feet and nothing was done to punish the offenders or to stop the plundering, the Captain was powerless and he appealed in vain for protection and assistance.

Later in an appendix to the report the 'Annie Jane' comes up again:

> Mr. Beatson expresses himself as being grateful that someone from Government has at last visited Barra. He hoped that something might be done to improve the administration of wrecks.
>
> He showed me a copy of a bill sent in by the farmers on whose land the "Annie Jane" was lost in 1853. It gives such a good idea of the manner the inhabitants benefit themselves by wreck that I copied it.
>
> It is as follows...
>
> Donald Maclellan Farmer
> Vatersay

Charge for drying ropes in the sands and frightening the cows	£360.00
Charge for cows that slipped their Calves – calves lost	£420.00
Black cattle so scared that they would not feed	£364.00
Surface damage	£100.00
Circuitous route which had to be taken for seaweed	£127.00
Burying the dead	£225.15.00
Damage to house	£20.00
15 days food and lodging to 68 people	£120.2.00

Total £1736.17

The case was tried in Edinbro or Glasgow and Mr Harper the secretary of the present Lloyd's salvage association was I believed engaged in it against the farmer. The sum awarded was £156.00 and this chiefly on account of lodgings and burials.

Beatson does not wish his name to transpire, his conduct presented a curious mixture of a strong desire to improve the state of things on Barra and a dread of the consequence of interfering, or having being recognised as having given any information. He came down to the miserable hotel where I was sleeping at 2am but could not make me hear, and returned home. I visited him quietly the next day.

Gray has a lot more to say in his confidential report about the conduct of the deputy receiver of wrecks, Neil Macdonald from South Uist, writing: *He allows wrecked property to be plundered in the most reckless manner, and himself in some instance shares the plunder.* He also had serious allegations to make about the Roman Catholic priest on Barra, William MacDonnel, claiming that he took a share of anything his parishioners acquired or received for working on wrecks, and that everybody in the community was terrified of him. The local policeman, Alexander Macleod, was not spared the cutting edge of his pen either, accused of being a drunken useless man. He had informed Gray that he would give the people 24 hours' notice when he would do a search, not surprisingly never finding anything.

After Gray's report Alexander Macleod and Neil Macdonald were sacked; both threatened legal action as they had not been told what the allegations were against them and had no chance to defend themselves. Macdonald's supervisor in Stornoway was dismissed as well. William MacDonnel, the Barra priest, published a pamphlet defending himself and the Barra people, parts of which were published in various newspapers in 1867.

Gray's report quite clearly implies that the Maclellans and Macgillivarys were involved in acquiring the jewellery that came ashore on the 'Annie Jane'. Undoubtedly emigrants, for whom the journey would have been intended to be one-way, would have left nothing of value behind them in their native land, and have been

The Gray Report and the Monument

carrying all they possessed with them. So valuables would have been hidden in the baggage and on the bodies, but it is unlikely that there would have been vast quantities. Wealthy people would not have been travelling steerage, with all the hardship that involved.

Probably the most compelling evidence of wrongdoing and the looting of the wreck is the song written by a native of Barra which is in Chapter 14 of this book. In the oral history of the islands a reliable way of recording history is in song, usually biting satire, but always relating true events. In a population of generally illiterate people, it was the most common way for the native population of recording history and would be sung and repeated, unchanged through the decades.

So this verse of song translated from Gaelic into English, Brogan Ur Bellag (Bellag's New Shoes), says everything:

The people of the island are cutting fingers,
Using knives when their teeth wear out;
Searching the bodies, feeling them all over,
We will see in the end, the guilty will be in prison.

Despite Gray's wish for a monument or fence around the spot where so many bodies were interred, it would remain unmarked for almost twenty years. In 1881, a granite memorial was put up on the spot where it still stands in a commanding position above the beach. Today it is still the only listed structure on Vatersay. There is no inscription recording who erected the memorial on it, but according to Ben Buxton's excellent book, The Vatersay Raiders[3]:

A visitor in 1887 informs us that "a few years ago Robert MacFie of Airds and Oban[4] was cruising among the Western islands in his yacht, and on hearing of the disaster resolved to commemorate it. He commissioned the memorial from a firm of masons who were working in Barra at the time, Cruickshank of Glasgow".

Robert MacFie of Airds and Oban was born in 1812 into a wealthy family of sugar refiners in Greenock, Glasgow. In 1851 he was sailing his yacht 'La Belle Anglaise' around the west coast of Scotland, and in September of that year he sailed into Airds Bay, Port Appin, just outside Oban; he saw and fell in love with Airds House, bought it and made it his home and also the base for exploring the

The Gray Report and the Monument

west coast of Scotland in the summer. It was probably on one of the expeditions from there that he sailed into Vatersay Bay, and heard the story of the 'Annie Jane'. Without the selfless actions of one man and his erection of the monument, there would have been nothing else to commemorate the tragedy.

---

1. Gray's confidential report, NA: MT(/153/1878)
2. Bent is a natural coarse grass.
3. Taken from The Vatersay Raiders by Ben Buxton, published by Birlinn Press, 2008.
4. http://www.oldappin.com/robert-macfie-of-airds

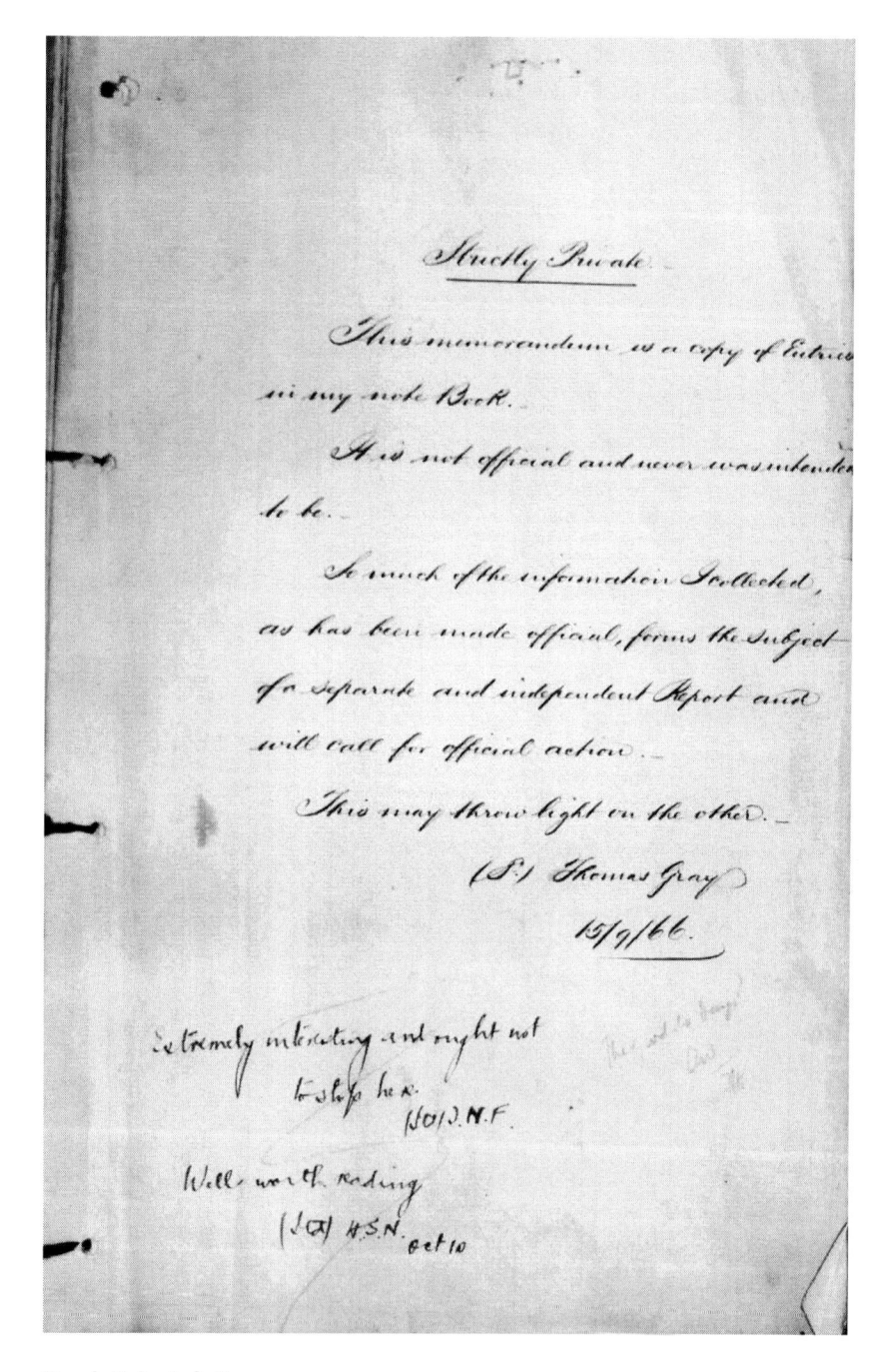

Gray's Private letter
Gray's private letter: with thanks to The National Archives.
© National Archives.

Gray's Private letter
Gray's private letter: with thanks to The National Archives.
© National Archives.

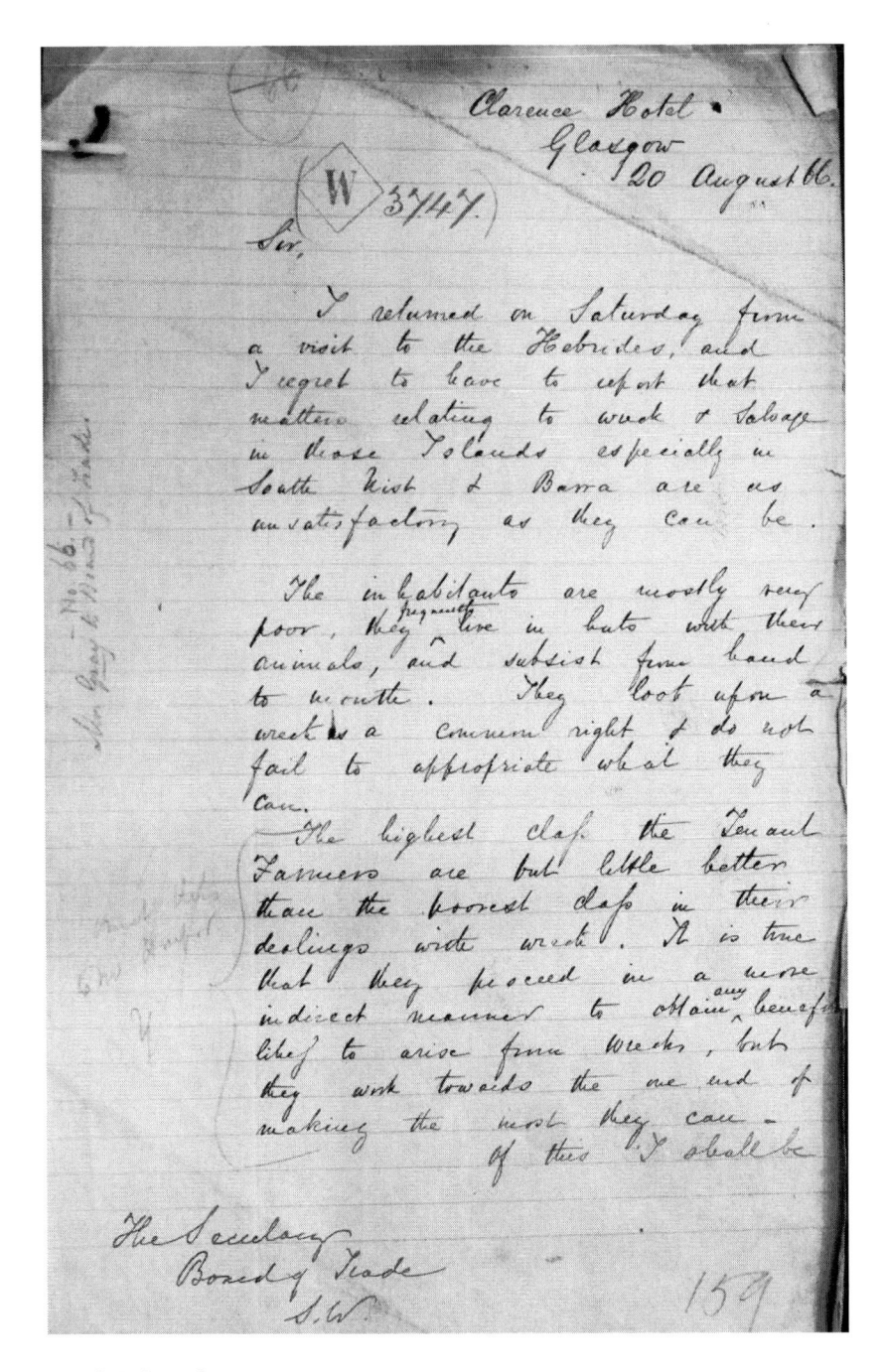

12

Freight is the Mother of Wages

Article in the Montreal Witness, 26th November 1853:

The "Annie Jane"– The surviving eight French-Canadians arrived in this city from Baltimore, on Saturday evening on their way home, some to Quebec, some below that port, and one for the Bay of Chaleur. The poor fellows look well and were in good spirits though they had lost everything, and ready for another voyage. The British consul of New York paid their passage to Montreal and gave them letters for Messrs. Culliver and Co for further assistance. A subscription should be raised to supply them with another kit.

There is no evidence of a subscription being raised for the poor survivors. In most cases, as noted earlier, a seaman did not get paid when a ship was lost unless he could prove negligence on the part of the owner or the Captain.

Did the first group of surviving seamen of the 'Annie Jane' to arrive at Liverpool get paid up to 11th October, the date of their discharge on the crew agreement? Legally, Thomas Holderness did not have to give them a penny, from the date of their initial employment in August 1853. Once the ship was declared a wreck, fifteen minutes before the end of 28th September, that was when all their wages disappeared, unless their employer was generous enough to want to pay them.

There is evidence from another court judgment of the period, in November 1853[1]

> **There is no question that the very basis of the owner and his seamen was, that the freight should be earned by a successful termination of the voyage. The principle *"freight is the mother of all wages"* is too fully recognized to be questioned. The contract for the mariner is a contract for the voyage and unlike most contracts for the hire of services, the wages are made dependent on the successful issue of the enterprise for reasons of policy. In order that the mariner's reward may be bound up in the safety of the vessel and cargo so that the motive to exertion may be drawn in part from his own interests. The owner therefore is absolved from the payment of wages by the total loss of the ship, however long the mariner may have been in his employment previous to such a loss. Unless the loss of the vessel was caused by the fraud or fault of the master or owner.**

Under British maritime law the same concept applied. This seems bizarre to the modern reader: what difference could one seaman make to the destiny of a ship? A Captain, yes, but would a seaman put his life in jeopardy by not striving to keep a ship from wreck?

Twenty-two-year-old Jean Baptiste Langlois, one of the survivors of the 'Annie Jane' was angered by this and felt a great injustice had been done to him. He had been engaged on the 'Sir Allan Mcnab' for what he thought would be a return journey, but it was chartered by the British government to make a trip to Australia. The captain arranged for Jean Baptiste Langlois and another sixteen French-Canadian seamen to make the return journey on the 'Annie Jane'.

Jean Baptiste thought, having being engaged by contract for a round trip, that he had detected a loophole in the system. He won the first round, in the circuit court, but the judgment was appealed to the Supreme Court. Given his pursuit of this case it looks as though Jean Baptiste and the other seamen had not received wages for the first trip on the 'Sir Allan McNab' or the return journey on the 'Annie Jane' and the subsequent wreck. Communications between Quebec and Liverpool were good, with business interests intertwined. It is doubtful that this case could have proceeded without the knowledge and avid interest of the Liverpool ship owners. A win for Jean Baptiste Langlois could have had serious implications for everybody involved in the maritime industry. It is the weight of those interests that might go some way to explain the verdict reached.

Superior Court – Quebec
Case No1066 Bernier et al Appellants.

Langlois Respondent.

Judgment rendered the 26th day of June 1855

This was an appeal from a judgment rendered in the circuit court, at Quebec, by Mr, Justice Power, on the 20th day of January 1855, in an action by the respondent against the appellants, the judgment of the circuit court was in favor of the respondent; the following are the facts of the case as exhibited by the pleadings and the evidence.

The respondent instituted his action against the Appellants for the recovery of the sum of 22 pounds 17 shillings currency, alleged to be due him for the balance of his wages as mariner, from the first of July to the 1st of December 1853, on a voyage in the ship Sir Allan Mcnab, from Quebec to Liverpool, in England and to return the same year, at the rate of 5 Pounds and 10 shillings a month, upon the express condition that if Bernier, the master, did not see fit to return to Canada with the said vessel, in that case he should be bound to procure to the respondent a berth, as mariner, on board of a vessel returning to Canada, in the Autumn of 1853, and in case the said master should be unable to place the respondent as mariner on board a vessel returning to Canada, then he would be bound to procure to the respondent a passage at his costs: as the whole had been agreed upon by deed before Glackameyer, and another, Notaries, on the fourth of July 1853; to which deed the appellants, Bernier, as master, and Dubord as owner, of the Sir Allan Mcnab, were parties, obliging themselves jointly and severally . The respondent declared that he had well and truly performed the said voyage, but that the appellants had neglected to provide a passage for him to Quebec, by means thereof he was obliged to return to Quebec without receiving any wages, and to pay his expenses up to the 1st day of December, 1853 the day of his arrival in Quebec.

The Respondent then concluded for judgment against the appellants, jointly and severally; to this action the Appellants pleaded the general issue and an exception, by which latter plea, after setting forth the agreement above stated, They alleged that the said Bernier, having sailed from Quebec with the Sir Allan Mcnab on a voyage of twenty four days, arriving at his destination Liverpool, England, in the month of August 1853, that having sold the Sir Allan Mcnab, he procured for the respondent a berth, as mariner on board a vessel returning to Canada that Autumn. In compliance with the covenants and stipulations contained in the contract above mentioned. The vessel was called the 'Annie Jane' coming to Canada, and that the respondent, on the 20th day of August 1853, had actually shipped on board of that vessel at the same rate of wages; and that the said vessel had sailed from Liverpool for Canada, with the respondent on board, but that the said vessel, on her voyage out had suffered shipwreck, and become a total loss. It was further proved that the respondent had been saved and had returned to Liverpool, from which place he had sailed on board of the Grecian, which brought him to Baltimore, and that he reached Quebec about the end of November. His passage on board the Grecian had been paid in England, but it was not ascertained by whom. This point however, was immaterial to the cause.

At the argument of the case in the Circuit court the Respondent had claimed wages, firstly, for his services from the 1st July to the

20th of August 1853 on board the Sir Allan McNab, 2ndly, from the 20th of August to the 1st day of December 1853, day of his arrival in Quebec.

The Appellants contended that they were bound to pay wages to the Respondent for his services on board of the Sir Allan McNab up to the 20th of August 1853, and that a judgment ought to be rendered against them for a small sum as balance of wages for those services, they having failed to prove all the payments as alleged, but that as to the surplus of wages from the 20th of August they were not liable having fulfilled their contract by procuring for the Respondent a berth aboard the Annie Jane; that from that day they were relieved from all liability incurred by their contract except what might be earned by the respondent aboard the Annie Jane.

And that, consequently, the Respondent had no action for wages from the 20th of August 1853, he being in the position of a shipwrecked mariner whose vessel was totally lost.

Such was the point submitted to the Circuit court.

The judgment of the Superior court was as follows:

Considering that by the agreement of the 4th July 1853 the Respondent, plaintiff in the court below, had engaged as a mariner for the voyage in the vessel called the Sir Allan McNab from the port of Quebec to Liverpool, and to return to Quebec, which engagement formed the principal agreement between the two parties: that it was, however, agreed that if the master of the vessel did not think proper of returning to Canada with the ship, he should be bound to procure for the said Respondent, together with other seamen engaged according to the said agreement, a berth as seaman on board of a vessel returning to Canada and make up the difference of wages, and that in the case the said Master, to wit Louis B. Bernier, one of the Appellants, and one of the defendants in the court below, should not be able to provide a berth for the respondent, he should be bound to procure a passage for him at his own cost; considering that the said Louis B. Bernier has complied with the condition of finding a return berth as seaman for the said Respondent, to wit: on board the vessel called the

Annie Jane, on board of which the respondent has been engaged, and that thus the Appellants have discharged, as well the said condition, as the subsidiary one of procuring a passage for the Respondent, the said Appellants remaining responsible for the difference in wages; and considering this last responsibility did not change the nature of the engagement of the Respondent, and that the Appellants could not be responsible for the difference of wages for the services of the Respondent on board of the Annie Jane, except in the same manner as they would have been responsible for the same services aboard the Sir Allan McNab, and under the same circumstances; considering by the shipwreck and loss of the said vessel the Annie Jane, the Respondent has by law, lost his return wages; considering also that the wages of the Respondent up to the time of his engagement on board the Annie Jane amounted to 8 pound 9 shillings currency, and that the payments on account alleged by the Appellants have not been proved; doth reverse the judgment appealed from with costs, and proceeding to render the judgment which ought to have been rendered in the court below, doth condemn the Appellants, Defendants in the court below, jointly and severally to pay to the Respondent the plaintiff in the court below, the sum of 8 pounds 9 shillings currency for the wages of the said Respondent, Plaintiff as mentioned in the declaration with interest &c with costs as in a second class non appealable case of the circuit court.

HELD: That freight is the mother of wages, and if during a voyage a vessel becomes a total loss the seamen cannot recover wages and that consequently the liability of a third party to pay them their wages will cease.[2]

Jean Baptiste Langlois lost the case and no appeal was allowed. One can only hope for his sake that 'no win, no fee' was a fashion that started in Quebec in the mid 1800's, or that he had a family member in the legal profession representing him.

Other than that, he would have been inflicted with yet another loss to his name.

1. New York Times November 10th 1853 copyright New York Times
https://uk-mg42.mail.yahoo.com/neo/launch?.rand=7nio4cjivc5mr

2. View the original document here:
 http://babel.hathitrust.org/cgi/pt?id=umn.31951d02284023h;view=1up;seq=430

Original from the University of Minnesota.

13

Persecution of a Clergyman for a Peccadillo[1]

The majority of the survivors of the 'Annie Jane' disappeared into obscurity never to appear in sensational newspaper headlines again. There was, however, an exception.

The passengers on the 'Annie Jane' were on the ship for many reasons. Some hoped to improve their lives, many to join loved ones. Most simply looked forward to a brighter and better future. Very few of them would have been dreading the voyage, but there was one young girl, Deborah Stanley, who ran down the gangway after the first voyage, her sister Catherine trailing behind her, eight-month-old baby daughter in her arms, desperate to get away from the ship. Like many others, she had lost all her provisions in the chaos of the storm. One can easily imagine her screaming with fear at every exaggerated lurch or roll of the vessel. She had been given £50 to make a journey to America and disappear from Ireland forever. The first voyage was enough for her: nothing would ever tempt her out to sea again.

Yet there was another kind of storm brewing for her.

At the Liverpool police courts on a Saturday in October 1856 a case was heard in which the plaintiff was the very same Deborah Stanley. The Rev Peter William Browne, Blackrod, near Chorley, was the named defendant.

It was a claim for affiliation[2] against a clergyman of the established church, and the small courtroom was crowded. The defendant was represented by Mr. Blair, barrister. Mr. Cobb was solicitor for the complainant.

Most of what follows is taken from contemporary newspaper reports of the case.

The defendant was described as a person of gentlemanly appearance, quiet, and self-possessed in his manner and perfectly grave in his demeanour. *'He appeared to be about fifty years of age but could be a lot less. Complainant was said to be young, of exceedingly sallow appearance, and by no means good-looking, her figure was not provided with a complimentary description. We are only told, she was "much under the usual stature".'*

Mr. Cobb, in opening the case, stated that in the month of March 1852 the affair between Mr. Browne and Deborah Stanley took place, when she was aged between 16 and 17. At this time she was residing in Dublin with her father, who maintained her. Her father was a coachman of some twenty years' standing. Deborah was in Mountjoy Square listening to some street music late in the afternoon, when the defendant came up and accosted her. They walked about the square for some time, and then the defendant asked her to accompany him to a house in the vicinity of Sackville Street where he said an Aunt of his resided. This, however, turned out to be 'a house of an improper description', and there, we are informed, 'the defendant effected the girl's ruin'.

For all this, Reverend Browne was perfectly satisfied that up to that time the girl had been perfectly virtuous. He promised to meet her the next evening, when he would give her a handsome present in lieu of a bonnet and a comb which his vigorous attentions had injured.

It does not appear that the complainant knew anything about the name, family, or residence of the gentleman she had encountered. The following evening, she was again in Mountjoy Square. The gentleman did not keep his appointment but, in her wanderings through the square, her attention was taken by a carriage at an open door, into which a gentleman was 'handing ladies'. She inquired who was doing this and was informed that it was the Rev. Browne of 12 Mountjoy Square who was acting this way. No communication took place between the parties from the month of March to the accouchement of the claimant. In about three months, her condition became such as to cause her to leave her father's house. He would not retain her at home. She then went to reside with a married sister and afterwards removed to a house on Clarendon Street in Dublin. It was here in the month of December, 1852 the complainant was confined of a female child, the subject of this claim.

Mr Cobb continued: She never spoke of her state to the defendant. Neither did she write to him or send him a message, nor received any from him. The defendant may in fact have forgotten her existence. About two months after the birth of her child, a letter was sent to him through the post. No answer was returned. She tried again several times but no response ever came. At length, she resolved to send a letter that her sister should convey. The letter was delivered by the sister to the defendant. Having perused it, he promised that he would call the following day. He did call at her lodging the next morning at an early hour, found her in bed, and having looked at and enquired the sex of the child, asked if three shillings a week would suffice for her purposes. Of course, his offer was not satisfactory, but he left assuring her that something should be done. He stated that if her landlady, who was her sister, would follow him to his solicitor, Mr. Worral's, she would receive a pound. She followed and had that sum from Mr. Worral or someone in his office.

An arrangement was made by which the complainant had seven shillings a week allowed her. This continued until the child was eight months old. In September 1853, a proposal was made to the plaintiff to go to America. She consented to this, upon which a sum of £50[3] was paid to her, by Mr. Fitzgerald (Mr. Worral's manager) with the understanding that she would leave Dublin immediately for Liverpool and take passage to America.

According to her solicitor's statement, this journey took place. The client actually sailed from Liverpool in the 'Annie Jane', a vessel that was compelled to return to Port damaged. Having lost her provisions, she refused to sail on the 'Annie Jane' again. She wrote to Fitzgerald describing the circumstances. He contacted her to say that something should still be done to enable her to go to America. Every effort was made to induce her to go there, and she would have voyaged west, but for the circumstance that her sister Catherine had gone out on the same vessel that she (the claimant) had taken passage before, that the vessel had again been wrecked and that 380 of the passengers were lost, her sister barely escaping with her life.

Mr. Cobb admitted at this point in his narrative, that it was to be regretted that the girl did not inform Mr. Browne of her determination not to go to America.

Having spent the £50 in one way or another, she again claimed support from Mr. Browne. Her claim was allowed. As a result, for a considerable time while residing in Liverpool, she obtained ten shillings a week for her own and the child's support.

This allowance was paid to her by a Mr. Fitzgerald, a conducting clerk of Mr. Worral, solicitor. It was again proposed to her that she should depart for America and a sum of £35 was given her, besides paying for her passage outwards. On this occasion to guard against mistakes, Fitzgerald was sent with the emigrant. He was to ensure she was on board, then give her the money. He came to Liverpool with the complainant, took her on board the vessel, and saw the ship in the river, and having paid the money, accepted a receipt. He left the ship on the river just as she was about to sail, and so did the complainant. He was scarcely on shore when she followed him back to land.

It was clear she had no intention of emigrating.

She took the money, but (Mr. Cobb himself admitted) misled Mr. Browne, remaining in Liverpool while the £35 lasted. She then went down to Chorley to remind Rev. Browne of her existence. He was so annoyed by her presence that he called a policeman, and the girl went away. Shortly afterwards the present proceedings were instituted. Mr. Cobb did not deny that the claimant was the mother of a second child which she had affiliated in this court, but this was not fathered by Mr. Browne and did not affect the proceedings.

Deborah Stanley was next called and corroborated by her evidence the statements of Mr. Cobb. In cross examination by Mr. Blair, the complainant denied that she had ever written a letter threatening to leave the child in the hall of Mr. Browne's home or that she had expressed the intent in a letter to expose him in his church and also threatened to visit his parish to see him. The letters to Mr. Browne had been written by acquaintances. She agreed that eight months after the child was born, she received from Mr. Brown a £50 lump sum, having received 7 shillings a week in the interim. In September, she received £35. Mr. Blair solicited that the letters sent by the complainant to Mr. Browne contained several wilful misrepresentations. He pointed out that the £50 was obtained from Mr. Browne on the understanding that she was emigrating and getting married. The £35 was obtained to pay her passage to New York.

Re-examined by Mr. Cobb, the complainant said she did not receive the £35 in satisfaction of all her claims on Mr. Browne. She would never have put her mark to the receipt had she so understood it at the time. Mr. Browne's objective all along had been to exile her to America.

The sister of the claimant was called, but before her evidence was proceeded with, Mr. Aiken who with Mr. Benn presided, said they should dismiss the case. (A murmur of approval throughout the court). Mr. Blair on behalf of his client begged to state, that although Mr. Browne did not deny the grievous error and mistake of which he had been guilty in regard to intercourse with the girl, there was abundant evidence to prove the child was not his. Since the child's birth, Mr. Browne had been the victim of persecution, which had gone on until it was perfectly intolerable. The fear of exposure through the press had hitherto induced Mr. Browne to meet demand after demand upon his purse, and Mr. Blair hoped the press in the exercise of its discretion, would disappoint the desire to make this a further matter of torture to the defendant and his family, "*had Mr. Browne but an opportunity of appearing in the box*".

Mr. Cobb, who now seemed highly excited, interjected "*I am instructed by a highly respectable gentleman to give notice of appeal, and then Mr. Browne shall have the opportunity of getting in the box and giving his version of events. If they were so desirous of examining him, why not put him in the box?"*

Mr Blair replied: *"Because the court has dismissed the complaint, else I have strong evidence which would prove perfectly to the court that it was quite impossible that this child could be the daughter of Mr. Browne. I don't think it is necessary now to state what that evidence is. This complaint has been dismissed."*

Mr Cobb: *"I think if there is any case where an appeal ought to be allowed it is in one such as this. If this girl is a perjured individual and a disgrace to society, the case ought to go on to have her punished. If so, it must be followed to its ultimate result."* He continued *"I have a person to prove..."*, but the bad-tempered exchange was cut short by a remark from the bench, and notice of appeal having been given, the magistrates proceeded with other cases.

For all Mr. Cobb's bluster, that seems to have been the end of the case, with no record of any further proceedings. What seems obvious to us today, and deeply relevant, is that Deborah was not able to read or write. The so-called receipt, or the absolution of Mr. Browne of all future responsibility for the child, should have been thrown out of court.

---

1. Peccadillo, small, relatively unimportant offence or sin. This title is taken from a contemporary newspaper report in the Preston Chronicle and Lancashire Advertiser of 25th October 1856.

2. A legal order in which a man who is not married to the mother of his child must pay money in support.

3. The sum of £50 then would be the equivalent of almost £4000 in 2017.

14

Songs and Ballads of the 'Annie Jane'

GEMS from the "Annie Jane"

"The boys that read the book"

"Good out of evil" is the aim of Christian men to bring;
"Good out of evil" is a theme for Christian bards to sing
And one amongst the humblest now essays, in simple strain,
Pearls from the lost ship to produce – gems from the "Annie Jane".

The "Annie Jane" was hurrying on, she would not heed the helm;
And the raging billows, roaring round, were threat'ning to o'erwhelm;
Yet, while the seamen watch'd her course, with dark despairing looks,
Two children from a ragged school were reading God's own book.

And spite of many a howling blast, and many a yawning grave,
They read of him the merciful, and the mighty one to save;
Whose sov'reign power, in days of old, performed his sov'reign will,
When he spoke to the Sea of Galilee, and bade its storms be still.

But, as they read, a fearful shout, and then a sudden shock –
The "Annie Jane" had ceased to sail – she was dashed upon a rock!
And many sank; but when they came to number up the band,
'Twas found the boys who read the book had safe escaped to land!

And one with spirit undismay'd, back to his school return'd,
With graphic pen has written down the lessons he has learn'd;
And, reckless of the past is gone, with fearless thoughts and free,
To tempt again the treacherous main, and distant countries see.

God speed thy course, thou gallant boy, depending on the truth
Which thou hast treasured in thy heart, in the days of early youth;
Then, shouldst thou die in quiet bed or 'midst the wild waves driven,
Where'er thy body is entomb'd, thy soul shall rest in heaven.

And ye who read the touching tale that gallant boy has told,
Do what you can to help the cause that made his heart so bold;
And give the compass and the chart that guide him on his way,

Ye who are humble on the earth, and ye who proudly live,
For the Bible and the ragged school your substance freely give;
And who can tell but you may meet on Canan's peaceful shore,
With the ragged boys who read the book, and many thousands more!

Temple, 1st May, 1854   J.P

Note: Taken from the Ragged School Union magazine VOL 6 1854 page 99

Looking up

"Though the waves and storms go over my head,
"I will look up" the psalmist said;
He did; and, e'en with such a look,
Gazed the poor "boy that read the book"
    On board the "Annie Jane"

A drop of water from above
Fell on his head: twas sent in love;
To make him raise his tearful eye,
And fix it on the starry sky,
    That lit the "Annie Jane"

He saw deliverance as he gazed,
And o'er the flood his form he raised;
And then a safe escape he found;
While those who look'd not up were drown'd;
    Lost with the "Annie Jane"

When troubles threaten to destroy,
Look up, look up, poor ragged boy;
Look up beyond the stormy wave,
To him who died mankind to save,
    From misery and pain.

Look up, and see the prospect clear;
Look up, and find deliverance near:
And while thou bind'st it to thy heart
The lesson to thy friends impart,
Learn'd from the "Annie Jane"

Temple, June 1854   J.P

Note: taken from the Ragged School Union magazine VOL 6 1854 page 137

An emigrant ballad about emigrants who didn't make it

The 'Annie Jane'

You landsmen all pray lend an ear, to this my dismal tale,
Concerning the wreck of the 'Annie Jane', which from Liverpool did sail;
It was for Quebec she was bound, across the raging main,
With four hundred and fifty souls aboard, the ill-fated 'Annie Jane'.

One hundred smiths and joiners, to Scotland did belong,
To work on the Quebec railway, they being young and strong;
From England and from Ireland, the rest of them they came,
They little thought they'd lose their lives in the ill-fated 'Annie Jane'.

With lightsome hearts we bore away, not thinking danger nigh,
Till the third day a storm arose, and dismal was the sky;
Our masts and rigging were blown away into the raging main,
Who can describe our suffering great, in the ill-fated 'Annie Jane'.

A petition from the passengers, the Captain did implore,
For to return to Liverpool and tempt the seas no more;
Our petition, by the Captain was treated with disdain,
In the dead of night he put about the ill-fated 'Annie Jane'.

On the morning of the twenty-ninth, our ship was run ashore,
The wind it blew a hurricane, and the billows loud did roar;
Each struggled hard amidst the waves, their lives to maintain,
But three hundred and forty eight were lost, with the ill-fated 'Annie Jane'.

Our vessel then to pieces went, whene'er she struck the ground,
Our cries for help did rend the air, but alas no help was found;
My language fails for to describe, the horrors of that scene,
Each wave swept hundreds to their grave, from the ill-fated 'Annie Jane'.

A mother held her infant twins, for hours to her breast.
Death at length claimed one of them to its eternal rest,
By the assisting hand of Providence, the mother the shore did gain;
And thus escaped a watery grave in the ill-fated 'Annie Jane'.

*How many a mother laments her son, and wives their husbands dear,
And many a pretty fair maid for her lover drops a tear;
And many do lament their friends, whom they'll ne'er see again,
Who alas have found a watery grave in the ill-fated 'Annie Jane'.*

*Now to conclude, and make an end, of this my dismal song,
The Captain should be taken, and placed in prison strong;
If our petition he had granted, and had turned back again,
Our precious lives would all been spared, and the ill-fated
'Annie Jane'.*

Air is given as "Mary Neal"

Mu23-yl:115,Murraycollection, Glasgow university.
http://www.gla.ac.uk/0t4/~dumfries/files/layer2/glasgow_broadside_ballads/mu23y1115.htm

Song to the 'Annie Jane'

It is believed that this song was composed in the Gaelic language by Donald MacLachlan (Domhnall MacLachlainn) many years after the disaster. He was a resident of Borve, a small village near the town of Castlebay on the neighbouring island of Barra.

An 'Annie Jane'

Tha Brogan air Bellaig gun tarraig gun iaruinn,
Thainag air Bharraidh air cladach Traigh Siar;
Bean Chaiptein Ros chaidh gu socair do'n siorruidheachd,
Thilg iad a corp, as an t-slochd roimh na ceudan.

Tha muinntir an eilean a gearradh nam meur dhiubh,
Gabhail na sgeanan nuair theirig ne fiaclan;
Rurach nam corp, gar robladh's ga feuchainn,
Chi sibh mu dheireadh gun teid a'choire do'n phrioson.

Nuair theid an insurance an taobh seo de Alba,
Chi sibh gu sgiursadh gach truileach is cealgair;
'S fhalbh thus a null is thoir do chul ris a' mheallaich,
Gheibh thu na guin a bha aig Una' san fhalchan.

Thainig an 'Annie Jane' a Bharraidh gun truaille,
Clann Nic Ill'Fhaolain nach dol dh'innis na fhuair iad;
Luchdachadh na cairtean a dol thairis gu Tuath leotha,
Lan fhainichean, ghriogagan is sioda nan uaislean.

Listen to a version of the song here:
http://www.tobarandualchais.co.uk/en play/6360;jsessionid =E68063E08F02A2CB08424A030269C118
Sung by Donald Campbell.
Reporter: Calum Ian Maclean.
Transcribed in the School of Scottish Studies.
Composed by Dòmhnall mac'ic Lochlainn of Borgh.

English translation

By Allan Murray, with Norman and Agnes Ann Macleod.

Bella wears shoes without iron or tacks,
That came to Barra on the shore of West Beach:
Captain Rose's wife that went peacefully to eternity,
Her body thrown into the pit before the hundreds.

The people of the island are cutting fingers,
Using knives when their teeth wear out;
Searching the bodies, feeling them all over,
We will see in the end, the guilty will be in prison.

When the insurance comes to this side of Scotland,
It is certain the rogues will be punished;
Go over and turn your back to the Mheallaich[1]
You will get the gowns that Una has hidden.

The 'Annie Jane' arrived in Barra without grief,
The MacLellans did not tell all that they got;
Loaded their carts and went over to the North with them,
Full of rings, beads and silk of the nobility.

---

1. The name of the area on the East side of Vatersay.

15

The Lean Years

The islands

Even in the present day, transport links with the island of Barra aren't wonderful. There is now a plane that lands on a beach at the north end of Barra; it is one of Barra's claims to fame is that it has the only scheduled landing strip in the country that is tidal and is washed twice a day by the sea. All flight timetables to Barra reflect that. The plane is a Twin Otter flying between Glasgow and Barra and on to the Isle of Benbecula. Operated by Loganair, it lands on a cockle beach when the tide is out. Go any time in the summer and there will be a line of tourists taking photographs of the plane, its wheels throwing an arc of salt water into the air as it lands. The event includes the enjoyable spectacle of the airport's Land Rover chasing away any stray livestock or tourists from the beach just prior to a landing.

If you are leaving the island by sea, the preferred option is to go to the picturesque little town of Castlebay; there, depending on the schedule, a Caledonian Macbrayne ferry docks in the harbour most days; it then sets off on a five-hour journey to Oban, sheltered behind the island of Mull.

The island of Vatersay is now joined to Barra by a short causeway which was built in 1991 at a cost of £3.7 million. Before the construction of the causeway Vatersay suffered from a declining population as it was dependent on a small ferry which ran from Castlebay in Barra. During severe weather the island could be cut off from Barra for days. The population has stabilised now; it had fallen as low as 65 and has now slightly risen in numbers to around 90. It is a pleasant green island, measuring three miles east to west by two miles north to south. Its most attractive feature comprises two beautiful crescents of sandy beaches directly opposite each other, nearly cutting the island in half, with the sand being eroded on one side and replaced on the other, continually leaving it in a state of change. Ironically, the east side creates a very safe natural harbour: I have spent nights anchored there, and always slept soundly, enjoying one of the most sheltered and picturesque spots in the Hebrides. The west coast, where the 'Annie Jane' came to grief, has a slightly smaller beach which is exposed to the open sea, and in winter the waves, with the full open reach of the Atlantic to propel them, come thundering onto the shore.

The island of Vatersay is at the southern end of the Outer Hebrides. It is the first of a chain of small islands, including Pabbay, Sandray, Mingulay (which is the largest of the group), and Berneray, the most southerly point, on which the Barra Head lighthouse, 693 feet above sea level, is situated at the end of the chain.

Probably the most notable and newsworthy event that has ever happened to Barra was another shipwreck, coincidentally, like the 'Annie Jane', also a ship that had sailed from Liverpool. That time, fortunately, no lives were lost.

When the 'SS Politician' ran aground in the Sound of Eriskay in February 1945, just a few miles away from Barra, it was carrying a cargo of 28,000 bottles of malt whisky. There is no doubt that descendants of the people who had so eagerly pillaged the 'Annie Jane' now approached the wreck of the 'Politician' with extraordinary enthusiasm: they had certainly not lost any of their ancestors' talents. Nowadays some might argue that it was nature, some might

The Lean Years

argue nurture, which left them so well-equipped and eager for the task. After a lot of careful consideration, I would maintain it was the malt whisky; during a period of wartime shortage it proved irresistible. The islanders are still inclined to be partial to a 'wee dram' today. The writer Compton Mackenzie came to live on Barra, heard the story, wrote about it in a book entitled 'Whisky Galore' and set the story on Barra: the rest, as they say, is history. A very successful film followed. Bottles still turn up to the present day, hidden in ingenious locations scattered the length and breadth of the island.

The remains of the wreck were dynamited eventually; the feelings of the Barra folk were summed up succinctly by Angus John Campbell, who commented, *"Dynamiting whisky. You wouldn't think there'd be men in the world so crazy as that!"*

The shipwrecked crew of the 'Politician' were looked after well by the islanders, with no recorded complaints about their accommodation or food.

During the period when the 'Annie Jane' was wrecked, the Isle of Vatersay was owned by a Colonel John Gordon of Cluny; he had bought the islands of Benbecula, South Uist, Barra and all the outlying smaller islands from the bankrupt hereditary owner, General MacNeil, in 1838. A notoriously parsimonious individual, the Colonel spent as little on his property as he could get away with. He had acquired islands that were grossly overpopulated and unable to support the population at the best of times. In 1846 the potato blight reached Barra and Vatersay, leaving the islanders with the almost total loss of what was their staple diet. Subsequent years were little better. In late 1850 a group of islanders left Barra, turning up in Inverness initially, starving, destitute and in rags, claiming they had been evicted from their homes, to make way for sheep, and then evicted again from the tents and shelters they had put up on the shoreline. Eventually they made their way to Glasgow, prompting an application to be directed to the Colonel, asking him what he was going to do for his tenants. His reply was short and to the point.

The Lean Years

Cluny Castle Dec 18

> Sir, – Your letter of the 14th being addressed to Edinburgh, missed me, and was forwarded here. Of the appearance in Glasgow, of a number of my tenants and cottars, from the parish of Barra, I had no intimation previous to the receipt of your communication, and in answer to your inquiry, *'What I propose doing with the people?'* I say nothing. – I am, sir with due consideration. John Gordon.

At the time if a tenant left a landlord's property, the landlord was still financially responsible for them; if they managed to claim poor relief in another parish, that parish could try to reclaim the cost from the original landlord. The Colonel was not to be moved, refusing to even contemplate assistance or compensation for the support of his former tenants. Other groups followed, driven from their homes by hunger and eviction; with no security of tenure they could be thrown out at any time from the land their families had lived in for generations. One group of 61 turned up in Inverness in February 1851.

Pressure came from Government and letter after letter was sent in to the papers pouring scorn on the Colonel's head. There was none in his defence: who could possibly bring themselves to defend the indefensible? The Edinburgh Evening Courant of 26th July 1851 carried the following, from a minute of the Parochial Board of Barra dated 11th April.

> We are acquainted with Barr Macdougall, Donald, McLean, commonly called Donald Hectorson, Roderick McNeill, senior and Roderick McNeill junior, who have been referred to in the papers as persons who had left Barra and gone to Edinburgh because of their inability to obtain the means of subsistence here. They were all provided with houses at the time of their departure. They were all either employed by the Relief Committee or might have been so at the time of their departure. With the exception of Roderick McNeill, senior who left this in the first week of September, all the others left Barra in July. Barr Macdougall was

notoriously lazy, and before Colonel Gordon had acquired this property, had voluntarily surrendered his croft at Greine, and subsisted therefore partly by begging, for which purpose he perambulated the country. On the failure of the potatoes, he became altogether destitute, and was received on the lists of the relief committee. Roderick McNeill, junior, was employed by Mr. Macallister at one shilling a day which he voluntarily relinquished, declaring that the wages were too low. He then applied to the inspector of the poor for assistance, and was refused, on the grounds that he had left Mr. Macallister's service, where he could have obtained the means of subsistence. He was an able bodied man.

Donald MacLean was an indolent man who never did much work, even when wages could be earned: whose wife perambulated the country begging from house to house.

Roderick McNeill senior was several times accused of theft, and once apprehended on a charge of sheep stealing, but was not convicted.

Of Ann McPherson, or McKinnon, nothing is known in Barra, unless she be a sister in law of Roderick McNeill senior, who had an illegitimate child to a person of the name of McPherson and whose own name was McKinnon.

We are of the opinion that the eleemosynary relief afforded to the people has had a prejudicial effect upon their character and habits; that it has induced many to misrepresent their circumstances with a view to participate in it; that it has taught the people to rely more on others and less on themselves; and we have reason to believe that, relying on this source of subsistence, some persons even neglected to sow their lands.

Signed Henry Beatson, Minister
D.W. McGillivary, J.P, Tacksman
William Birnie, manager for Colonel Gordon
Donald N Nicholson, M.D, Tacksman
Archibald Macdonald, Elder, Tenant

To obtain poor relief, first of all you had to get rid of every possession and be left with nothing; cattle had to go, probably at a reduced rate in lieu of rent owed; if you had any seed corn or potatoes you would have to eat them; then and only then could application be made for poor relief. The myth of the lazy highlander was commonly used as an excuse for their mistreatment; but how could you plant crops in the spring when you had no money to buy seed?

Press reports about the starvation and deprivations of the inhabitants of all the islands and growing pressure from Government finally forced the Colonel to do something about it. His solution was radical and cost-effective. Throughout 1851, in one of the most shameful episodes in Highland history, ships were sent to his properties and 1681 of his tenants were encouraged by the threat of financial penalties or physically rounded up by police and estate officials to be placed aboard ships. Many of them, it must be said, were willing emigrants, believing that nothing could be worse than their present existence. Some of the tenants who had been wandering around the Highlands, begging, returned to the islands to seek passage. The last shipload, comprising 413 people, mostly from Barra, were sent on the 'Admiral', the reluctant rounded up on Barra with the enthusiastic support and active participation of the local Church of Scotland minister, Reverend Henry Beatson. The pitiful group on the 'Admiral' were described as *"having survived on shellfish and seaweed from the shore, that there was danger of them surfeiting on the rations of an emigrant ship"*. The ship's rations had to be doled out sparingly to them in case any fell ill. Only a few could speak English.

Dr Douglas, the medical superintendent at Grosse Isle[1] reported, *"I never saw a body of emigrants so destitute of clothing and bedding. Many children of nine and ten years old were completely naked without even a rag to cover them. Mrs. Crisp the wife of the master of the Admiral was busily employed all the voyage in converting empty bread bags, old canvas, blankets, flour bags, into coverings for them. One full grown man passed my inspection with no other garment than a woman's petticoat".* They arrived in Quebec on 1st October 1851, just at the beginning of the Canadian winter.

When the emigrants reached Quebec they made a statement which was published first in Irish newspapers – most of the British newspapers avoiding the story. This is from the Limerick and Clare Examiner, 17th December 1851:

> We the undersigned passengers, per Admiral from Stornoway in the Highlands of Scotland, do solemnly depose to the following facts: That Colonel Gordon is proprietor of estates in South Uist and Barra; that among many hundreds of tenants and cottars, that he has sent this season from his estates to Canada, he gave directions to his first factor, Mr. Fleming of Cloyne Castle, Aberdeenshire, to ship on board of the above named vessel a number of nearly 450 of said tenants and cottars, from the estate in Barra. That accordingly, a great majority of these people, among which were the undersigned, proceeded voluntary to embark aboard the "Admiral" in Lochboisdale, on or about the 14th of August 1851, but several of the people who were intended to ship from this port to Quebec, refused to proceed on board and in fact absconded from their homes, to avoid the embarkation.
>
> Whereupon Mr. Fleming gave orders to a policeman, who was accompanied by the ground officer to the estate in Barra and some constables to pursue the people who had run away among the mountains, which they did, and succeeded in capturing about twenty from the mountains, and from other islands in the neighbourhood; but these only came with the officers on an attempt being made to handcuff them, and that some of those who ran away were not brought back, in consequence of which four families at least have been divided, some coming in the ship to Quebec, while other members of the same families are left in the Highlands. The undersigned further declare that those who voluntarily embarked did so under promises to the effect that Colonel Gordon would defray their passage to Quebec; that the Government Emigration agent there, would send the whole to upper Canada, where on arrival,

the Government officers would give them work, and furthermore grant them land on certain conditions. The undersigned finally declare that they are now landed in Quebec so destitute, that if immediate relief be not afforded them, and continued until they are settled in employment, the whole will be liable to perish with want.

**Signed Hector Lamont
and 70 others**

Between 1850 and 1851 Colonel Gordon cleared Vatersay of almost all of the cottars and fishermen who made up its population. At least one of these families ended up on the 'Admiral'. The whole island was leased to the farmer Donald McClellan; his was the only substantial house on the island. There were a couple of smaller houses, black houses, barns, stables and byres scattered round the house in which seasonal workers and farm labourers lived. In 1853 there were said to be only seven or eight men on the island; besides that there would have been female farm servants, dairy maids and possibly the wives and children of some of the workers.

One of the newspaper reports of the time state that 'the survivors were given reluctant hospitality', being told to mind the pigs as they settled down for the night. Given that there was only one house of any consequence on the island, this is hardly surprising. The tenant of the house was not at home, so his brother had to assume the responsibility and make the decision to accommodate and feed all the 102 survivors.

In the Elgin Courant of 21st May 1858 is Colonel Gordon's obituary: he is described as the richest commoner in Scotland, possessed of lands and funds worth between £200,000 and £300,000, with not a single mortgage or debt of any kind.

Some people would say that was the extent of the Colonel's legacy, but was it? An argument could be made that the Colonel left behind a much more enduring legacy, in the collective memories of his tenants; even today if his name is mentioned in Barra the people remember the poverty and desperate straits he reduced the local population to.

A case could be made that the islanders were as good as they could be to the 'Annie Jane' survivors, in the light of their own exploitation at the hands of the individuals who had been allowed to wield power in this remote part of Scotland unchecked. Nobody who could read or write dared to complain or stand up for the tenants; the only legal authority they could appeal to were the people carrying out the abuse. The islanders had lived through a period where they had to turn a blind eye to their neighbours being dispossessed, pushed into smaller and smaller plots of land, till they had nothing, then watching them roaming the shore stripping the coast of shellfish. A contemporary account describes them: '*I have never witnessed such countenances – starvation on many faces – the children with their melancholy looks, big looking knees, shrivelled legs, hollow eyes, swollen-like bellies – God help them, I never did witness such wretchedness.*'[2]

Then fellow islanders had to witness the same individuals rounded up and shipped overseas. This was a small community where everybody was known: they had all grown up together. This must have had a dehumanising effect on those who were left behind. The individuals in the boats at the wreck of the 'Annie Jane' were mostly ex-cottars who had been forced off the land and reluctantly had to make a living from the sea to survive. It is hard to feel empathy when you have become hardened to the sufferings of others, as you see those in power enriching themselves at the expense of everybody else. Colonel Gordon, by allowing his managers to squeeze every penny out of his tenants, had created a dog-eat-dog society, where the weak were sacrificed and compassion for the poor was non-existent.

In the circumstances, it was not surprising that the island people descended on wrecks like vultures: the example had been set long before, by those who should have known better.

---

1. https://personal.uwaterloo.ca/marj/genealogy/reports/report1851.html

2. Hunter, James, *The Making of the Crofting Community*, Birlinn Ltd, 2010.

16

Epilogue

I had no intention of ever writing a book, but the story of the 'Annie Jane' always intrigued me. I began to ask questions and the answers on the whole were not what I expected, every answer leading to another question. I realized very quickly that the real story of the 'Annie Jane' and her passengers had never been told, so, in a sense, this book was thrust upon me.

At the end of my research, many of the puzzles are still unsolved, but they proved beyond me. I tried to locate the origins and ages of as many of the casualties and survivors as possible, but that on the whole proved impossible. For the Scots and English at least I had hope, but for the Irish no chance at all. I was handicapped by the destruction of the census records in the fight for independence and the sheer size of the Irish diaspora, as well as by the death toll in Ireland during the famine years of the 1840s and 50s.

Another problem is that when people die prematurely they normally do not leave descendants who are looking for them: whole family groups are interred somewhere in the sand dunes of Vatersay.

With ages and origins a researcher has a good chance of finding people using census results, but the passenger lists were only names, very often misspelled names; to find someone you need to locate an exact family group, but in most cases this proved impossible. With lots of help from enthusiastic amateur genealogists I managed to find the origins of all but ten of the 102 survivors. We also now have the names of 309 people who are interred on Vatersay, the rest, and the exact number of casualties, known only to God.

Why was the 'Annie Jane' not remembered? Firstly, the passengers were generally poor, Irish, Scottish and English working class, and the majority of the cabin class were foreigners. Secondly, you could have hardly picked a more remote spot in the British Isles to wreck a ship: the vast majority of the British public did not know where the island of Vatersay was

The sale of the items from the 'Annie Jane' dragged on for many years: notification of sales regularly appeared in the Glasgow newspapers through 1855 and the last advertisement appears in the Glasgow Herald on 29th September 1856, exactly three years to the day after the survivors lined up in Vatersay Bay to be counted.

Wreck of the 'Annie Jane'
EXTENSIVE PUBLIC SALE OF
ABOUT 110 TONS MALLEABLE IRON RAILS
SPRINGS, KNEES, ANCHORS &c;
ROPES, COMPOSITION METAL, IRON SCRAPS, &c;

(On account of whom it may or doth concern)
THERE will be sold, by Public Auction, at our Public
Stores, Elliot Street, Lancefield Quay, on Friday, 3rd
October, at Twelve o'clock noon

About 80 Tons MALLEABLE IRON RAILS, each 6 and 7 Yards in length
   "   10 Tons RAILWAY SPRINGS
   "   10   " IRON KNEES
   "   10 Cwt COMPOSITION RODS
   "   30   " ROPES
   "   30   " ANCHORS

The whole may be seen any time prior to the sale at the stores.
LAUGHLAND & BROWN, Brokers 91 Buchanan Street
JOHN & JAMES MORRISON, Auctioneers 11 Virginia Street

And if you think the passengers who 'escaped' from the 'Annie Jane' and took passage on the 'Sarah Sands' had it easy, please think again; the following is from steerage passengers who steamed from Liverpool on 16th September 1853.

Quebec, 14th Oct, 1853

Perceiving the cabin passengers of the Sarah Sands have given to Capt. Isley a very flattering testimonial, to which we beg to attach our names, as we fully concur in acknowledging the Captain an able seaman, but the treatment received by the steerage passengers requires an investigation to prevent in future a recurrence. Firstly we were stored in berths to contain three with barely sufficient room for two and provisions served of such an inferior quality that they could not be partaken of the, greater part being entirely rotten, consequently unfit for human food, and calculated to generate disease and all its terrible consequences...

The passengers were divided into messes, and frequently three or four persons were served with more provisions than eight; the officer's attention was frequently called to this point and when applying to the galley nothing but oaths and abuses were to be received from that official. The passengers were generally stowed or berthed irrespective of sex, which tends greatly to promote immorality in all its demoralizing effects.[1]

Captain William Mason did not long outlive the passengers whom he had let down so badly, dying on the ship 'Alliance' of Liverpool on a voyage to Singapore on 8th July 1857.

If I have achieved anything I would like to think that when you stand at the monument overlooking the magnificent West beach on Vatersay, you will now know some of the people who lie interred there under your feet, somewhere among the dunes, and the story of how they got there.

Now I will give the final words to Bob Charnley who inspired me with his booklet *Shipwrecked on Vatersay*, published in 1992. His final paragraph will also be my own:

Should you ever visit the beach a moment of private reflection or prayer would not be inappropriate. However calm the sea or flower-

Epilogue

strewn the machair, the bay before you contains the wreck of the "Annie Jane", whilst the white sand below your feet is the grave-yard for the mortal remains of her dead. May they always be remembered, and allowed to Rest in Peace.

---

1. Montreal Chronicle October 21st 1853, page 3. http://collections.banq.qc.ca/ark:/52327/1841600.

Epilogue

> **WRECK OF THE ANNIE JANE.**
>
> **EXTENSIVE PUBLIC SALE OF**
> ABOUT 110 TONS MALLEABLE IRON RAILS,
> SPRINGS, KNEES, ANCHORS, &c.;
> ROPES, COMPOSITION METAL, IRON SCRAPS, &c.,
> (*On account of whom it may or doth concern.*)
>
> THERE will be Sold, by Public Auction, at our Public Stores, Elliot Street, Lancefield Quay, on Friday, 3d October, at Twelve o'clock Noon,
> About 80 Tons MALLEABLE IRON RAILS, each 6 and 7 Yards in length.
> " 10 Tons RAILWAY SPRINGS.
> " 10 " IRON KNEES.
> " 10 Cwt. COMPOSITION RODS.
> " 30 " ROPES.
> " 30 " ANCHORS.
> The whole may be seen any time prior to Sale at the Stores.
> LAUGHLAND & BROWN, Brokers,
> 91 Buchanan Street.
> JOHN & JAMES MORRISON, Auctioneers.
> 11 Virginia Street, 22d Sept., 1856.

'Annie Jane' salvage auction
Glasgow Herald 29th September 1856
With thanks to The British Newspaper Archive (www.britishnewspaperarchive.co.uk);
©The British Library Board.

> **British America.**
>
> **STEAM BETWEEN**
> **LIVERPOOL AND CANADA.**
> The first-class Screw Steam-ships
> SARAH SANDS......Capt. LISLAY.
> LADY EGLINTON..Capt. WALTER PATON.
> CLEOPATRA ....Capt. ——
> Are intended to be despatched as under:
> From Birkenhead Dock,
> **FOR QUEBEC AND MONTREAL,**
> SARAH SANDS....................Thursday, 15th September.
> Cabin passage, exclusive of wines or liquors ...20 Guineas.
> Second Cabin passage..............................12 Guineas.
> Ditto, Intermediate ....14 Guineas.
> Steerage, including provisions properly cooked.. 6 Guineas.
> These rates include steward's fee and provisions, but not wines or liquors, which can be obtained on board at moderate rates.
> Freight 60s., and five per cent. Coarse goods per agreement.
> Apply to   M'KEAN, M'LARTY, & CO., 21, Water-street.
> Goods are now being received at the Dock Company's Transit Sheds, Birkenhead, or at the Duke's Dock, Liverpool. Shippers paying carriage across.

Voyage on the 'Sarah Sands'
Liverpool Mercury, 14th September 1853.
With thanks to The British Newspaper Archive (www.britishnewspaperarchive.co.uk);
© The British Library Board.

199

Appendix 1:
Those who died in the Wreck of the Annie Jane'.

Cabin passengers drowned

1. Mr. John Potter Cattley: aged 13, Stillington, York, England
2. Mr. Louis Kempf, Canton of Uri, Switzerland
3. Mrs. Louise Kempf, Canton of Uri, Switzerland
4. Louis Kempf, aged 12, Canton of Uri, Switzerland
5. Louise Kempf, aged 10 or 11, Canton of Uri, Switzerland
6. Lieutenant Charles Rose R.N., aged 60, Melbourne East, Quebec, originally from the town of Nairn in Scotland[1]
7. Mrs. Miriam Rose, aged 56, Melbourne East, Quebec, originally of Devonport, England
8. Reverend Jean Vernier, aged 31, Pointe-Aux-Trembles, Quebec, Originally of Blamont Doubs, France[2]

Steerage passengers drowned

9. Elizabeth Allan
10. Alfred Allan
11. Jane Allan
12. Eliza Barry, County Cork, Ireland.
13. Mary Barry, County Cork, Ireland.
14. Harriet Belcher
15. Kyrow Benyan
16. Margaret Benyan
17. Bridget Benyan
18. James Benyan
19. Mary Brooks
20. John Bryan
21. Ann Bryan
22. Kate Bryan

Appendix 1

23. Mary Bryan
24. Ann Bryan
25. Edward Bryan
26. Alice Bryan
27. Isabella Calders
28. Isabella E Calders
29. Dennis Camere
30. Catherine Camere
31. John Campbell; single ticket
32. Thomas Campbell; single ticket
33. John Campbell
34. Ann Campbell
35. Mary Campbell
36. James Campbell
37. Anne E Campbell
38. Johanna Campbell
39. William Campbell
40. John Carr
41. Mary Cassidy, aged 20, Kilmarnock, Scotland, Mill worker[3]
42. Daniel Cassidy, aged 5 months, Kilmarnock, Scotland
43. Peter Catarnagh
44. Thomas Cavonna: London, England, Ragged school boy.[4]
45. John Chambers
46. William Charles
47. William Chisholm, Lyne of Gorthleck, Inverness, Scotland
48. Magdalen Chisholm, Lyne of Gorthleck, Inverness, Scotland
49. Isabela Chisholm, Lyne of Gorthleck, Inverness, Scotland
50. John Christopher
51. Archiebald Clark
52. Dennis Clinton
53. Fredrick Cohen
54. Johanna Cohen

201

Appendix 1

55. Sophia Cohen
56. Ferdinand Cohen
57. Amelia Cohen
58. Morice Coller
59. James Collin
60. Bell Collin
61. Margaret Connolly
62. Charles Connolly
63. Thomas Cook
64. Jane Cook
65. William Corbet, blacksmith, Glasgow, Scotland
66. Catherine Corbet, née Reekie, Glasgow, Scotland
67. Helen Millar Corbet, aged 9, Glasgow, Scotland
68. William Corbet, aged 7, Glasgow, Scotland
69. Catherine Costigan
70. Hannah Costigan
71. Susan Costigan
72. Richard Dempsey
73. J. C. Denkins
74. Mary Desmond
75. Thomas Dirrom
76. Mary Dirrom
77. Honor Dirrom
78. Patrick Dirrom
79. Margaret Dirrom
80. Martha Donohoe
81. Thomas Dover
82. Mary Dover
83. Mary Dowens
84. Hugh Dowens
85. Bess Dowens
86. Johnson Dowler

Appendix 1

87. Lucy Drury
88. Mary Drury
89. Lochallan Drury
90. Johanna Duffy
91. Ellen Duffy
92. Betsy Duffy
93. Patrick Duffy
94. William Dunlop
95. James Ewart
96. Maria Ewart
97. Walter Fannen: London, England, ragged school boy?[4]
98. James Farrel, Bellaghy, County Derry/Londonderry, Ireland
99. Kitty Farrel, Bellaghy, County Derry/Londonderry, Ireland
100. Sally Farrel, Bellaghy, County Derry/Londonderry, Ireland
101. David Farrel, Bellaghy, County Derry/Londonderry, Ireland
102. Female infant Farrel, Bellaghy, County Derry/Londonderry, Ireland
103. Male infant Farrel, Bellaghy, County Derry/Londonderry, Ireland
104. John Faulkner: London, England, ragged school boy?[4]
105. Michael Fawley
106. Ellen Ferns
107. Catherine Flanagan
108. Catherine E Flanagan
109. Thomas Flanagan
110. Rose Flanagan
111. Daniel Flanagan
112. Mary Flanagan
113. Thomas Galbraith
114. Jane Genlee
115. James Genlee
116. Charles Genlee
117. Michael Genlee

Appendix 1

118. Martha Gibney
119. William Gibney
120. John Gibney
121. Robert Gibney
122. Margaret Gibney
123. Jane Gibney
124. Alexander Gibney
125. George Golding: London, England, ragged school boy?[4]
126. Alexander Graham
127. William Gray: London, England, ragged school boy?[4]
128. Robert Henderson
129. Ellen Henelstone
130. J H Henelstone
131. John Henrick
132. Thomas Hogan
133. Patrick Hogan
134. Margaret Hogan
135. Mary Howley
136. Christy Hygendorf
137. Bridget Johnson
138. James Johnson
139. Ellen Johnson
140. Mary Jones
141. Samuel Jones
142. Mathew Jones
143. Sarah Joyce
144. Martin Joyce
145. William Joyce: London, England, ragged school boy?[4]
146. Patrick Kane
147. Catherine Kane
148. Johanna Kennedy
149. Anna Kennedy

Appendix 1

150. Maria Kent
151. Peggy Kingston
152. Gilbert Kinneard
153. John Lamb
154. Thomas Lea
155. Anna Lea
156. Jane Ann Lea
157. Daniel Leaky
158. Bridget Leaky
159. Fredrick Lhanation
160. Henry Linton
161. August Lloyd
162. Betsy Logan
163. Peggy Logan
164. Stewart Logan
165. Julia Loneham
166. Julia Loneham
167. Margaret Loneham
168. Edward Lonelly
169. Timothy Macarthy, Crookhaven, County Cork, Ireland
170. Katherine Macarthy, Crookhaven, County Cork, Ireland
171. Female infant Macarthy, 4 months old (twin brother and mother survived)
172. Margaret Macartney
173. Alexander Macdonald
174. John MacDougal
175. Duncan Maclellan
176. Mary Maclellan
177. Mary Macleod
178. Houston Macleod
179. James Macleod
180. Robert Macleod

Appendix 1

181. James Maclynatt
182. Mary Macmillan
183. Bernard Macminnia
184. Peter Macpherson
185. Alexander Macrae, aged 24, blacksmith, originally from Fort Augustus, Scotland
186. Janet Macrichmon
187. Catherine Macrichmon
188. Jessie Macrichmon
189. Mary Macrichmon
190. Eliza Macrichmon
191. Malcolm Macrichmon
192. Ellen Mahoney, County Cork, Ireland
193. Jenny Mahoney, County Cork, Ireland
194. James Maxwell
195. Rose Mcael
196. Alexander Mcael
197. Mary Mcael
198. Peggy Mcael
199. John Mcael
200. Francis Mcael
201. Nancy Mcael
202. George McChelan
203. John McConnell
204. John McCormack
205. Betty McCormack
206. Jessie McKechnie, Kiln Lane, Paisley, Scotland, aged 36, travelling with five children[5]
207. Catherine McKechnie, aged 13, Kiln Lane, Paisley, Scotland
208. Mary McKechnie, aged 11, Kiln Lane, Paisley, Scotland
209. Jessie McKechnie, aged 9, Kiln Lane, Paisley, Scotland

Appendix 1

210. Eliza McKechnie, aged 5, Kiln Lane, Paisley, Scotland
211. Malcolm McKechnie, aged 2, Kiln Lane, Paisley, Scotland
212. James Moran
213. Bridget Moran
214. Honore Morgarty
215. Martha Morrison
216. Hugh Munro, rail contractor and builder, Loan of Tulloch, Scotland[6]
217. Margaret Munro, née Maculloch, Balnagown, Scotland
218. Female infant Munro[6]
219. Robert Murray, joiner, Scotland
220. Thomas Neale
221. Catherine Oates, aged 32, née McEwen, originally from the island of Lewis[7], Scotland
222. Margaret Oates, aged 6 months, baptised in Haddington, East Lothian, Scotland
223. Francis O'Bryan
224. Jerry O'Bryan
225. Michael O'Donovan, West Cork, Ireland
226. John Parker, London, England, ragged school boy?[4]
227. John Power
228. Ann Power
229. Margaret Power
230. James Power
231. James Prates
232. Thomas Ralphis
233. Mary Reilly, first group
234. William Reilly
235. Mary Reilly
236. Mary Reilly
237. Eliza Reilly
238. Mary Reilly, second group.

207

Appendix 1

239. Bridget Reilly
240. Thomas Reilly
241. William Reilly
242. Eliza Reilly
243. Henry Reynolds, Church St, Lyme Regis, Dorset, England, Carpenter, aged 51
244. Sarah Reynolds, Church St, Lyme Regis, Dorset, England, aged 40
245. Maria Reynolds, Church St, Lyme Regis Dorset, England, Dressmaker aged 23
246. Albert Reynolds, Church St, Lyme Regis, Dorset, England aged 8
247. Sarah Richards
248. Martha Robinson
249. William Charles Rodgers, Kilbirnie, Ayrshire, Scotland – father and brothers survived – originally from County Clare, Ireland
250. Alexander Ross, Gorbals, Glasgow, Scotland, Engineer aged 25
251. Marian Ross, Gorbals, Glasgow, Scotland, aged 21
252. Francis Ross, Gorbals, Glasgow, Scotland, aged 1
253. David Ross, Rosskeen, Rosshire, Scotland, Shoemaker aged 36
254. Christy Ross, Rosskeen, Rosshire, Scotland, aged 32
255. John Ross, Rosskeen, Rosshire, Scotland, aged 8
256. Isabella Ross, Rosskeen, Rosshire, Scotland, aged 5
257. Alexander Ross, Rosskeen, Rosshire, Scotland, aged 3
258. John Ryan
259. Henry Searl, London, England, ragged school boy [4]
260. Catherine Slater
261. Mary Slater
262. Daniel Smith
263. Catherine Smith

Appendix 1

264. John Snow
265. John W Snow
266. Patrick Sullivan
267. Ann Sullivan
268. William Sutherland
269. George Thomas, London, England, ragged school boy?[4]
270. Ann T Townsley, County Antrim, Ireland
271. James Townsley, County Antrim, Ireland
272. Mary Townsley, County Antrim, Ireland
273. John Townsley, County Antrim, Ireland
274. William Townsley, County Antrim, Ireland
275. Robert Townsley, County Antrim, Ireland
276. Joseph Townsley, County Antrim, Ireland
277. Elizabeth Townsley, County Antrim, Ireland
278. Andrew Townsley, County Antrim, Ireland
279. Eliza Townsley, County Antrim, Ireland
280. James Twidle
281. Jane Twidle
282. Martha Twidle
283. Charles Twidle
284. Agnes Twidle
285. David Wakeley
286. Mary Wakeley
287. John Walker
288. Margaret Walker
289. Margaret Walker
290. Margaret Walker
291. Mary Ann Walker
292. John Weir
293. David William
294. Rachael Wilson, first group
295. Joseph Wilson

Appendix 1

296. Thomas Wilson
297. Edmund Wilson
298. William Wilson, second group
299. Margaret Wilson
300. Letitia Wilson
301. James Wood
302. Catherine Yewell
303. Thomas Yewell

---

1. Served in the Royal Navy, seeing action at Algeciras and the blockade of Cadiz. Was granted 105 acres of land in Canada in 1837. Described himself as a farmer in the 1852 census, with a farm in Melbourne, East Quebec. Left four adult children, two born in England and two born in Canada.

2. On 1st May, 1855, the Reverend Jean Vernier's widow remarried the Reverend Jean Antoine Vernon. One would imagine with five children to support she had little choice; she had one more child from her second marriage.

3. Mary is the writer of the poignant letter home to her mother.

4. Ragged school boys' identities have been established from a passenger list that was published in the Quebec Morning Chronicle. The list does not give individual names but family groups. It looks as though the first eleven names on it are the ragged school boys as it contains the two known survivors. They would have been booked as a group so that seems to be highly likely.

5. Jessie's husband, Malcolm, settled in Sherbrooke, Quebec, remarried a Jean Younie two years later and went on to have another seven children.

6. In Hugh's marriage certificate of 2nd March 1852 he is described as a farmer. In the Liverpool birth announcement he has graduated to rail contractor and builder. Unfortunately, as was the fashion of the time, in the birth announcement no name was given to his daughter. Births at sea were meant to be registered, but I can find no record of this being done.

7. A researcher, Linda Hall, found Catherine McEwen, aged 20, in Church St., Stornoway in the 1841 Census, working as a maid for the Falconer family. Unfortunately, place of origin was not required for that census. By 1851 she is no longer there, the Falconers now having fallen into hard times Mrs Falconer is now a widow and a pauper. The next link is more tenuous as there is a maid working for the Smith family in Garrabost, Point, whose name is badly transcribed, but it is 'McE...' or something

Appendix 1

similar; Place of Birth, parish of Barvas on the island of Lewis, aged 28 – a slight discrepancy. What is certain is a baptism at Haddington in March 1853, Mother: Catherine McEwen. Father: Bernard Oates. Daughter Margaret, illegitimate. Bernard a surveyor from Ireland is working in Lewis in 1851. The census has him at Galson Farm as part of a working party creating the first ordnance survey map of Lewis. So that is very likely where they met, as the Ordnance Survey party would have explored every part of Lewis. Surveyors were much desired by the Canadian railway companies in their rapid expansion. Catherine was probably travelling to re-join Bernard, as she was travelling under the name of Oates. They may even have married between the months of March and September but I can find no record of the union. Registration of marriage was not compulsory in that period.

Crew drowned

304. Charles Bell, First Mate, aged 23, Goole, England, register number 142941

305. Thomas Callaghan, passenger cook, aged 38, Wicklow, Ireland, register number 316447

306. John Dunlop, Bo's'un, aged 28, Ayr, Scotland, register number 211004

307. Pierre Chevanelle, seaman, aged 29, Québec, register number 99969

308. Andre Drapeau, seaman, aged 24, Québec, register number 100033

309. Uhalt Gagnon, seaman/carpenter, aged 24, Canada, register number 105641

310. Joseph Jalbert, seaman, aged 19, Québec, register number 100012

311. Samuel Langlois, seaman, aged 28, Québec, register number 100310

312. Elie Levesque, seaman, aged 28, L'islet, Québec, register number 684021[1]

313. Napoleon Mercier, seaman, aged 24, L'islet, Québec, register number 1056640

314. Amable Morin, seaman, aged 25, L'islet, Québec, register number 100046

315. Unnamed Apprentice

Appendix 1

1. A baptism took place on 1st November 1853 at Sainte-Anne-de-la Pocatière, Quebec of Theophile Levesque, father marked as absent. The news of his death would not have reached the family. As well as his newborn son Elie Levesque also left behind a twenty-nine-year-old widow, Marie Adelaide, and a daughter, Adelaide, who was three years old.

Appendix 2:
Those who survived

Cabin passenger survivors

1. Marc Ami, aged 19, Geneva, Switzerland, 1834–1902
2. Fredrick Lammert Van Buren, aged 29, Holland, 1824–1888
3. Jean Francois Cornu, aged 30, Switzerland, 1823–1891
4. John Morgan

Steerage passenger survivors

5. Alexander Allen
6. Michael Barry, labourer, County Cork, Ireland
7. Abraham Brooks, aged 21, joiner, Perth, Scotland[1]
8. John Brooks, aged 17, farm servant, Perth, Scotland
9. Catherine Burke, Servant, County Tipperary, Ireland
10. Mary J Caruthers
11. David Caulder, ropemaker, Edinburgh, Scotland
12. Gerry Clifford, labourer, County Kerry, Ireland
13. Mary Clifford, wife of above, County Kerry, Ireland
14. Rosina Cohen
15. Johanna Cohen
16. Edward Donnelly, labourer, Ireland
17. Patrick Donnelly, labourer, Balingarry, County Kilkenny, Ireland
18. Martha Donohoe, Cahersiveen, County Kerry, Ireland
19. James Edmundson, County Antrim, Ireland
20. Jane Farrel: Bellaghy, County Derry/Londonderry, Ireland
21. Walter Farrier, labourer, County Waterford, Ireland
22. Donald Fraser, joiner, Inverness, Scotland[2]

Appendix 2

23. William Fraser, labourer, Inverness, Scotland
24. Thomas Galbraith, joiner, Scotland
25. Mary J Getty
26. John Grogan, aged 14, labourer, London, England, ragged school boy
27. John Häberli, Switzerland[3]
28. Thomas Hawkins, labourer, London, England
29. Mathew Hayes, labourer, County Clare, Ireland
30. Thomas Kavanagh, labourer, Ireland
31. Patrick Kelly, labourer, County Waterford, Ireland
32. Ellen Kelly, wife of above, County Waterford, Ireland
33. William Kelly, Bellaghy, County Derry/Londonderry, Ireland
34. Mary Kelly, Bellaghy, County Derry/Londonderry, Ireland
35. Amelia Kelly, Bellaghy, County Derry/Londonderry, Ireland
36. Rachael Kelly, Bellaghy, County Derry/Londonderry, Ireland[4]
37. James Kelly, labourer, Ireland
38. George Kingston, County Cork, Ireland
39. John Kingston, County Cork, Ireland
40. George Lennox, potter, Portobello, Edinburgh, Scotland
41. Julia McCarthy, Crookhaven, County Cork, Ireland
42. Infant Macarthy (four-month-old-boy – the other twin was lost)[5]
43. Margaret Macaulay
44. Cornelius Mahoney: County Cork, Ireland
45. Martha Marah
46. Angus Mathieson: blacksmith, Dornoch, Scotland
47. Thomas McCarty, labourer, Ireland
48. Alexander McCormick, County Armagh, Ireland
49. John McNamara, labourer, County Tipperary, Ireland
50. John O'Brien, Ireland

Appendix 2

51. Timothy O'Donovan, West Cork, Ireland[6]
52. John Parry, sawyer, Liverpool, England
53. William Reynolds, aged 22, mason, Church St, Lyme Regis, Dorset, England
54. Timothy Rodgers, aged 38, Kilbirnie, Ayrshire, originally from County Clare, Ireland[7]
55. James Rodgers, aged 13, Kilbirnie, Ayrshire, Scotland, originally from County Clare, Ireland
56. John Rodgers, aged 16, Kilbirnie, Ayrshire, Scotland, originally from County Clare, Ireland
57. William Shack, labourer, County Tipperary, Ireland
58. Edward Shanehan, labourer, County Waterford Ireland
59. Patrick Shea, labourer, Cahersiveen, County Kerry, Ireland
60. Mary Sheridan
61. Charles Smith, joiner, Grantown-on-Spey, Scotland
62. Catherine Stanley, Dublin, Ireland
63. Elizabeth Bridget Sullivan
64. Mathew Toumaway, County Cork, Ireland
65. John Townsley, labourer, County Antrim, Ireland
66. Alexander Walker, labourer, County Antrim, Ireland
67. Robert C Walters, London, England, ragged school boy

215

Appendix 2

1. Abraham never made that Atlantic crossing, settling down in Scotland and raising a family.

2. Donald and William may have moved to Aberdeen, but both give their place of birth as Inverness.

3. On the passenger list of the 'America', grouped with the missionaries, was a young man of 17, transcribed this time as Hacherlin. He is probably the same survivor helped out in Portree by Professor Albert Necker.

4. Captain Mason's list composed on the morning of the 29th September had 101 names plus Julia Macarthy's child. He missed one, that was Rachael Kelly from Bellaghy in Ireland. So the total of survivors has been revised to 103.

5. A story is told in Barra, recounted in a book, Vatersay and its People, by Mairi Ceit MacKinnon. It is of a young man John Sinclair (Iain Dhonnchaidh) engaged in seasonal fishing in Ireland years later, encountering this young man there.

6. The last mention I can find of any survivor is a newspaper article in 1904, after the sinking of the 'Norge', which ran into Rockall, an uninhabited granite outcrop in the North Atlantic Ocean. Timothy is mentioned as a survivor of the 'Annie Jane' living in West Cork.

7. This family all made it to America, settling in Boston. Timothy lost one son in the shipwreck; he subsequently had another child who he called William. One would assume he was named after the lost son.

Appendix 2

Crew survivors

68. Captain William Mason, aged 47, Liverpool, England, register number 513851[1]
69. Surgeon Francis Goold, Goolds Hill, Cork, Ireland
70. Thomas Markham, Second Mate, aged 18, Hull, England, register number 106107 (Captain Mason's brother-in-law)
71. Thomas Mason, carpenter, aged 26, Hull, England, register number 99511
72. William Lewis, carpenter's mate, aged 29, Liverpool, England, register number 346147
73. William Moore, sailmaker, aged 21, Liverpool, England, register number 486383
74. Mathew Irwin, apprentice, aged 13, Liverpool, England, register number 99483
75. Charles Lee, apprentice, aged 16, indentured for 5 years, register number 99478
76. Edward Roberts, apprentice, aged 14, indentured for 6 years, register number 99424
77. William Anfield, first steward, aged 25, Hull, England, register number 486695 (Captain Mason's son-in-law)
78. James Taylor, second steward, Canada
79. James Allen, seaman, aged 30, Pembroke, England, register number 470338
80. Pierre Damase Bernier, carpenter/seaman, aged 26, L'islet, Quebec, register number 99924, working his passage
81. James Boyd, carpenter/seaman, aged 33, Belfast, register number 105900, working his passage
82. Charles Brown, seaman, aged 23, New York, America
83. Charles Burnett, seaman, aged 26, Forfar, Scotland, register number 115590
84. Theodore Charest, seaman, aged 21, Quebec, register number 100037
85. Joseph Dion, seaman, Quebec, register number 100004
86. Edward Delwain, carpenter/seaman, working his passage[2]

Appendix 2

87. Jacques Faillow, seaman, aged 19, Quebec, register number 100042
88. Charles Garrett, seaman, aged 23, Bay of Chaluer, Quebec, register number 100022
89. Celestin Gruimont, seaman, aged 16, Quebec, register number 99927
90. Thomas Halcrow, seaman, aged 20, St Johns, Newfoundland, register number 82452
91. James Hood, seaman, aged 19, Dundee, Scotland, register number 175345
92. John Hutchinson, seaman, aged 19, Ayr, Scotland, register number 416024
93. John Jackson, seaman, aged 20, St Johns, Newfoundland, register number 202921
94. Archibald Jamieson, cook/seaman, aged 33, Fillaford, Sandness, Shetland Isles, Scotland, register number 1777253[3]
95. Christopher Kelly, seaman, aged 22, Rush, Dublin, Ireland register number 571632
96. William Lancaster, seaman, aged 18, Liverpool, England register number 586287
97. Jean Baptiste Langlois[4], seaman, aged 20, Quebec, register number 105888
98. Odulphe Lemieux, seaman, aged 25, Quebec, register number 105655
99. Joseph Leuniel, aged 24, seaman, Quebec, register number 99972
100. Antoine Lizotte, seaman, Lower Canada, register number 100043
101. James Marshall, carpenter/seaman, aged 34, Sunderland, England, register number 105887, working his passage
102. Richard Stevens, seaman, aged 24, London, England, register number 564519
103. Francis Walsh, seaman, aged 20, Dublin, Ireland, register number 483296

Appendix 2

1. Died on a voyage to Singapore, 8th July 1857. The funeral service aboard the ship 'Alliance' conducted by the first mate, his son John.

2. Ship register has 'don't know' against place of birth and no register number. Called Durrant at the inquiry by Richard Stevens. Because their names were unpronounceable by English speakers many of the French-Canadians had two names, increasing the confusion.

3. Later emigrated to Australia.

4. Respondent in Quebec court case.

While every effort has been made to ensure the accuracy of this book, if you are using the information contained within for family research, you are advised to check against other sources. Surnames were fluid during this period, with different spellings for some of the survivors at every interview.

In the two main casualty lists spellings vary: Cohen, Kohen, Hohen and Roher depending on which list you consult; Kerr could be Carr and Curr. The Irish O' as a prefix is dropped regularly. So please try variants of surnames if searching for long-lost relatives among the passengers on the 'Annie Jane'.

(M)   RELEASE AT T

Name of Ship.	No. and Date of Register.	Port of Registry.	Name
Annie Jane	373 / 1853	Liverpool	

WE, the Undersigned Members of the Crew of the said Ship, do hereby release the said Ship and the Master the said Crew from all Claims in respect of the said Voyage.

Dated at *L'pool*, the *11* day of *October*, 185*3*.

Crew Signatures

Signatures or marks of some of the surviving crew members on the discharge document. With thanks to The National Archives.

© National Archives.

...MINATION OF A VOYAGE.

...e of Crew.	Description of Voyage.	Date and Place of Commencement of Voyage.	Date and Place of Termination of Voyage.
...Westerner	Foreign	L'pool 24th August	L'pool 27 Sept

...thereof from all Claims for Wages or otherwise in respect of the above-mentioned Voyage; And I, the Master...

(Signed) for Wm Mason
Wm Down

Signatures of Crew.	No. of Register Ticket.	Shipping Office or Home No. if any.	Signatures of Crew.	Regis...
Charles Garrett			French Canadians	
(various signatures with "his mark")				
Joseph Dion				
(additional crew signatures)				

...ave release in my presence,

(Signed) J.W. Walker

List C.
No. 2410

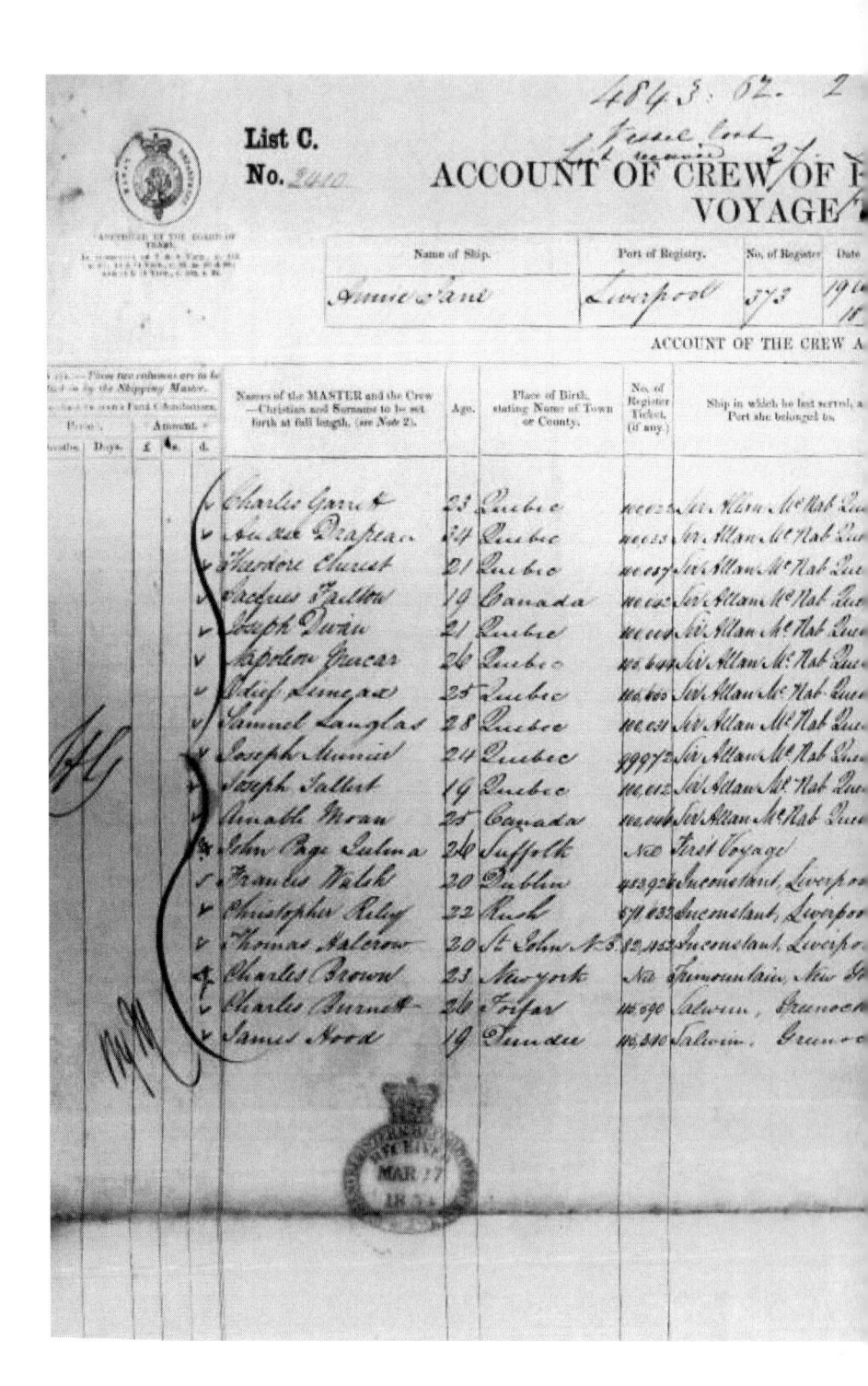

ACCOUNT OF CREW OF [ ]
VOYAGE

Name of Ship	Port of Registry	No. of Register	Date
Annie Jane	Liverpool	373	19[ ]

ACCOUNT OF THE CREW A[ ]

Names of the MASTER and the Crew—Christian and Surnames to be set forth at full length.	Age	Place of Birth, stating Name of Town or County.	No. of Register Ticket (if any.)	Ship in which he last served; Port she belonged to.
Charles Garret	23	Quebec	00017	Sir Allan McNab, Que
Peter Papeau	24	Quebec	00015	Sir Allan McNab, Que
Theodore Churet	21	Quebec	00017	Sir Allan McNab, Que
Jacques Fullon	19	Canada	00019	Sir Allan McNab, Que
Joseph Duran	21	Quebec	00018	Sir Allan McNab, Que
Napoleon Guicar	26	Quebec	00 box	Sir Allan McNab, Que
Oliff Longeas	25	Quebec	00102	Sir Allan McNab, Que
Samuel Langlas	28	Quebec	00013	Sir Allan McNab, Que
Joseph Munier	24	Quebec	9972	Sir Allan McNab, Que
Joseph Tallet	19	Quebec	00012	Sir Allan McNab, Que
Amable Moan	25	Canada	00014	Sir Allan McNab, Que
John Page Latina	24	Suffolk		First Voyage
Francis Walsh	20	Dublin	132932	Inconstant, Liverpool
Christopher Riley	22	Rush	149132	Inconstant, Liverpool
Thomas Halcrow	20	St John N.B.	82113	Inconstant, Liverpool
Charles Brown	23	New York	No	Hermountain, New Y[ ]
Charles Burnet	26	Forfar	116090	Calvin, Greenock
James Hood	19	Dundee	116310	Calvin, Greenock

OF Liverpool

GOING SHIP, TO BE DELIVERED AT THE END OF
SHIPPING MASTER AT THE ABOVE PORT.

Name of Master	No. of his Certificate	First Port of Departure	Date of Departure	Final
William Mason	51385	Liverpool	24 August 1853	Liv

PARTICULARS REQUIRED BY LAW, IN RESPECT OF THE ABOVE-MENTIONED VOYAGE.

Date and Place of joining this Ship		In what Capacity Engaged, and, if Mate, No. of Certificate (if any)	Date, Place, and Cause of Death, or Leaving this Ship			Report of Character	
Date	Place		Date	Place	Cause	Ability	Conduct
19 Aug 53	Liverpool	Seaman	11 October 53	Liverpool	Paid Off	G	G
19 Aug 53	Liverpool	Seaman	28 Sept 53	Para	Believe to be drowned		
19 Aug 53	Liverpool	Seaman	11 October 53	Liverpool	Paid Off	G	G
19 Aug 53	Liverpool	Seaman	11 October 53	Liverpool	Paid Off	G	G
19 Aug 53	Liverpool	Seaman	11 October 53	Liverpool	Paid Off	G	G
19 Aug 53	Liverpool	Seaman	21 Sept 53	Para	Believe to be drowned		
19 Aug 53	Liverpool	Seaman	11 October 53	Liverpool	Paid Off	G	G
19 Aug 53	Liverpool	Seaman	28 Sept 53	Para	Believe to be drowned		
19 Aug 53	Liverpool	Seaman	11 October 53	Liverpool	Paid Off	G	G
19 Aug 53	Liverpool	Seaman	28 Sept 53	Para	Believe to be drowned		
19 Aug 53	Liverpool	Seaman	28 Sept 53	Para	Believe to be drowned		
22 Aug 53	Liverpool	Surgeon	2 Sept 53	Liverpool	Left the Ship		
7 Sept 53	Liverpool	Seaman	11 October 53	Liverpool	Paid Off	V G	V G
7 Sept 53	Liverpool	Seaman	11 October 53	Liverpool	Paid Off	V G	V G
7 Sept 53	Liverpool	Seaman	11 October 53	Liverpool	Paid Off	V G	V G
7 Sept 53	Liverpool	Seaman	11 October 53	Liverpool	Paid Off	V G	V G
7 Sept 53	Liverpool	Seaman	11 October 53	Liverpool	Paid Off	V G	V G
7 Sept 53	Liverpool	Seaman	11 October 53	Liverpool	Paid Off	V G	V G

Glossary

A1 at Lloyd's: First Class vessel in Lloyd's Register of Shipping.

Accouchement: the confinement of childbirth.

Affiliation: a maintenance order to support a child.

Aft: stern or back of ship.

Bent: type of coarse grass.

Bilge: internal area of a ship's hull, curving inwards towards the bottom.

Binnacle: wooden stand, very often ornate, for locating ship's compass.

Bo's'un (Boatswain): ship's officer in charge of sails and rigging.

Bowsprit: spar jutting out in front of the ship to allow it to carry headsails, which were similar in shape to modern yacht sails, also used to attach the forestay.

Brail: small rope on sail edges, used for stowing or tying the mast when rolled up.

Brougham: type of horse-drawn carriage, a boxlike structure for four people with the driver perched outside.

Bulkhead: upright partition separating sections of a ship.

Capstan: revolving barrel shape, worked by men walking round pushing horizontal bars, used for winding cable, lifting the anchor.

Companionway: internal stairway on a ship.

Compass: instrument for navigation showing true North.

Cottar: peasant occupying cottage with little or no land.

Davits: overhanging cranes, usually in pairs, for lowering or raising a ship's boat.

Deal: a sawed plank typically three inches thick, in various widths and lengths, normally seven inches wide and at least six feet long.

Deckhead: ceiling on a ship.

Deckhouse: structure bolted to main deck.

Double-reefed: use of two ropes at each reefing point when reducing sail.

Eleemosynary: charitable.

Fathom: measure of six feet in length, usually used for measuring depth of water or length of rope.

First Mate: officer directly under the Captain, always referred to as Mr. (Mister), first name never used.

Flake (vb): to coil or lay out a rope so it is ready to run freely.

Fo'c'sle (Forecastle): forward part of ship containing sailors' accommodation.

Forehold: hold in the forward part of the ship.

Foremast: furthest forward mast.

Galley: cooking area aboard a ship.

Gig: light narrow, clinker-built wooden boat.

Graving dock: dry dock.

Grieve: farm manager or overseer.

Guano: bird excrement, used as fertiliser.

Gybe (vb): to bring the wind from one quarter to another by passing the stern of a vessel through the wind.

Hardtack: a simple type of biscuit or cracker, made from flour, water, and sometimes salt. Inexpensive and long-lasting, it was and is used for sustenance in the absence of perishable foods, commonly used during long sea voyages.

Heel to: to list or lean over.

Jib: the furthest forward sail.

Jib boom: the extension of the bowsprit.

Jury-rigged: temporary or makeshift set of sails.

Glossary

Larboard: old expression, changed to Port to avoid confusion with starboard, and meaning the left side of a ship looking forward.

Lie to: to stop the progress of a vessel, by reducing sail so she will make little or no headway, but to lose as little ground as possible in the desired direction of travel.

Mainmast: largest mast in the centre of the ship.

Mizzenmast: mast nearest the stern/rear of the ship.

Molasses: thick brown syrup made from sugar refining process, similar to treacle.

O.M.: Overall Mass, or total weight.

Ounces: measure of weight, equivalent to 480 grams.

Pease meal: roasted yellow peas, milled into a flour for cooking.

Peccadillo: small or minor sin.

Plimsoll Line: painted marking on ship's side, showing legal submersion level.

Poop, poop deck: stern of a ship, aftermost and highest part, thus deck at stern.

Port side: left side of a ship, looking forward.

Porthole: round glass window on a ship.

Pound: measure of weight, 16 ounces, equivalent to 453 grams; not to be confused with the unit of currency.

Quart: unit of measurement of fluid, two pints or a quarter of a gallon, almost equivalent to a litre.

Rigging: the system of ropes used to support and control the masts, spars and sails of a ship.

Royal sails: a small sail flown above the topgallant sail.

Saloon: public room for first class passengers.

Second Mate: third officer in command of a merchant ship.

Sheet: a rope attached to one of the lower corners of a sail.

Shilling: unit of currency, 20 shillings in a pound.

Sovereign: gold coin, worth one pound sterling.

Spar: stout wooden pole, used to carry and support a sail.

Spurtle: rod-shaped wooden tool for stirring porridge.

Starboard: right side of a ship looking forward.

Steerage: part of ship allocated to passengers travelling on the cheapest tickets.

Tack: change direction of ship to take advantage of side wind, to make forward movement in the direction of the wind.

Tacksman: a leaser of land from the clan chief or landowner, sub-letting the land in smaller parcels to crofters or smallholders.

Tamarack: A tree also known as Eastern Larch and in Canada as Hackmatack.

Topgallant: the sail immediately above the topsail.

Topsail: a sail set above the course sail or mainsail.

Tweendeck, twixt deck: area between decks, below the main deck, occupied by the steerage passengers.

Wear ship: to turn the ship away from the wind in order to change direction.

Weather deck: top deck, the one exposed to the weather.

Weather (vb): to get to windward of, or to come safely through.

Windlass: another word for capstan.

Acknowledgements

There are many people who in one way or another contributed to the research and writing of this book. They are not in any order here as each of them made important additions to the book that eventually made up the whole.

I would like to thank Mairi Ceit Mackinnon of the island of Barra for checking this book over to make sure there were no glaring local historical errors. She has asked me to point out, and I am very glad to do so, that the inhabitants of Vatersay in the present day have no connection to the people who were present in 1853 when the 'Annie Jane' came to grief. Vatersay was settled by people from the island of Mingulay in the early part of the 20th Century.

I enlisted the help of the online community to research this book: many of them are retired or have been forced into early retirement. Others have a fascination with genealogy, with research skills I can only marvel at and that they are just dying to use. Without the members of the *rootschat* website community, a free genealogy website, none of this would have been possible. They have embraced the search for people, documents, newspaper articles, and given up their own time to search libraries in Canada, London and all points in-between. Thanks are due to the moderators of the site for permission to use the information sourced by their members.

My special and heartfelt thanks to Linda Hall from Ottawa, Ontario, who was a one-woman research team once she discovered the ragged school orphans and all the Scottish and Irish emigrants on the Annie Jane. She was inspired by her great grandfather, James Clark, a Barnados orphan from London, who sailed to Canada from Liverpool in 1890, and her Scottish grandmother, Janet Mathieson Mckay Dorman. Her grandmother's Irish ancestors were originally from County Down and as a young girl with her mother and siblings, she emigrated to Quebec to join her father who had gone ahead six months earlier in 1913. Both of those brave immigrants began her Canadian family tree. Linda found the Ragged School Boy account, the Quebec court case and the 'Rosetta Stone' of the casualty list: an article in the Montreal Chronicle. Linda also found the origins of so many of the lost passengers and the survivors and the family gravestone of Alexander Macrae in Fort Augustus. She also supplied the factual information trawled from the pages of Canadian newspapers. Without her passion, unstinting and generous efforts, this book in its present form would not exist.

Thanks to all the other *rootschat* members who replied to any of the posts I put on the site. Deserving of special mention is Marylin (Bunkie), second name unknown, who found Marc Ami's published book,'Le Naufrage de l'Annie Jane'.

I posted many technical questions on the website *Ships Nostalgia* and offer my thanks to their members for the answers I was given. The website *Genealogy Specialists* helped me to establish the origin and identity of Captain Mason.

Alan W. Blackwood, merchant ship heritage specialist, whom I met at the Tall Ship on the riverside in Glasgow, provided invaluable advice and information, and read drafts of the early chapters of the book, which has benefited greatly from his knowledge.

My thanks to Anelizia, my wife, for putting up with the other woman: my passion for the 'Annie Jane' meant she was neglected at times. Thanks also to my daughter Rebecca for the art work for the cover of the book and other illustrations. Special thanks to my daughter Anna for acquiring Gray's report from the National Archives, and, in the last hour of her visit to London, deciding to check among the 1854 crew agreements and rather amazingly finding the crew agreement for the 'Annie Jane'. What a thrill, to actually hold copies of those documents in my hands and to see the signatures or marks of the crew, and what a priceless tool it became. Before the discovery of those documents, no accurate list of the crew survivors existed. Even more important, no list of the crew who died existed, as none had ever been issued. Anna also undertook the laborious and challenging task of translating 'Le Naufrage de l'Annie Jane' for me.

Thanks are due to my son-in-law Craig Johnstone, who set up the 'Annie Jane' website through which I was contacted by many relatives, both of those who died and of those who survived.

Thanks to my editor and friend David Green for proof-reading and correcting the book and also sorting out my grammar and punctuation: months of work.

My friend Arnaud Rué, occasional chemist and official offshore translator, is also due special thanks.

Acknowledgements

I acknowledge the following with gratitude:

Google Books for digitizing the Beechey report, the Ragged School Boy Magazine and the Quebec court case and making them available online;

the University of Ottawa for digitizing 'Le Naufrage de L'Annie Jane' and putting a copy of the book online;

the British Newspaper Archive for access to a fully searchable database of British newspapers covering that period and beyond;

the always-helpful staff at the Mitchell Library, Glasgow, for access to the North British Daily Mail and other Glasgow papers of the period;

Tobair an Dualchais for the valuable historical recordings they have online and permission to mention Ann MacKinnon's recollections of the 'Annie Jane' and the wonderful singing of the Annie Jane song by Donald Campbell.

When I went to re-visit the 'Annie Jane' monument in 2016 it was to find it in a neglected and pitiable state: my thanks to Macinnes Brothers Construction for providing the materials to in fill and repair the site.

The staff of the Stornoway library for their help navigating the interlibrary loan scheme.

The ever professional staff at the National Archives for their help locating documents.

The Scottish National Archives for access to genealogy records and the interim interdict served on Captain Mason.

The staff of the Jeanie Johnston in Dublin for a personal tour of the reproduction famine ship berthed at Dublin docks. http://jeaniejohnston.ie/

Finally, many thanks to Acair for taking this from manuscript form to published book.

Select Bibliography

Ami, Marc: *Le Naufrage de l'Annie Jane, Episode de l'Histoire des Missions Franco-Canadiennes*, Le Fidèle Messager, Manchester N.H.,1891. Digitizing sponsor, University of Ottawa.

Beechey, Frederick W., Captain R.N.: *Report of an investigation into the loss of the "Annie Jane"*, made by the direction of the Board of Trade, Eyre, George Edward and Spottiswoode, William, 1854. Original from Harvard Library, digitized by Google books.

Branigan, Keith: *Barra – Episodes from an Island's History*, Amberly Publishing, 2012.

Buxton, Ben: *The Vatersay Raiders*, Birlinn Ltd., 2008.

Campbell, John Lorne, editor: *The Book of Barra*, Acair Ltd., 2006.

Campey, Lucille H: *After the Hector*, Dundurn Press, 2007.

Charnley, Bob: *Shipwrecked on Vatersay*, Maclean Press, 1992.

Fry, John: *A Mind at Sea*, Dundurn Press, 2013.

Gifford, Ann: *Towards Quebec*, HMSO, 1981.

Harper, Marjory: *Adventurers and Exiles: The Great Scottish Exodus*, Profile Books, 2003.

Hunter, James: *A Dance Called America*, Mainstream Publishing, 1994.

Hunter, James: *The Making of the Crofting Community*, Birlinn Ltd., 2010

Hutchinson, Roger: *Polly*, Mainstream Publishing, 1990.

Jones, Nicolette: *The Plimsoll Sensation*, Little, Brown & Co., 2006.

Lower Canada reports: *Decisions Des Tribuneaux 1854/1855*. Public domain, digitized by Google Books.

Lundy, Derek: *The Way of a Ship*, Knopf, 2002.

Mackinnon, Mairi Ceit: *Vatersay and its People*, self-published, 2017.

The Ragged School Union Magazine, Partridge & Oakey,1854. Original from Ghent University, digitized by Google Books.